Geology Hikes of Northern California

by

Robin C. Johnson

and

Dot Lofstrom

California Venture Books

2018

Acknowledgements

There are many people to thank for the production of this guide. The geology presented is not based on original research, but has been assembled in bits and pieces from the great mass of published literature on California geology. In particular, we would like to acknowledge Deborah Harden's outstanding *California Geology*, a solid text providing an excellent starting place for the reader who wants to pursue a more detailed study. We would also like to thank the National Park Service, the U.S.D.A. Forest Service, the U.S. Geological Survey, the California Department of Parks and Recreation, and the Bureau of Land Management for the many informative maps, brochures, and reference materials that were made available to us regarding California's public lands. Numerous rangers and other park employees have generously offered information and advice, providing a well-informed resource for anyone looking for a rewarding hiking experience.

We gratefully acknowledge our friends and family members for their support and encouragement throughout this project, which has taken us up, down, and across the state of California for many years in a most thrilling exploration of the remarkable ground beneath our feet.

Dedication

To my father, in memory, who successfully instilled in me his great love and respect for the natural world.

—Robin C. Johnson

To my instructors at Southwest Missouri State University. Thank you for so graciously inviting me in to this wonderful world of geology.

—Dot Lofstrom

Contents

INTRODUCTION

In the context of the everyday, it seems as though we are standing on fairly solid footing and that the earth beneath us is stable and immutable. And, except for the occasional significant earthquake, the ground generally is a reliable perch. However, taken in a larger context, speeded up significantly like a time-lapse photography sequence, the earth's crust is a constantly changing and evolving system. Over the course of millions of years, land masses have split and merged, oceans have encroached on the land and receded again, mountains have grown and eroded away, and masses of living organisms have arisen and returned to the dust.

It is easy to forget about all of the activity that the earth is busily engaged in while we scurry to and from work each day. And although we cannot speed the process up enough to see it in any tangible sense, the earth's busyness is visible to those who go looking for it. That is the purpose of this book, to help you explore the hundreds of millions of years of earth's evolution up until now. (See Appendix B, the geologic time scale, to see a summary of that entire history and familiarize yourself with how geologists talk about the periods of earth's development.)

Thinking about all that has come before, most of which had nothing to do with humans, is one of the most humbling experiences we can imagine. Observing evidence of past geologic processes is the means to achieving that experience. All over the globe there are pieces of the puzzle of earth's story. Collecting and fitting together those pieces is the job of geologists. Our job, or rather our pastime, is to understand and marvel at the resulting composite. One of the best ways to do that is to strap on our boots and go for a walk on that deceptively still surface of the earth. And one of the best places to do it, for both geology and hiking in general, is California.

There are many hiking guides for California, most of them featuring trails to beautiful alpine lakes, stately redwood forests, bird-choked marshes, lush fern canyons, and palm oases. And, although we love those hikes, we've noticed an absence of guides to California geology trails, that is, hiking trails leading to something of geologic interest. Since California occupies one of the most geologically entertaining settings on Earth's surface, we think a guide to those sites is in order.

This is not a rock hounding or fossil collecting guide, nor is it an in-depth study of geology. This is a walking and hiking guide, focusing on trails that showcase the natural history of California. If you thrill at caves, want to climb a volcano, are awed by the power of time to sculpt natural works of art in stone, you will find many great trails in this guide.

This book, in tandem with *Geology Hikes of Southern California*, will provide a comprehensive story of the geologic history of our state on the trails. Just as California boasts habitats ranging from alpine forests to low desert, so it can offer us just about every type of geology lesson there is. There is tectonic action of monumental proportion, major earthquake faulting, fascinating volcanoes, glacially-carved peaks and valleys, geysers, bubbling mud pots, lava flows, mines, caves, fossils, and more. The problem in compiling trails for this guide was not the effort of finding them, but the unhappy process of eliminating many. For, truth be told, geology is all around us, as long as you know what to look for.

If you sometimes think of the world's biota as getting in the way of seeing the good stuff, you will be overjoyed with the trails in this guide. But there are enough beautiful plants and animals to satisfy your hiking buddies as well. Quite frequently, a geology trail is just as interesting historically and biologically as it is mineralogically. We have certainly taken these other attractions into account in assembling this collection.

For geologists, the earth is divided into naturally-occurring sections based on the type of material and topography found on its surface. These are called geomorphic provinces (see the figure on the following page), and, because of the convoluted and dynamic history of the West Coast, California has more of them than any other U. S. state. The provinces do not obey our artificial boundaries, of course, so they range where they will, crossing county, state and even national boundaries. The Basin and Range, for instance, is a large province that includes parts of California, Nevada, Colorado, Utah, and Arizona. The Klamath Mountains province, found in the far north of California, continues on into Oregon. We will be taking advantage of these divisions in the arrangement of this guide. Beginning with the Klamath Mountains in the northwest corner of the state, each chapter will represent one of the six geomorphic provinces of Northern California. The five remaining provinces are covered in *Geology Hikes of Southern California*, another collection of geologically-exciting walking and hiking opportunities for the southern half of the state.

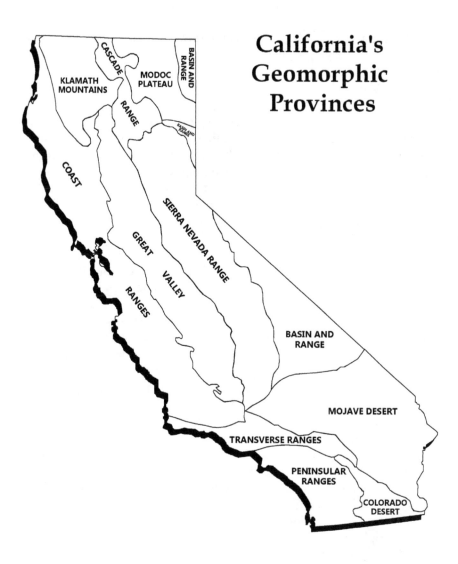

California's
Geomorphic
Provinces

KLAMATH
MOUNTAINS

CASCADE

RANGE

MODOC
PLATEAU

BASIN AND
RANGE

COAST

SIERRA NEVADA RANGE

GREAT

VALLEY

RANGES

BASIN AND
RANGE

MOJAVE DESERT

TRANSVERSE RANGES

PENINSULAR
RANGES

COLORADO
DESERT

Major Geologic Features of California

What are these earthly glories that spring up along our hiking trails? Here's a short overview of the kinds of attractions we're about to see.

Tectonism

A cursory glance at a topographic map of California will show that it is bounded on west and east by mountain ranges enclosing a huge central valley. These features dominate the way in which the geomorphic provinces are assigned. Several mountain ranges occupy the state, almost all of them oriented in a north-south pattern, such as the Coast Ranges and the Sierra Nevadas. Around San Luis Obispo, though, a different mountain system appears, the Transverse Ranges, which run generally east-west.

In the case of the California mountain ranges and mountains in general, the force at work is tectonism. Plate tectonics, once thought of among the scientific community as just a well-coddled egg in the mind of half-baked German geophysicist Alfred Wegener, is now accepted as the fundamental explanation about how the earth came to look as it does today. When Wegener first proposed his idea of continental drift in the early twentieth century, it met with widespread ridicule. What could he expect from a species still reeling from the idea that the earth was not the center of the universe? But the evidence began to stack up and the notion that vast land masses moved and shifted around the globe grew and gathered momentum. Today, the moving plates have been mapped and named and are known to be responsible for creating mountains on land, the deep basins of the oceans, the ring of fire in the Pacific Ocean, and the Mid-Atlantic Ridge in the Atlantic Ocean. Without the drifting plates, we would be living on a very flat, uniform, and boring ball, probably standing in ankle-deep water.

There are seven major plates and several minor ones on the Earth. They are rigid pieces of crust and upper mantle, together known as the lithosphere, that move over a softer cushion beneath them called the asthenosphere. Depending on where you live in California, you're either moving westward or northward at this very moment.

The movement of the tectonic plates is responsible for many of the dramatic features of California, including rugged mountain ranges and low deserts. There are also even more obvious bits of evidence to be found in the Golden State. At Pinnacles National Monument, for instance, a bit of Southern California now sits displaced in Central California, far from home. How did it get there? This is one of the mysteries we will explore.

Glaciation

As in much of North America, ice ages have brought vast quantities of ice down into California at various times throughout the history of the earth. Evidence of the scraping action of the ice is visible in the Sierra Nevada mountains and elsewhere. Where the glaciers have moved through, they have carved lakes and deep gorges and polished hard bedrock. They have left "islands" of resistant rock in place and carried huge boulders far from their origin. They have given us alluring formations such as the turrets of Castle Crags. And they have given us the breathtaking beauty of Yosemite National Park.

At the highest elevations in the Sierras and Cascades, remnants of old glaciers still exist, such as the one on the northern side of Mt. Lyell in Yosemite or the several glaciers fringing the top of Mt. Shasta. But most of the trails showcasing glaciation will travel to places where the ice receded long ago, leaving tracks on the faces of the rocks.

Mineral Deposits

Without gold, California's human history would be dramatically different. On January 24, 1848, when California belonged to Mexico, gold was discovered in Coloma on the South Fork of the American River. This event sparked the 1849 Gold Rush, a sudden and dramatic influx of people from all over the world—miners, of course, and an entire support system geared towards serving their needs. Bars, brothels, hotels, bookstores, supply stores, legal offices, laundries, merchants of every type, shipping, railroads, an entire civilization sprung up wherever there was gold being coaxed from the rivers or pried out of the mountains.

The gold primarily originated in vast quartz veins in the Sierra Nevadas and was discovered in the many waterways washing eroded particles down into all parts west of the mountains. Many who came for gold eventually settled in California and plied the trades they brought along, such as farming, ranching, and many more. Likewise, many foreigners arrived from countries near and far and some of them remained, contributing to a highly diverse population that exists to the present day.

When the gold fever cooled, the region had been radically transformed from a sparsely-occupied Mexican territory of Catholic missions and ranches to the bustling and burgeoning 31st state of the union (1850).

Gold mining has continued into modern times, but is an entirely different kind of operation now. Still, in the area where gold was first discovered, along the American River, you will still see people panning today. And on public land throughout the state, you will see rock cairns marking someone's mining claim. There is still some gold in them thar hills.

In addition to gold, other minerals have been successfully mined in the state, including silver, tungsten, borax, salt, and chromium, to name a few. We will visit several historic mining sites and even venture into some of the abandoned mines.

Earthquake Faults

California is well known for its earthquakes, a fact of life that leaves natives almost apathetic, but creates tremors in the bones of visitors riding the trains of Bay Area Rapid Transit (BART) under the San Francisco Bay. Earthquakes are nothing to be blasé about, to be sure, but as is customary, people tend not to fear the familiar. California has dozens of earthquakes daily, most of them so small that no one notices except geologists and seismologists monitoring such things. Occasionally, however, such as in the Loma Prieta quake of 1989 and the Northridge quake of 1994, the earth delivers us a major jolt, and then all of us pay attention.

It is no mystery to scientists why we have this activity. The most interesting geology worldwide occurs along tectonic plate boundaries, and California is a perfect example of this process.

California is where the North American and Pacific Plates meet, a dynamic boundary that runs roughly along the largest earthquake fault in California, the San Andreas. This plate collision is responsible for the mountainous coastal terrain and most of the earthquake activity throughout the state. On the trails, we'll explore how this plate boundary dramatically affects the topography and mineralogy of California.

Volcanoes

The numerous volcanoes of California have been quiet for a long time now, so much so that those of us living here almost never think about the possibility of an eruption. But evidence of past volcanic activity is easily observed, particularly in the northeast section of the state, where huge volcanoes poured lava out over the landscape as recently as 1917. And even today, there is enough geothermal activity just under the surface to create the fascinating spectacles in Lassen National Park—bubbling mud pots, steam shooting out of holes in the ground, and hot springs and creeks. In the Cascades, there are several volcanoes that are considered dormant, but not extinct, including Medicine Lake, Mt. Shasta, and Lassen Peak. The Long Valley Caldera and the Mammoth Lake area are also active volcanic regions.

All over the state, we see evidence of our volcanic past. There are cinder cones dotting the Mojave Desert, and the entire Sierra Nevada range is made of granite that was once molten material underground. There are lava flows so pristine that they look as though they happened yesterday, but, in geologic time, of course, a few thousand years ago was about when you started reading this paragraph.

We will be exploring numerous remnants of this activity, as well as many surface features that hint at the turmoil still brewing just below the surface.

Caves

In California, caves are generally one of two types, either lava tubes or dissolved limestone. Many limestone caves are located in the Sierra Nevada Range and feature typical cave formations, such as stalactites, stalagmites, flowstone, draperies, etc. One of the caves, Black Chasm, also has large collections of rare crystal formations called helictites. These caves have been created by ground water dissolving the calcium carbonate over a long period of time. A cave is considered living if it is still being formed, if water is still present. It is a dead cave if it is dry.

Lava tubes are an entirely different sort of cave. They are created by highly liquid lava flowing downhill in such a way that the outer area cools and forms a crust while insulating the liquid lava within. The still-liquid lava flows through the hardened crust, eventually draining out when the eruption ceases, leaving a hollow tube behind. Lava tubes are often found when a portion of the ceiling caves in and exposes an opening. Hundreds of these tubes are located in Lava Beds National Monument. They are common elsewhere as well, and we will visit several. There are no crystalline formations in these caves, but they have their own particular charms. They are not quite so daunting as other caves to explore because they are often a single tube or limited branching tubes, difficult to get lost in.

Fossils

Because California contains huge tracts of land that were once at the bottom of ancient seas, a good percentage of the known fossil beds contain the remains of sea creatures, with some notable exceptions such as the La Brea tar pits in Southern California. There are several ammonite sites, and many places where clam shells and the like can be viewed. In the round old hills south of Tracy, the gigantic marine reptile, ichthyosaurus, has been found. Many important Miocene mammal fossils have been discovered in the Blackhawk area of Mount Diablo.

Most of the fossil sites we will visit are protected in parklands, so you will only be able to look, but there are places where collecting is allowed. There are few things more exciting that holding something in your hand that was living millions of years ago.

For those of us attracted to rocks and fossils, it's natural to want to take some home. It's important that you know the rules regarding the taking of natural objects. Collecting is prohibited in national and state parks, with occasional exceptions. Leave your rock hammer at home when visiting these places, but bring your hand lens. You can usually collect rocks and fossils on land overseen by the Bureau of Land Management. Make sure you check with the local BLM office, however. Most sites have a 25-pound collecting limit. As an example, these guidelines are issued by the Barstow Field Office for rock collecting:

> Part 8365 of Title 43 CFR (Code of Federal Regulations) provide for the collecting of "reasonable" quantities of rocks, minerals, semiprecious gemstones, and invertebrate and plant fossils of non-scientific importance, for personal use. With respect to rockhound material, the Field Office considers a "reasonable quantity" to be not more than can be carried in a daypack. Regulations do not allow collecting on "developed recreation sites and areas," or where otherwise prohibited or posted. Care should be exercised not to collect minerals on mining claims.

There are other rules regarding collecting of fossils and other objects. Some protected wilderness areas are completely off limits for collecting of any kind, and some allow personal collecting. Check with the agency overseeing the area. As always while visiting nature's wonderland, stay on established trails, respect wildlife, bring out everything you took in, and leave no trace.

Hazards of the Trail

By far, the most hazardous of animals you will likely encounter is the rattlesnake. Most animals will stay away from you, including snakes, but be careful where you put your hands among rocks. Mountain lions live in the areas you will enter, but you will not normally see one. And bears are mostly interested in your food, so, if you camp, keep your food items locked up or tied high out of the way. Some of the animals living in Northern California are very large, such as elk and elephant seals, and can be dangerous just because of their size, not because they are especially ferocious. Give wild animals plenty of space and don't ever corner them.

Poison oak is very common along these trails. Learn to recognize it and stay away from it. In spring, it has glossy, three-part leaves. The best defense is to stay on the trail. The same advice applies for avoiding ticks.

Wearing long pants and sleeves can also help protect you from ticks. Mosquitos can be a problem in wetter areas. It's a good idea to take an insect repellent along in your pack. And to avoid accidents, wear sturdy boots and always watch your footing.

Always carry water, a first-aid kit, snacks, matches in a waterproof container, a mirror for signaling, a map, an extra jacket or sweatshirt, and your cell phone, turned off. Forest Service maps, which can be purchased at ranger stations, through the mail, or from the Forest Service web sites, are a valuable resource, and a handheld GPS receiver can be a real lifesaver if you wander off the trail.

Using This Guide

The trails here are ordered by geomorphic province so you can locate those in your neighborhood or can target a particular area for a hiking trip. There is a thematic cross-reference in Appendix A to let you easily locate your particular favorite attraction. So if you're just wild about volcanoes, for instance, flip to the back of the book to find the trails that satisfy your passion.

Each section begins with an overview of the geology of the area, a description of the forces that shaped it, and what sort of landscape dominates as a result.

The trails are described in detail, including the round-trip distance, the difficulty level, what you'll see on the trail, and directions to parking and the trailhead. Most of these hikes are easy to moderate and last no more than a few hours. The goal is to see interesting geology, not navigate the outback. With your kids, on a Sunday afternoon, you can hike these trails and have a healthy, educational, and joyful outing. Another bonus is that a lot of them are free. If you pack sandwiches, it's cheaper than a movie.

Spotting maps show the distribution of the trails. They are keyed to the numbered hikes in each section.

We hope you enjoy traversing these paths as much as we have. So let's get to it!

Redwood National Park

SECTION 1
KLAMATH MOUNTAINS & NORTH COAST

The northwest corner of the state is primarily known for its magnificent, ancient redwood forests. Not only can you not see the forest for the trees, but neither can you see the rocks. So geology trails are a little scarce in this province. But there is geology underneath it all, and we can glimpse it, especially at the seashore and in the higher elevations.

There is no way to talk about the Klamath province (or, indeed, California in general) without referring often to the theory of plate tectonics. In fact, it was this very region that provided important clues to the development of the theory. The rocks of the Klamath Mountains puzzled geologists for a long time. Resembling rocks that formed in the deep ocean, they seemed to be out of place, as if they had just been dumped here at the edge of the continent. In a sense, that is exactly what happened. Before we talk about these mystery rocks, however, a brief review of plate tectonics will be helpful.

It was the German geophysicist Alfred Wegener who first proposed the idea of continental drift in 1912, citing as one example that the east coast of South America seemed to fit the west coast of Africa like the piece of a puzzle. At the time, his idea that continents moved around the globe was viewed in the scientific community with widespread ridicule. What could be expected from a species still reeling from the idea that the earth was not the center of the universe? Many scientists reluctantly agreed that the shape of the continents suggested they had once been part of a single, larger continent, but how could rigid, rocky slabs move around? The answer lay in the theory of plate tectonics, proposed in the 1960s and now universally accepted. We now know that it is not only land masses that move, but the entire surface of the Earth, which is composed of several distinct segments called plates. The moving plates have been mapped and named and are known to be responsible for creating mountains on land, the deep basins of the oceans, the ring of fire in the Pacific Ocean, and the Mid-Atlantic Ridge in the Atlantic Ocean. Without the drifting plates, we would be living on a very flat, uniform, and boring ball, probably standing in ankle-deep water.

There are seven major plates and several minor ones on the Earth. They are rigid pieces of crust and upper mantle, together known as the lithosphere, that are carried on a softer cushion beneath them called the asthenosphere, a layer with the consistency of modeling clay.

You can think of the plates as riding on a conveyor belt. Where they move away from one another at sea-floor spreading centers, magma surfaces in the rift to create new oceanic plate material. The plates move out from these spots, their leading edges moving toward other plates, often continental or dry land plates. Where the plates meet, interesting things happen. Like automobiles plowing into one another in slow motion, they either crash head-on together, side-swipe each other, or one of them ends up shoved underneath the other. The land at these boundaries responds in the way you'd expect to such violence collisions—it breaks, shears off, gets crumpled up, gets pushed upward or downward, gets crushed, melted and transformed in a variety of ways. In the case of crustal plates, when an oceanic plate encounters a continental plate, the denser oceanic plate dives under the lighter, more buoyant continental plate. This is called "subduction." The subducted plate goes deeper into the earth, remelting into the mantle and becoming magma once again. However, pieces of it, just as in a violent car crash, end up being left behind, sutured onto the edge of the continental plate. This process is known as the theory of "accreted terrane," or more poetically, "suspect terrane," where pieces of other continents or ocean crust are merged onto a continent as the result of tectonic plate movement.

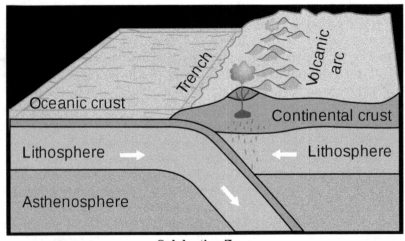

Subduction Zone

That is exactly what happened in California up until about 30 million years ago because coastal California occupies the boundary between two massive tectonic plates—the Pacific and the North American. For millions of years, subduction occurred at the edge of California, but the boundary changed into a transform fault boundary about three million years ago. That boundary is now known as the San Andreas Fault. Both plates are moving westward, but the Pacific Plate is moving faster, an average of three or four inches per year compared to the one inch movement of the North American Plate. For this reason, the Pacific Plate is sliding northward along the North American Plate. Depending on where you live in California, that is, which side of the San Andreas Fault, you're either moving westward or northward at this very moment. This type of plate encounter is called a "transform fault" or "strike-slip" boundary.

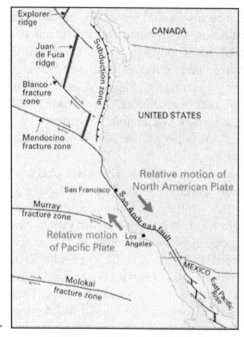

California's Tectonic Plates

When you're talking about something as bulky as huge land masses, they don't slide past one another in a smooth and civil manner. There's incredible pressure and tension involved, and this unrest is the source of earthquakes and volcanic eruptions. The plate boundary is what makes California such an interesting place, geologically, and is also what makes it so diverse and beautiful.

Plates have been colliding here for millions of years. Some smaller plates have been eaten up in the meantime, leaving behind tell-tale signs of themselves in the rocks. Geologists believe that oceanic material was plastered onto the continental crust at least five separate times in the Klamath Mountains province. Each sequence is known as a *terrane*, and the terranes get increasingly younger as you move from east to west. The subduction of the oceanic plate is still occurring in at the Oregon coast and in the northernmost reaches of California, creating an unstable coast where earthquakes and landslides are common. We'll see evidence of that on the coastal trails.

If you're interested in reading more about this process, celebrated writer John McPhee wrote an entire book about it called *In Suspect Terrain*, book two of his masterpiece, *Annals of the Former World*.

Plate tectonics provides an explanation of the origin of the rocks of the Klamath region, but does not explain their dramatic beauty. For that, we must turn to a much more recent episode of glaciation.

This province encompasses several mountain ranges, including the Trinity Alps, Siskiyou Mountains, Marble Mountains, and Salmon Mountains. There are many places in these mountains where evidence of glaciation is on view, such as the unique and dramatic outcrop of eroded granite spires called Castle Crags. We will visit Castle Crags State Park for three hikes.

One of the more interesting formations in the Klamath Mountains is the McCloud limestone. It's made of calcium carbonate and full of fossils from the Permian ocean. The fossils include corals, brachiopods (which resemble clams), and fusulinids, small one-celled organisms that go by the nickname of "footballs" based on their shape. Limestone is easily dissolved by groundwater into caverns and sinkholes, a characteristic observable at the magnificent Shasta Caverns. The limestone was originally a coral reef surrounding the volcanic mid-oceanic islands of the early Klamath Mountains. Whenever you encounter fossiliferous limestone, you know you're standing in a place that was once a warm, shallow sea.

Redwood National Park is located here, as are five state parks, all featuring dense coastal redwood forests. When the Hudson Bay Company fur traders came to this stretch of California, they were astounded at the abundance of beaver. Unlike those earlier visitors, we will be taking photos instead of pelts. Among other early explorers here was the famous mountain man Jedediah Smith in 1828. The Smith River and a state park are named after him. Russian fur traders also made their way through the north coast area, establishing camps and villages. Their presence has been preserved in place names such as Russian Wilderness, Russian Gulch, and, further south, Russian River.

As in the rest of northern California, gold was found in the Klamath area as well. The town of Happy Camp was founded in 1851 by miners who were happy with the local pickings. Today, Happy Camp is a base for a variety of recreational activities in the extreme north of the state. But even such pivotal destinations in the Klamath are still small towns in this minimally populated region.

There are three wilderness areas located here, the Russian Wilderness Area, located along a major ridge dividing the Scott and Salmon River watersheds, Siskiyou Wilderness between Happy Camp and the coast, and the Marble Mountain Wilderness Area, 250,000 acres of thick forests, tall peaks, glacial lakes, and plenty of solitude.

Perhaps because of all this wilderness, Bigfoot has managed to hang on here, in legend at least [see inset]. In California, there have been reports of Bigfoot on Mt. Shasta and even further south, but his (or her) real domain is in the forests around the Klamath and Trinity Rivers. There is even a road named after the elusive creature, the Bigfoot Scenic Byway, 85 miles along Highway 96. The tiny town of Willow Creek (Highway 96 and Highway 299) has declared itself "the Bigfoot capital of the world." You can visit the Willow Creek-China Flat Museum there to see casts of Bigfoot footprints and photos, as well as a Gigantopithecus (Bigfoot?) skull. And don't forget to take your camera when you go hiking in the Klamath Mountains. What a shame if you ran into Bigfoot and had no proof.

BIGFOOT

Almost everyone has heard of Bigfoot, or Sasquatch, or Yeti, or the Abominable Snowman, the huge primate who walks on two feet and lives in the forests of the American Northwest, Canada, or the Himalayas. Legends of the creature's existence go back hundreds of years, and even in modern times, thousands of sightings have been reported. But, so far, no firm evidence has been found to prove its existence. No bones have turned up and no bodies have ever been seen. Footprints have been found, but some appear to have been faked and there is no definitive test of authenticity for the rest.

Descriptions of Bigfoot all over the world are fairly consistent—an ape-like creature walking bipedally with a loping gate, covered in dark, often reddish hair, standing between eight and eleven feet tall. This description is remarkably close to a known animal thought to be extinct. *Gigantopithecus* lived between one and nine million years ago in central and southeast Asia. Its closest modern relative is the orangutan. Some scientists postulate that this ancient ape migrated to North America the same way humans did, over temporary land bridges, and somehow has survived in North America to this day.

With all of the interest in Bigfoot, however, many people believe that it could not have remained hidden from us for so long. Skeptics suspect that well-intentioned people who report sightings have actually seen a bear standing on its hind legs.

No doubt the legend, if not the actual creature, will remain alive for a long time to come.

Trails of the Klamath Mountains

1. Myrtle Creek Trail
2. Coastal Trail – Enderts Beach Segment
3. Rim Trail
4. Heart Lake Trail
5. Vista Point Trail
6. Crags Trail
7. Pacific Crest Trail – Castle Crags Segment
8. Samwel Cave Nature Trail
9. Lake Shasta Caverns
10. Natural Bridge Interpretive Trail

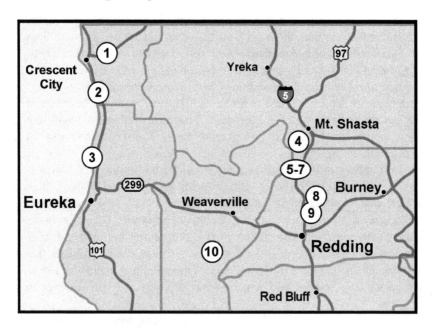

1. Myrtle Creek Trail

EFFORT: Minimal
LENGTH: 2.0 miles
GEOLOGICAL FEATURE(S): Mining
LOCATION: Smith River National Recreation Area

Description: A 15-stop self-guiding interpretive trail along Myrtle Creek, this trail visits a site of intense mining activity during the latter half of the nineteenth century. The creek marks a boundary between typical local soils supporting the redwood and Douglas fir forest and serpentine soils rich in iron and magnesium and therefore reddish in color. This area is designated as a special Botanical Area to protect its unique environment. Because serpentine soils are uncommon, plants growing in them are often rare.

On this trail, you will visit the remains of mining operations dating from 1853 when gold was discovered here by Louis Gallise. The gold was mined for some time by panning until 1890 when a huge, 47-ounce gold nugget was discovered, bringing a lot of attention to the site. Around 1894, a group of investors from Crescent City formed the Myrtle Creek Mining Company and constructed a ditch to allow hydraulic mining. Gold and silver were successfully mined here until the 1920s.

As evidenced by the different plant communities on either side of the creek and the different soils supporting them, this is the location of a fault. Faults are often not obvious on the surface, so geologists study aerial photographs for suggestions of lines, called "lineations." Like the name suggests, lineations are an alignment of surface features as a result of a fault. People are usually too close to the earth to be able to see the lineations on the surface, which is why aerial photographs are needed. Even on the photographs, though, the shadowy suggestion of lineations aren't easily seen.

It's not a coincidence that this mine has been situated in the area of a fault. Both faults and cooling magma result in the formation of cracks that go deep into the earth, possibly even into the mantle. These are very narrow cracks, from a centimeter to a few inches, and they don't extend to the surface, so don't worry that you're going to fall into them. Nor do they go straight down. They usually branch, one to another, like a series of twigs. When the cracks occur, hydrothermal fluid (hot, mineral-laden water) is able to move through them, first as steam and later as water. As the fluid moves upward through the cracks, minerals (including gold and silver) begin to precipitate out on the walls of the cracks, gradually filling them in. Usually, the last mineral to crystallize out is quartz. You see evidence of these cracks all the time when you see quartz veins in boulders or in road cuts. Mines cannot be located just anywhere it's convenient. They have to be located in an area where the minerals were deposited, and that means an area of volcanic or tectonic activity.

Before your hike, pick up a trail guide at the Forest Service office in Eureka or at the Smith River National Recreation Area office in Gasquet. The well-established trail will bring you through the ditch system dug by the miners and remnants of a ground sluicing operation. It will also explain how the surrounding flora was affected by the mining activity. In addition to the diversion of the creek, downing of timber for construction, and moving of soil, the miners also burned the vegetation down to get a better look at the geology (a temptation generally avoided by modern geologists). The landscape still shows scars from the intensive and long-term mining, but healing is ongoing.

Start out on an easy trail through a forest of coast redwood, tanoak, rhododendron, azalea, evergreen huckleberry, redwood sorrel, wild ginger, California hazel, milkmaids, thimbleberry, sword fern, five-finger fern, maidenhair fern, licorice fern, and Port-Orford cedar. Also making an appearance is the Oregon myrtle, for which the creek is named. We usually call this tree a California bay or laurel. Break one of its leaves to

California pitcher plant

smell the distinctive aroma. Near the creek, big leaf maples and alders enjoy the water provided by the year-round stream.

The trail follows the old mining ditch. It was used to transport large amounts of water for washing soil through sluice boxes. Next you will come to a footbridge, a wooden gate and one of the metal pipes used to divert the water into the ditch. This system was designed to discharge up to 15,000 gallons per minute.

At stop five, you'll be able to see the different plant communities of the serpentine soils. The reddish soil across the creek supports manzanita,

Labrador tea, California coffee berry, huckleberry, oak, beargrass, silk tassel bush, and the rare Bolander's lily.

The carnivorous California pitcher plant can be found in the boggy areas along the creek. The brochure brings them to your attention at stop seven. The rare Pitcher Plants (Darlingtonia californica) are able to live in wet, serpentine soils devoid of nitrogen and phosphorous because they obtain these nutrients from the insects and other small organisms they trap in their Cobra-like hoods. They are sometimes called "cobra plants." They produce an abundance of nectar to attract insects inside their single leaf (pitcher). The insects drown in the nectar and decay through bacterial action. These plants are protected and it is illegal to pick them. The pitcher plant grows in marshy areas along the California and Oregon coast where cold, moving water is present. Since it is almost always found in poor quality soils where the parent rock is serpentine, it is considered a serpentine indicator.

Other rare, beautiful flowers growing here are the California lady's slipper and the Vollmer's lily.

You'll come to a place where the serpentine is exposed alongside the trail. It is gray-green in color and feels somewhat waxy or soapy to the touch. Since serpentine is unstable, ditches were not dug through it. Instead, the miners built flumes to carry the water over it. Remnants of these flumes can be seen below the trail.

Continue through the moist riparian environment along the creek. Ferns dominate the understory as you approach the trail's end at the creek bed. You might want to stop here for a while to enjoy the serenity of the cool forest and running stream before heading back. Return along the same path.

Serpentine

Serpentine is an attractive, mottled greenish metamorphic rock derived from igneous rocks with a low silica, high iron, and high magnesium content like peridotite. It is common in California and is California's state rock. However, it is not common in other places. Serpentine occurs in a particular type of environment at a tectonic plate boundary in which one of those plates is an oceanic plate. The presence of sea water is a critical factor in making serpentine, created by hydration and low-temperature metamorphosis.

Soils derived from serpentine are toxic to many plants because of high levels of nickel, chromium, and cobalt. Growth of many plants is also inhibited by low levels of potassium and phosphorus.

Serpentine got its name from its likeness to a snake, either in color or in the waxy feel of its surface.

Directions: On Highway 101 in Crescent City, go three miles north to Highway 199, then turn east and go seven miles across the Myrtle Creek Bridge to the parking area on the river side of the road. Cross the road to the trailhead. Access is free.

2. Coastal Trail – Enderts Beach Segment

EFFORT: Minimal
LENGTH: 2.0 miles
GEOLOGICAL FEATURE(S): Erosional Features
LOCATION: Redwood National Park

Description: Take binoculars, your camera, and a picnic on this short seaside stroll through Monterey cypress and wildflowers to Enderts Beach and the Hidden Beach tide pools. Between the geology, flowers, animals, and surf, there is something to entertain everyone on this trail.

The intense seismic activity and rapid uplift of the North Coast leads to frequent landslides, shifting rivers, and dramatic coastal erosion. In the 1990s, at least nine magnitude 6.0-plus earthquakes jolted the North Coast. This incidence of large quakes was higher than in any other decade within the last century. We've already discussed the causes of this activity in the introduction to this chapter. Now, let's take a look at the results.

The Coastal Trail runs up and down the length of this coastline through Redwood National Park and the state parks contained within it. The trail's north end can be found at Crescent Beach in a short section leading to Enderts Beach where Little Nickel Creek runs into the ocean. The trail to Enderts Beach is only a half mile, but we're going to take a short side trip along the way and then extend the hike by walking on to the tide pools.

From the beginning of this trail, there is ample evidence of the powerful forces chewing into the landscape. Near the first parking area you'll see a dramatic landslide, an obvious indicator of how wave action is cutting into the shoreline. In 2017, another landslide occurred here, burying Lakeshore Blvd. and cutting off access to Crescent Beach.

Follow the old road south, noting how it has been partially reclaimed by the sea and is no longer usable. This sort of action is occurring all along the ocean edge to varying degrees. But it is especially pronounced here because of the type of rock underlying the park. Later, down on the beach, we'll get a close-up view of that unstable foundation.

As you walk, enjoy the lovely seascapes and excellent wildlife viewing. Among the birds you may see here are brown pelicans, murres, cormorants, and gulls. Dolphins, killer whales, and gray whales may be passing by offshore. The gray whale watching is best from March to May during the spring migration. Harbor seals may be frolicking closer in.

The path, wide and gently sloping downhill, routes you between hedges of greenery and a profusion of springtime wildflowers.

Views out to sea are good in clear weather from the upper trail. In any weather, your walk will be accompanied by a distant foghorn. Looking back, you'll see the long sweeping curve of Crescent Beach leading out to Battery Point and Crescent City, and you'll see how the beach got its name. As you drop down from the high points, you'll become enclosed by arbors of dense vegetation and lose the views. These sections are brief, but quite enjoyable.

Continue the easy walk downhill to a junction. Left is a nature trail along Nickel Creek and right is the path to Enderts Beach. South the Coastal Trail continues. If you want to, detour to the Nickel Creek nature trail (recommended). It's only a quarter mile long and displays licorice ferns overwhelming the trunks and branches of the trees. It's sort of eerie, especially for those of us more accustomed to looking at rocks. The trail follows Nickel Creek inland through a very dense forest smothered in green moss and ferns. You can hear the creek beside you, but can't see much of it. Be careful not to step on banana slugs here on the moist creekside trail.

Continuing into the dense tree cover, you may be reminded of Hansel and Gretel. It can get a little scary with all these vines reaching toward you. Once you've covered over half of this little side trip, you'll begin to see the licorice ferns growing on the trees. As you go further, you'll come to a huge branch across the trail, high enough for you to walk under. It's overwhelmed with ferns. Look up and around you to see how the ferns are colonizing the trees. From here, it's only a few steps to a broken bench. The legs of the bench have rusted through and the bench is now sitting directly on the ground. The bench marks the end of the trail.

Returning to the junction, go straight toward the beach. From the grassy cliff top, head down the steep slope on a narrow, rocky path. You'll pass a trail left that leads to the campground. You want to continue straight toward the beach. Going steeply down between walls of thick plants, you'll come out on a sandy platform above the beach. Clamber down the rocks to the beach and turn left to reach the spot where Nickel Creek carves a narrow channel through the sand on its way into the ocean.

Enderts Beach (National Park Service)

Facing the eroded cliff face, you can see the different layers of the unstable rock foundation we mentioned earlier, the Franciscan Mélange. Melanges consist of mixtures of rocks of all different sizes in a shale or serpentine matrix. Notice that the bottom visible layer is dark with much lighter layers above it. This is an excellent opportunity to observe the Franciscan formation, one of the most complex and famous rock formations in the United States. The Franciscan Mélange includes fine-grained, deep-sea sedimentary rocks (greywacke) with large blocks of oceanic crust along with blue and greenschist metamorphic facies. This type of conglomerate forms at convergent plate boundary subduction zones where the deep-sea sediments are dragged down with the oceanic crust as it is subducted beneath the continental crust. The result is a complicated mixture of Jurassic and Cretaceous sedimentary, metamorphic, and igneous rocks. You can see fine examples of the Franciscan formation around San Francisco, where it has been bent into lovely chevron folds, made starkly visible by the alternating beds of chert and shale. But we digress. Here in the North Coast, this formation underlies most of Redwood National Park, and is composed primarily of sandstones and mudstones, with some serpentinite and greenstone, sheared, altered and highly fractured.

Generally, the Franciscan formation is highly unstable, largely because of the presence of both small and very large faults and shear zones often hundreds of feet wide. These inherently weak structural features, combined with high rainfall and prolonged storms on the north coast account for the instability and easy erodibility of this shoreline. As you observed at the start of this trail, catastrophic landslides, stream bank erosion, and soil creep are common. In the previous hike (Myrtle Creek Trail), we noticed that miners avoided digging ditches in this type of rock for these very reasons and built flumes to carry water instead. Miners know what they're doing when it comes to geology. At least the successful ones do.

Hop the creek and continue walking southward and notice the many black stones in the sand. These have washed out of the dark layer visible at the base of the cliff. Many of them have white stripes (quartz veins) in them. Some are crisscrossed many times with these veins, creating some quite interesting black and white striped rocks. The high stresses at the plate boundary create more highly fractured rock than we are accustomed to seeing. Facing the cliff wall, notice that the rocks exhibit obvious bending patterns, yet more evidence of the forces at work here, and the separate layers of sandstone, siltstone, and shale are easy to distinguish.

Ahead, you can see where we're going, where the sandy beach gives way to jagged black rocks that jut out and appear to form a barrier between this beach and the next. Climb among the rocky shoreline to take advantage of some of the most fertile tide pools we have ever seen. They are teeming with green and pink anemones, acorn barnacles, snails, sea urchins, limpets, sea stars, and sea palms. Be careful to step only on the rock, which is difficult here. Every little crevice in the surfaces is a home to small sea creatures.

It's rewarding to find a good tide pool and sit still and peer into it. The details of its contents will reveal themselves gradually. Hundreds of sea stars can be seen here, including the brilliant orange leather star.

Make your way across the rocks to the incipient arches (arches in the making). You are witnessing a particular stage in the process of coastal arch formation. At this stage, the resistant rock you're climbing on has remained in place while the softer cliff of Enderts Beach has eroded further inland. But even this material will eventually succumb. For now, the ocean has managed to punch a couple of holes into it. Over time, the waves will work the walls and ceilings of these caves, increasing the size of the holes. Someday, a delicate arch may result. And then, someday further into the future, the center of the arch will collapse, leaving behind a couple of sea stacks. As we visit more coastal trails, we'll observe these other stages of arch formation.

You can pass through the first cave, which is somewhat narrow and partially blocked by a large branch, but easily maneuvered. Coming out the other side, you'll find a treasure trove of tide pools and another beach, Hidden Beach. No doubt the rich abundance of sea creatures here will hold your interest for a while.

Okay, it looks like your friends are impatient to break out the sandwiches. Back on Enderts Beach, you'll find some nice smooth logs to perch on. After your picnic, return by the same path.

Directions: From Crescent City, take Highway 101 south two miles. Turn right on Enderts Beach Road and proceed to the end of the road and a parking lot overlooking Crescent Beach. Access is free. There are picnic tables, but no other facilities at the trailhead. You will find portable toilets further along on the trail.

3. Rim Trail

EFFORT: Moderate
LENGTH: 4+ miles
GEOLOGICAL FEATURE(S): Rock Collecting, Erosional Features
LOCATION: Patrick's Point State Park

Description: In addition to dramatic shorelines, sandy beaches, sea stacks, and tide pools, this park offers a reconstructed Yurok village to investigate. Consider walking the Sumeg Village trail near the visitor center before or after this one and spend the entire day in the park.

The Rim Trail runs for two miles along the ocean bluffs, connecting several of the popular stops and terminating at Agate Beach where we will do some poking about for pretty rocks. If your time is limited, you can pick up the trail at Patrick's Point or Mussel Rock to shorten the hike. Be forewarned that the coastline is often fogbound in summer. Sometimes beach hikes are best done in winter when other places may be less hospitable.

At the edge of the Palmer's Point parking area, you will find an interpretive panel explaining the gruesome discovery of over 1,000 sea lion skulls on offshore Cone Rock, each with a hole drilled in it. Archeologists deduce these to be the remnants of hunting rituals. One of the skulls is mounted inside the case.

Before hiking the featured trail, you may want to wander out to Palmer's Point for a look-see. It's doubtful that you will hike only the length of the Rim Trail proper, so the length of your hike will be determined by how many side trips you take.

To find the beginning of the trail, walk back down the road a short distance. It's located on the left of the road. The trail heads north, following the coastal bluff, giving you commanding views of the rugged coast and Trinidad Head to the south. Offshore, sea stacks provide resting places for sea lions, seals, cormorants, gulls, brown pelicans, black oystercatchers, and pigeon guillemots. Sea stacks are isolated rock pillars located near shore that project above sea level. They're usually the remnants of an arch or natural bridge. A natural bridge occurs when the waves erode softer sediments away from more resistant rock in such a way as to wear right through the middle. As the process continues over a long time, wearing the "legs" of the bridge thinner, the top collapses under its own weight, leaving two sea stacks. This evolution is well demonstrated at Natural Bridges State Park near Santa Cruz. When the park was established, there were three bridges, but today there is only one, as the other two have succumbed to the waves.

Vegetation along the bluff includes alder, spruce, Douglas fir, pine, Douglas iris, salal, trillium, rhododendrons, and azaleas. Ferns line the trails and berry vines and wildflowers are prolific in summer. Vegetation piles up on itself in places, so don't be surprised if you start to imagine yourself in Jurassic Park on some stretches of this trail.

As you hike, you'll encounter many spur trails leading to overlooks and beaches. Enrich your experience by taking these side trips. The windy trails down to Abalone Point, Patrick's Point, Wedding Rock, and Mussel Rocks make for a delightfully varied hike. Abalone Point is just 0.4 miles from the trailhead. Next will be Lookout Rock and Patrick's Point. After 1.5 miles, you come to the spur trail leading to Mussel Rock. Go out towards it through a natural arbor and notice that a huge fracture has developed on the left side. Imagine that massive chunk of rock breaking free and falling into the sea. Someday, that is exactly what will happen. Erosion can be an extremely slow process, but moments do occur where a great change takes place instantaneously, like when an arch collapses or rocks break off and fall.

Clamber around the steps of Mussel Rock where stone walls have been erected to keep visitors from plummeting off. If you train your binoculars on the large sharp rock to the left, you'll probably see birds roosting there, pelicans or cormorants.

Return to the Rim Trail and continue. You'll reach the end of the trail at Agate Beach Campground after two miles.

From the parking area, take the steep trail down to a staircase that leads to Agate Beach. Once you're on the beach, look back at the cliff face. You can easily see the various bedding layers revealed there. On the bottom is the dark greenstone layer and then gravel above it. The top layer is sandstone.

Allow some time to search for agates, jade, and red jasper in the gravel bars. Most people do find agates if they have a little patience. You can walk along in the surf and look for them where the rough gravel lies, or you can sift through the dry sand up higher on the beach. The agates are glassy, translucent, and nearly white. They vary in size, but are normally about the size of a dime or smaller. There are plenty of quartz pieces here as well. You can distinguish the agates from them easily enough, as you cannot see into the quartz.

Agate

Agates, or banded chalcedony, are semi-precious gemstones that vary greatly in form and color and were once highly prized. Chalcedony is a type of cryptocrystalline quartz, which means that the crystals are too small to be seen even with a microscope. Agates are formed in vesicular volcanic rocks by a process that is not completely understood. The volcanic rocks have cavities (vesicles) because of escaping gases. The agate forms when groundwater percolates through the volcanic rock, leaving behind a micro layer of precipitated silica in the vesicle. The vesicles in the host rock are often round; thus, the precipitated layers will be seen as concentric bands. This banding creates beautiful patterns in a polished agate. If you're familiar with the game of marbles, you've probably played with some made from agates (aggies). Although the agates found here are generally white, agates occur in many different colors, depending on what other dissolved chemicals happened to be in the groundwater.

Time your visit to coincide with low tide, so you'll be able to find the newly deposited stones. Agate collecting is best after a winter storm. Also, some people suggest looking for discarded agates at the base of the stairs leading to the beach. After a day at the beach picking up rocks, some folks toss them out before they leave.

Agate Beach has many pretty surf-polished stones in addition to agates. If you're a rock hound, you will find this a rewarding spot to visit.

When you're ready, head back the way you came.

Directions: From Eureka, proceed 30 miles north on Highway 101 (Redwood Highway), to just north of the town of Trinidad. Exit on Patrick's Point Drive and follow it to the park entrance. Follow the signs to Palmer Point, about 0.25 miles past the entrance. There is a day-use fee. Restrooms are available.

4. Heart Lake Trail

EFFORT: Moderate
LENGTH: 2.2 miles
GEOLOGICAL FEATURE(S): Glaciation
LOCATION: Shasta-Trinity National Forest

Description: This is a short, gratifying trail in the Eddy Mountains with magnificent alpine views and great swimming opportunities. For many people, this will be an easy trail, but for those of us who are acclimated to sea level, the continual climb here was tiring and required several stops to catch our breath. Most of the trail courses through open sun, so wear a hat and sunscreen.

Even if you don't make it all the way to Heart Lake, the surrounding views are gorgeous and well worth climbing up part of the way.

Before you start hiking, let's take a moment to introduce the geology you're about to experience, a landscape sculpted by glacial ice. Pleistocene glaciers covered much of northern California from 1.8 million years ago to 10,000 years ago, advancing and retreating during that time as temperatures fluctuated. Later, around 1350 A.D., the climate began to cool again. This Little Ice Age, as it is known, persisted until about 1850. Permanent patches of ice (glaciers) still exist in high elevation areas of California, including the Sierras, the Klamath Mountains and on Mt. Shasta. These Shasta glaciers will be visible to you on this trail once we get higher up.

As for Castle Lake, it was created by glacial ice. It sits within a glacial cirque (bowl-shaped valley) with a high granite cliff at its southern end, something like a castle wall, hence its name. *Cirques* form when the head of a glacier is situated in that area for some time. They have three tall steep sides and then an open side, which is the direction the glacier flowed. Two cirques close together form an *arête*, a steep-sided ridge, and three together form a *horn*, such as the world-famous Matterhorn in the Alps. You'll encounter cirques often on the trails here and in the Sierras.

From the parking lot, head to the edge of Castle Lake where interpretive panels stand on the shore. Follow the trail across the lake's outlet, boulder hopping, and climb along the lake's east side among glacially-carved granite and sparse conifers. Take the Little Castle Lake Trail.

Views of Castle Lake are inspiring as you climb to a better vantage point for taking it all in. Watch your footing, as this is a rocky, uneven path. With the continuous climbing, this narrow section of trail will get your heart pumping.

This is a popular trail and you'll probably find yourself greeting several other hikers on the way. Seeing small children scampering back along the trail, we were lulled into a false feeling that it would be easy going. We later discovered that not everyone on the trail had the same destination. For families, the large beautiful meadows above Castle Lake seemed to be the draw. For a couple looking for a more secluded spot, Little Castle Lake was their choice.

Climbing higher, you'll reach open areas with full sun. We sampled some wild raspberries along the way and thoroughly enjoyed the blooming wild roses and Indian paintbrush.

When you reach a ridgetop saddle and trail junction, bear right uphill. This junction is hard to find and is indistinct over the ridge because the landscape is dominated by boulders and bare rock. Since we missed the trail ourselves, we positioned some cairns here on the way back. If you can't find the trail, just climb up on the ridge ahead and keep climbing in a southwest direction. Then, from a high point, turn around and look back. The trail is quite visible from the other direction, looking back down on it.

If you miss the junction and continue on the trail to Little Castle Lake, you'll be heading east instead and will pass by a lovely grassy meadow on your right. Also, the Little Castle Lake Trail will descend beyond the meadow. Our trail climbs the entire way, so you'll have no doubt if you heed this description about whether or not you're on the right trail.

Having made it over the ridge, walk the rocky path in the open sun, enjoying a profusion of wildflowers in spring and summer. Along this section of trail, it's easy to spot the glacial striations in the flat surfaces of the rocks. (The views, flowers and butterflies were so enchanting, you forgot we were here for geology, didn't you?) Look for patches of green and then examine them closely to see the polished, scratched surfaces where moving ice scraped over the rock. Glaciers carry soil, gravel and boulders along as they advance. It's this material that serves as the polishing agent on the underlying rock. Make sure to run your hand over the surface of this polished rock to marvel at its smoothness. Remember, striations point in the direction of glacial movement.

You will want to stop (maybe you will have to) often to look around you in every direction to take in the breathtaking views. Mt. Shasta is to the northeast, a stunning companion along most of this hike. Notice the glacial ice around its summit. There are seven named glaciers on that mountain. In subsequent hikes in this guide, you'll have the opportunity to get much closer to them.

Still climbing steeply, you'll finally scale another ridgetop to see tiny Heart Lake below you. It's hard to believe that it's only been a mile to get here. The lake is small and warm in summer and shaped like a heart.

Drop down to the lake shore and proceed to its northern edge. From here, look north to enjoy the highlight of this trail, the fine expansive view. All at once you can see Castle Lake shimmering below you, Mt. Shasta, Black Butte (Hike #15), and, in the distance to the northeast, The Whaleback (Hike #12), a huge cinder cone. Taking in this view, you have no doubt you are in the midst of a fairly young volcanic region.

Around the shore of Heart Lake you will find a few nice boulders to perch on after you take a dip. This is a perfect spot to spend some time, so bring a picnic lunch. If you're lucky, you'll have some solitude here in this special place which reminds us of the idyllic pools frequently seen in Tarzan movies. No, there is no waterfall tumbling down to the lake, but it is blissful swimming hole anyway.

Return the way you came, all downhill, sometimes steeply, but with great views spreading out ahead of you all the way.

Directions: From Interstate 5, take the Central Mt. Shasta exit and turn left onto N. Old Stage Road. Turn onto W.A. Barr Road, following the signs to Lake Siskiyou. Cross the Box Canyon Dam at Lake Siskiyou and turn left 0.2 miles further onto the paved road to Castle Lake, 7.2 miles along. At the 6-mile point where the road turns sharply right, there is a pullout on the left with a magnificent view of Mt. Shasta. It's worth a stop. Park in Castle Lake parking lot at the end of the road. There are restrooms. Access is free.

5. Vista Point Trail

EFFORT: Minimal
LENGTH: 0.3 miles
GEOLOGICAL FEATURE(S): Erosional Features
LOCATION: Castle Crags State Park

Description: This little trail to a fantastic view of Castle Crags is a good place to start your exploration of this park because this may well be the best view you'll get of its namesake rock formation.

The Crags, easily viewed from Interstate 5 between Dunsmuir and Castella as they jut up to 6,000 feet high, are dramatic granite spires named for their likeness to the turrets of a castle. The pluton (body of intrusive igneous rock) that formed the Crags about 170 million years ago resulted from magma welling up underground and cooling slowly.

It is here that the North American plate overrides several smaller oceanic plates. As this subduction occurs, rocks are heated and scraped off of the oceanic plate, mix with sea water and form California's state rock serpentine.

Later yet, glaciers moved through the area, carving the rock into the interesting jagged forms we see today.

During the nineteenth century, this formation was called *Castle del Diablo*, Spanish for Castle of the Devil. Earlier than that, however, the local Indian legends identified the Crags as home to an evil spirit.

The earliest European visitors to this area were fur traders, and included Michael La Framboise, who led parties of Hudson Bay Company trappers from 1830 to 1843 through the Shasta Valley and Sacramento River Valley. He founded the base of French Camp near present-day Stockton and established a well-used trail leading north into Oregon, known as Michael's Trail. The trails followed by the fur trappers would later be used by immigrants and miners pouring in from the east and cattle ranchers in the Great Valley. La Framboise mapped the area and named some of the features. One such map has been preserved, in which he named Castle Crags the "Needles" and Mt. Shasta, "Sasty Peak."

After the Gold Rush brought a large influx of white men, relationships with the Native Americans became strained. In 1855, the Battle of Castle Crags broke out, marking the beginning of the long and disastrous Modoc War that we'll talk more about in the Modoc Plateau chapter. The primary site of fighting was at the northwest end of the Crags between Battle Rock and Castle Lake.

Gold wasn't the only mineral mined in this area. Chromium mines were operated here as late as the 1950's. In the Castella area, you'll find a few historic buildings dating from the days when Castle Crags was a flourishing resort area. The mineral springs here attracted many visitors in the late 1800's and early 1900's.

Castle Crags

Walk up the steep trail to a picnic area and the lookout where you'll see the cream of the landmark crop—Mt. Shasta to the north, Castle Crags to the west, and Grey Rocks to the southwest—three neighboring landmarks made up of distinctly different materials and geologic histories. Mt. Shasta is a beautiful Cascade-range stratovolcano of andesite and dacite that we'll get much better acquainted with in the next chapter. Grey Rocks are metamorphic greenstone and slate that has been thrust upward at a dramatic angle. The Crags, as we mentioned earlier, are granite that was formed by magma cooling underground.

This is an inspiring place for lunch, but be prepared for sweat bees if you have food. They were particularly infuriating and persistent when we were here in August.

Directions: From Redding, go north 50 miles on Interstate 5 to the Castella exit. Or go south about six miles from Dunsmuir. Follow the signs to the park and pay a day-use fee. Just past the entrance kiosk, turn right towards the campground and continue past the campground until the road becomes a single lane winding up the side of the mountain. Honk when you come to blind corners, as traffic goes both directions, and proceed slowly. Park in the Vista Point parking area at the end of the road. There is a toilet adjacent to the parking area and a couple of picnic tables at Vista Point above the parking area. The trail begins on the east side of the parking lot.

6. Crags Trail

EFFORT: Difficult
LENGTH: 5.4 miles
GEOLOGICAL FEATURE(S): Erosional Features
LOCATION: Castle Crags State Park

Description: If you want to get close to the Crags rather than just look at them from a distance, this is your route, as it's the only trail that goes into their realm. It goes steeply up to the base of Castle Dome to a height of 4,900 feet with an elevation gain of 2,250 feet. You must be strong and sure-footed for this climb, but the payoff at the top is well worth the effort. Views up there among the bare rock are staggering.

From the parking area, look up at the Crags and locate the tall, dominant, rounded spire, distinctive among the other spiky ones. That's Castle Dome. Like other granite domes in California, particularly in Yosemite National Park, this one was created by a process called "exfoliation" or sheeting. Exposed to rain, wind, and cold, they shed layers. The result, after several layers are removed, is a rounded boulder.

Walk back up the road about 40 yards to the trailhead. The trail starts at the south side of the Dome and follows a crack up along the east side to a saddle below the granite turrets. Begin in a shady forest of Douglas fir, giant incense cedar, and a few oaks on a needle-carpeted path. In spring, you may pass blooming shooting stars and Indian warrior. A wide variety of plant and animal life can be found in the park, including over 300 species of wildflowers, one of which, the Castle Crags harebell, is found nowhere else.

After a quarter mile, you'll reach a trail junction. The trail heading dramatically upward is your path, the Crags Trail.

Continue through the forest. After 1.3 miles, you come upon a sudden view of the Crags. From here an optional quarter mile spur trail on the left leads to Indian Springs at the southern edge of Castle Crags. There, a cool spring provides some relief among bigleaf maples and dogwoods.

Continue climbing up above the tree line and into the Castle Crags Wilderness. Enjoy breathtaking mountain views along this trail, dominated by Mt. Shasta. As you climb into the Crags, you'll leave the shade behind and enter switchbacks up the stark granite cliffs. What you'll notice as you near them is that there are an infinite number of spires, not just the handful you notice from a distance. And soon you're walking among them.

Castle Dome (California Geological Survey)

Finally you'll reach a saddle at the western base of Castle Dome. This is the end of the trail. Gaze triumphantly over your dominion with a fine view of Mt. Shasta to the north. One of the nearby rock towers is Mount

Hubris, a popular rock climbing destination. Just west of trail's end is a cluster of smaller domes. One of these is known as Observation Deck, as it gives particularly splendid views. You can get on top of it with some careful maneuvering.

Return by the same path.

Directions: From Redding, go north 50 miles on Interstate 5 to the Castella exit. Or go south about six miles from Dunsmuir. Follow the signs to the park and pay a day-use fee. Just past the entrance kiosk, turn right towards the campground and continue past the campground until the road becomes a single lane winding up the side of the mountain. Honk when you come to blind corners, as traffic goes both directions, and proceed slowly. Park in the Vista Point parking area at the end of the road. There is a toilet adjacent to the parking area and a couple of picnic tables at Vista Point above the parking area.

7. Pacific Crest Trail – Castle Crags Segment

EFFORT: Moderate
LENGTH: 4.0 miles
GEOLOGICAL FEATURE(S): Erosional Features
LOCATION: Castle Crags State Park

Description: Ten miles of the Pacific Crest Trail runs through Castle Crags State Park. You can hike a fairly easy section with great views of Grey Rocks and the Crags from Vista Point to Winton Canyon, the route we have chosen to describe here. It's a tame two miles to our destination. There are no good picnic spots on this trail, so we recommend leaving your lunch behind to enjoy at Vista Point upon your return.

Walk back down the road about 40 yards to the trailhead. Walk through the forest for 0.25 miles on a smooth, shady trail. At the junction where Crags Trail (previous hike) veers off up and left, turn onto it and climb some steep switchbacks. You will soon reach a four-way junction. Turn left onto the Pacific Crest Trail. Right, the PCT continues on down to Interstate 5.

Generally uphill, steadily, but not too steeply, this trail takes you through a mixed conifer and oak forest. After a while, views open up on the left, giving you a sweeping panorama of the surrounding mountains to the south. Reaching a junction with Bob's Hat Trail at about a mile, continue on the PCT. Bob's Hat joins you for a moment, and then veers off to the right. At about this point, you'll be able to see Interstate 5 down below. The traffic hum from that major artery will be noticeable on this trail for a while as you walk parallel to it.

Round a bend and get an eyeful of Grey Rocks at 1.3 miles. Continuing, you get your first view of Castle Crags. The trail curves around a bend, turning to head north. You'll notice that the dirt underfoot and on the hill to your right turns red at this point due to iron in the soil. Along this red dirt trail you'll have some of your best views of the Crags. With intermittent views of the granite spires through the trees, you'll notice the sound of rushing water nearing.

At 1.5 miles, enter the Castle Crags Wilderness (signed). A few more feet brings you to the edge of a creek, amusingly signed "No Name Creek." If you need to take a break, this is a good spot to sit on a log in the shade and rest.

Continuing on the trail, you'll notice that the path is getting rockier and hotter as you traipse past manzanita on an open hillside. This open area gives good views of Grey Rocks. Notice the granite outcrop beside the trail just before you reach a wooden bridge at 1.7 miles. This is the same rock that comprises Castle Crags. The bridge spans Winton Canyon, which is flanked by blackberry bushes. A thin ribbon of water falls down a sheer bank here before ducking under the bridge through a narrow channel on its way down the hill.

Soon you will cross a creek bed, dry if you're here in summer, and then arrive at pretty Indian Creek at just under 2.0 miles. Rest a moment and enjoy this lovely spot. The creek is clear and cool. Picturesque leafy plants growing among the rocks in the creek make it seem more like a landscaper's creation than a natural stream.

You can turn around here if you've gone far enough, but if you continue for just a short distance further, you will get one last good view of the Crags from a different angle than you normally see them. Just past the creek, you emerge into the open sun on a granite cliff. Turning to look behind you, take in the Crags high above.

You can continue further if you like, but, having come for views of the Crags, we turned back here after two miles. For the duration of this hike, we met no one else until we were on our way back and passed a PCT hiker on his way into the wilderness.

Directions: From Redding, go north 50 miles on Interstate 5 to the Castella exit. Or go south about six miles from Dunsmuir. Follow the signs to the park and pay a day-use fee. Just past the entrance kiosk, turn right towards the campground and continue past the campground until the road becomes a single lane winding up the side of the mountain. Honk when you come to blind corners, as traffic goes both directions, and proceed slowly. Park in the Vista Point parking area at the end of the road. There is a toilet adjacent to the parking area and a couple of picnic tables at Vista Point above the parking area. The trail begins on the east side of the parking lot.

8. Samwel Cave Nature Trail

EFFORT: Minimal
LENGTH: 1.5 miles
GEOLOGICAL FEATURE(S): Caves
LOCATION: Shasta-Trinity National Forest

Description: Samwel Cave is a Permian limestone cave once visited as a holy place by the native Wintu who believed the cave was inhabited by bear spirits. They knew it as "Sa-Wal" (Grizzly Bear Cave). Artifacts have been found here that are even older, from an unknown prehistoric culture. The remains of a prehistoric giant ground sloth, cave bear, and eagle bones were found at the bottom of a 75-foot pit in the cave. Also found there was the skeleton of a girl. One of the Wintu legends tells of three girls who went into the cave to bathe in the pool on advice of an old woman who promised they would find strong, brave husbands if they did so. One of the girls fell to her death in the dark. Considering the skeleton, perhaps there is some truth to this tale, which gave the cave the alternative name, Cave of the Lost Maiden.

The trail offers some fine views of Lake Shasta along with the history and geology lesson. You can walk the trail to the entrance of the cave where a gate bars entry into the interior of the cave. However, if you have the skill and experience, the cave may be explored with a permit from the Shasta Lake Visitor Center at Mountain Gate. This is a rare and exciting spelunking opportunity in California. Unfortunately, most of the crystalline formations inside have been removed by souvenir hunters, but squeezing through muddy passages underground is still tremendous fun. If you choose to enter and explore the cave, make sure you're prepared with the proper equipment and a couple of companions. Never go caving alone.

This is a self-guiding interpretive trail explaining the Wintu legends surrounding the cave. The trail starts at the lakeshore. Keep in mind that in historical times, the McCloud River ran through this canyon and there was no Lake Shasta. The cave entrance lies 355 feet above the original riverbed in a limestone cliff, making it harder to get to in earlier times.

Above the McCloud Arm of the lake are towering grey limestone mountains formed from ocean sediments that accumulated 200 - 300 million years ago. The Grey Rocks, as they are known, contain the fossilized remains of corals, snails, clams and other sea creatures that existed in prehistoric times.

If you're approaching this trail by road, you'll use an informal route to get to it. Take the steep trail from the parking area down to the interpretive trail. You will alight shortly before the trail reaches the cave, but to do the trail as intended, you need to walk back to its start. From the trailhead, walk southeast toward the cave, reading the signs as you go. The trail ends at a locked gate inside the cave antechamber, open enough to the outside to explore without a flashlight. The sign here tells of the important archaeological finds deeper in the cave. This is the end of the interpretive trail.

Return to the spot where you first reached the trail and climb back up to the parking area.

Directions: From Interstate 5, exit at Gilman Road 18 miles north of Redding. Go east 16 miles to McCloud River Bridge. Cross the bridge and continue on gravel Fenders Ferry Road 2.8 miles to a turnout on the right. There is no sign and no facilities. An alternate approach to this trail is by boat at Point McCloud just south of the McCloud Bridge Campground. The McCloud River day-use area on Gilman Road is a great place for a picnic, by the way.

9. Lake Shasta Caverns

EFFORT: Moderate
LENGTH: N/A
GEOLOGICAL FEATURE(S): Caves
LOCATION: Shasta-Trinity National Forest

Description: For a very different caving experience from that of the previous hike, visit this beautiful limestone show cave on a guided tour. For the price of admission, you get a boat trip across Lake Shasta and a bus ride up the steep mountainside with scenic lake views along the way. These caverns were first opened to the public on May 30, 1964. Prior to that, around the turn of the century, this cave and nearby Samwel Cave were studied extensively by the Department of Anthropology of the University of California.

In summer (Memorial Day to Labor Day), tours depart every half hour, 9:00 am to 3:00 pm and take about two hours. The rest of the year, daily but fewer tours are conducted. Bring your camera, as photos are allowed inside the cave. Purchase tickets at the visitor center and then walk downhill on a dusty road to the boat dock. You will be rafted across the lake on a short cruise amid the roar of the boat engine. On the other side, walk up a steep hill to the staging area and bus stop. There is a picnic area here. We decided that these two short, steep hikes are designed to get you ready for the stairways in the cave.

The bus ride takes you up a precipitous one-lane road overlooking the McCloud arm of Lake Shasta. You are dropped off in a waiting room with information about the caverns and area wildlife. There are restrooms here. A tour guide will take charge of your group and lead you to the cavern entrance, a doorway into the lower levels of the cave. During the tour, you'll climb through the caverns and exit up above.

The cave is quite wet and has a humidity level of 95%, so it is not very comfortable. Wear light clothing and anticipate perspiring. Even though the cave is cool, you will not need a jacket. Normally, you can expect to have a diverse mix of people on a cave tour, with a varying level of fitness, so the pace is usually driven by the slower folks. But our particular group turned out to be quite spry, racing up the narrow staircases with alacrity, so we got a workout and had time to spare at the end of the tour.

As you're led through the cave, you will see gorgeous examples of flowstone and draperies. The typical cave formations are here—stalactites, stalagmites, soda straws, angel wings, cave bacon—along with a small group of the rare crystalline formations known as helictites in the Discovery Room. As always, you are warned against touching any of the crystals. This is a living cave and the speleothems are still forming. The guide will point out the different types of crystal structures and explain how they are formed, and will also shine a light on the formations that resemble Santa Claus, animals, etc., to entertain the kids.

On one wall you'll see where the first known white man in the cave signed his name, James A. Richardson, November 3, 1878, with the carbide from his lamp.

The tour proceeds through several rooms and up lots of stairs to the final chamber, which is magnificent and a fitting climax for the tour. This room houses huge formations that you can admire from benches as you rest up after the climb.

After exiting the cave, you'll make your way down many flights of stairs with a view of Lake Shasta below to the left. The trail ends back at the waiting room. From here, a bus takes you back down the hill, and then you walk down to the boat dock. After another boat excursion across the lake, a bus takes you up the steep dirt road to the visitor center.

Directions: From Interstate 5 in Redding, drive north across Lake Shasta to the Lake Shasta Caverns exit. Turn off and proceed east, past Bailey Cove and Holiday Harbor to the large parking lot outside the visitor center. There are restrooms, a gift shop, and a tour fee is charged.

10. Natural Bridge Interpretive Trail

EFFORT: Minimal
LENGTH: 0.5 miles
GEOLOGICAL FEATURE(S): Erosional Features
LOCATION: Shasta-Trinity National Forest

Description: This is an interpretive trail to a natural limestone arch, somewhat of a rarity in California. Pick up a pamphlet at the trailhead, which will explain the natural and human history of the area.

The native Wintu tell of a man with a huge bundle of hides coming along, tired and hungry, and slipping off the bundle. It rolled into Hayfork Creek and formed the natural bridge, or "bundle of hides," "Kok-Chee-Shup-Chee" to the Wintu. The color and texture of the bridge inspired this legend.

Names and dates etched into the limestone tell of early pioneers passing by. The ravine over which the arch stands has also given its name to a bloody confrontation between the local law enforcement and a band of Wintu. The Bridge Gulch Massacre took place in 1852 after a group of Wintu murdered a local rancher. The sheriff and his party traveled through this canyon to the tribal camp and shot everyone they found there, including women and children. According to the story, only three children survived the massacre.

You begin the trail at the picnic area and continue straight at the fork. You reach the arch almost immediately. It has a span of over 200 feet across the narrow ravine. Its opening is about 50 feet high. Over time, water has carved out the soft limestone below the arch to form this bridge. The trail brochure covers the geological, mythical, and historical aspects surrounding the arch. Unfortunately, this site has been marred in recent years by graffiti.

Continuing up Bridge Gulch, you'll come to the site of the historic massacre. This is halfway along. The trail then loops back on the other side of the canyon. You'll come to a place where a scout from the sheriff's party stood on the arch and spotted the Wintu encampment. Past this, you will encounter a steep section of the trail, and then be returned to the trailhead.

Directions: From Hayfork, travel about 4 miles east on Highway 3 to its intersection with County Road 302 (Wildwood Road). Turn south onto County Road 302 and travel about 4 miles to Forest Service Road 31N11 and on to the Natural Bridge Picnic Area a mile further. Parking, toilets, and picnicking are available at either end of the arch. Both parking areas are reached off of the same road. Access is free. This site is open from May 20 through November 1.

SECTION 2

THE CASCADES

The Cascade Range is a string of volcanoes extending from Mt. Garibaldi in British Columbia down to Mt. Lassen in Northern California. These volcanoes are the distinguishing characteristic of the Cascade Province, most of which is located in Oregon and Washington. Only the southern tip of the chain is present in California. However, of the twelve major volcanoes within the range, California's beloved Mt. Shasta, at 14,162 feet, is the second highest, coming in second only to Mt. Rainier in Washington. The two major California cones, Mt. Shasta and Mt. Lassen, are spectacularly beautiful landmarks on view from many miles around.

Visible geology is everywhere in this province, primarily in the form of relatively recent volcanic activity and glaciation. Mt. Shasta has been a very active volcano, erupting about every 600 years. Four of its major eruptive episodes have occurred since the last glaciers retreated, in the last 10,000 to 12,000 years, the most recent eruption being only 200 years ago.

Mt. Lassen has the distinction of being one of only two volcanoes to erupt in the twentieth century in the continental United States with a series of eruptions between 1914 and 1917. The other eruption was Mt. St. Helens in Washington, an event many of us remember.

The source of the Cascade Range activity lies deep beneath the mountains and is a continuation of the story of plate tectonics we introduced in the previous chapter. The geology throughout California is dominated by the stressful meeting of the Pacific and North American Plates. As the dense oceanic plate dives beneath the lighter, more buoyant continental plate, the oceanic material begins to melt. This molten rock then begins to rise to the surface, making its way through the cold, brittle continental crust. The result on the surface is a volcano.

As the molten rock rises to the surface, it interacts with the pre-existing continental rocks, producing different magmas with varying chemical compositions. The ultimate result of this interaction is different types of rocks. If the molten rock finds its way to the surface with very little interaction with pre-existing rocks, the rock formed at the surface will be the same composition as the original melt, *basalt*. You've probably used basalt in your backyard grill and may have referred to it as "lava rock."

A different type of rock is formed if the oceanic crustal melt interacts with pre-existing continental rock. The composition of the magma changes as the pre-existing rock partially melts and mixes with the original magma. Molecules of seawater, carried deep into the earth by the subducting plates, are released from the minerals in which they are trapped, lowering the melting point of the continental rocks and helping the melting action along. The resulting rock type from this sort of interaction is called *andesite*, named for the Andes Mountains. Andesite is commonly light gray in color, lighter than basalt because of its higher silica content, which results in the formation of light colored minerals such as quartz and potassium feldspar. Andesite is the most common volcanic rock in the Cascades.

Mt. St. Helens, 2 years after eruption (USGS)

A third type of rock results when the original melt is formed strictly from continental crust. This melt does not involve oceanic crust at all, and there is so much silica in the rocks that free quartz may form. This type of rock is called *rhyolite*. If it cools very quickly, too quickly for individual minerals to form, the rock is *obsidian*, a type of volcanic glass. Glass Mountain and Little Glass Mountain in the nearby Modoc Plateau are examples of obsidian lava flows. If the magma never reaches the surface but stays deep underground, it will cool slowly and large minerals will form, resulting in the familiar rock *granite*, the type of rock that forms the bulk of the Sierra Nevadas, as well as Castle Crags on the border of the Cascade and Klamath provinces. These are the main types of volcanic rocks we'll find in the Cascades and in the next chapter, the Modoc Plateau. Though the types of rocks are similar in the two provinces, we'll soon see how their formation varied greatly because of the differences in the types of volcanoes that produced them.

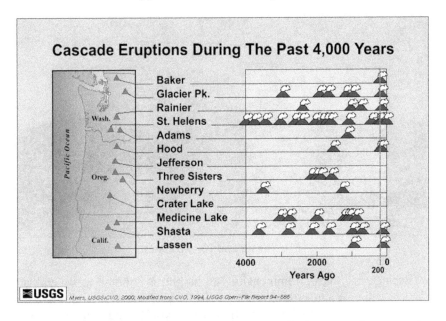

The major volcanoes in the Cascades are called *stratovolcanoes*, also known as composite cones. Stratovolcanoes are classic steep-sided volcanoes like Mt. Hood and Mt. Fuji in Japan. A sequence of eruptions over thousands of years results in layers building from the lava flows and pyroclastic debris. Also visible within the Cascades are cinder cones, small cone-shaped landforms composed of fragments thrown from a central or secondary vent. You can easily see two of these in wide vistas of the region—Black Butte near Mt. Shasta and the Whaleback to the north. A third type of volcano, a shield volcano, forms a broad, gently sloping mountain. A shield volcano slopes so gently that it is often not even visible to the person on the ground. A well-known California example is the Medicine Lake volcano, which is discussed in the Modoc Plateau chapter.

Mt. Shasta is a huge stratovolcano built by eruptions from four main volcanic events issuing from four separate vents. It has taken approximately 200,000 years for the present-day Shasta to form, with major cone building, including the summit, taking place within the last 10,000 years. But this site has been volcanically active for much longer. Shasta sits atop much older basalts and andesites, indicating that lava has been flowing here for at least 600,000 years. The two most active volcanic cones on Mount Shasta have resulted in two distinct and easily visible peaks—Shastina on the western flank and Hotlum Cone at the summit. The main rock type is andesite, although Shastina is composed primarily of dacite, a rock with a higher silica content than andesite, but not so much silica as to be considered granite.

Mt. Shasta and its two cones

Because of Shasta's immensity and height, it is home to several old glaciers, the Wintun, Konwakiton, Bolam, Whitney, Hotlum, Mud Creek, and Watkins. Above the timberline, you'll find stark rock, few plants, ice, rugged canyons, and cold winds. But the mountain also offers an astoundingly beautiful wild landscape of colorful volcanic rock, delicate wildflowers, sheltered green valleys, waterfalls, pure, natural springs, and the best views you could dream of. And even if you aren't interested in climbing into the glaciers' domain, many of these wonders are also available with just a couple of hours investment for the day-hiker.

If peaks are your thing, there are also plenty of striking cinder cones in this region, and, since it is human nature to want to climb every mountain, those who came before you have blazed trails to the tops of them all. But there are flat trails as well, so everyone will be happy walking in the beautiful Cascades.

Trails of the Cascades:

11. Pluto Caves
12. The Whaleback
13. Avalanche Gulch Trail
14. Brewer Creek Trail
15. Black Butte Trail
16. Squaw Meadows Trail
17. Burney Falls Loop
18. Subway Cave
19. Spattercone Trail
20. Cinder Cone Trail
21. Lassen Peak Summit Trail
22. Bumpass Hell Trail
23. Cold Boiling Lake Trail
24. Chaos Crags
25. Devils Kitchen Trail
26. Boiling Springs Lake Trail
27. Terminal Geyser

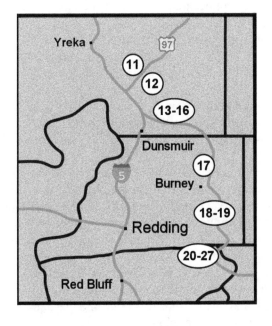

11. Pluto Caves

EFFORT: Minimal
LENGTH: 1+ mile
GEOLOGICAL FEATURE(S): Volcanism, Caves
LOCATION: Klamath National Forest

Description: Pluto Caves are large lava tubes created by Mt. Shasta eruptions. You'll find a discussion of lava tube formation in the introduction to this guide if you need a refresher, but the process boils down to this: liquid lava flows and the air-exposed lava cools and hardens, creating a shell through which liquid lava continues to flow and eventually drains out, leaving a hollow tube. These channels come in all sizes. The one here is quite large. The main tube has collapsed in three places to provide portals into the tunnel. If you're in the area and don't have time to detour out to Lava Beds National Monument, this is a good example of a tube more easily reached, but get out to Lava Beds (next section) when you can because it's one of the best places in the world to see lava tubes.

Whenever you go caving, bring more than one light source and don't go alone. Even in an easy to navigate cave like this, there is still danger from the uneven floor and the likelihood that nobody will be nearby if you need help.

From the parking area, you'll see a rock-edged walkway leading to the cave entrance. It's about a half mile to the cave. The trail is level and easy. The cave entrance will appear before you, fifteen feet high—no stooping required.

Walk into the cave on a sandy floor and notice right away that the temperature is much cooler than outside. Where the ceiling has collapsed, you'll have to climb over rocky debris. Wear sturdy shoes.

The tube is extremely large, sometimes as wide as 90 feet and as high as 50 feet. Marvel at this lava channel as you proceed about 250 yards into it, imagining it filled with molten rock coursing downhill. Examine the ceiling for signs the drip features known as *lavacicles*. As the lava begins to drain out of the tube, the still-liquid material left on the ceiling and walls runs and drips until it cools and hardens mid-drip. These features are common in lava tubes.

You may encounter bats and will no doubt see graffiti. When you reach a wall of rock, you've gone as far as you can. Turn around and go back.

Lavacicles

Directions: From Weed, take Highway 97 north and drive 12 miles to County Road A12. Turn left and drive 3 more miles, and turn left. There is a telephone post signed for Pluto Caves to mark the road. Drive down the dirt road about 0.2 miles to the parking area. Access is free. Note: While you are in the area, the imposing metal sculptures of the Living Memorial Sculpture Garden are worth a visit. You'll find the garden one mile beyond where you turned off Highway 97 on Road A12.

12. The Whaleback

EFFORT: Difficult
LENGTH: 3.0 miles
GEOLOGICAL FEATURE(S): Volcanism
LOCATION: Klamath National Forest

Description: This is a hike up to the top of the Whaleback, named for its resemblance to a diving whale. It is an 8,528-foot high volcano, a cinder cone with a collapsed center that sits prominently in the high desert landscape just south of the Oregon border. It is located north of Mt. Shasta, so the views of that majestic peak from the summit are unrivaled. And because the Whaleback stands alone, looming high over its territory, the views in all directions are unobscured from the summit. The higher you go, the more fantastic they get.

Cinder cones around the world look very similar, especially if they are recent enough that vegetation hasn't had time to gain a foothold. The cone is created when the lava explodes into the air and solidifies into rock before reaching the ground. The ejecta from a cinder cone is typically scoria, a lightweight volcanic rock riddled with *vesicles*, pockets that contained gas bubbles during eruption. Scoria can come in black, brown, gray and red. Because scoria resembles ash produced in a coal furnace, it was historically called cinders. A volcano that produces such cinders has become known as a cinder cone. Scoria resembles another vesicular volcanic rock, pumice, a type of volcanic glass whose gas content renders an extremely lightweight final material and can be used to polish your calloused feet or, when finely ground, your teeth. Once ejected into the air, the cinders fall back down around the central vent, building a conical mass of loose material. It grows higher and steeper as the cinders rain down, eventually causing the slopes to slide under the weight of the new material. The debris comes to rest when the sides of the cone reach a stable angle of steepness. This angle, about 35 degrees, is called the *angle of repose*. Most cinder cones have that same angle of repose, since they are composed of the same type of material, which is why they all look more or less the same, varying mainly in size.

The cinder cones in this area are extremely symmetrical and relatively young. They have sparse vegetation and are covered with loose debris. You'll find a similar mountain nearer Mt. Shasta in Black Butte (Hike #15), which is even more classic in appearance. But what this mountain has that you won't find there is a well-defined crater at the top. Some volcanoes get covered up, choked and smothered by their own ejecta or they literally blow their tops off so you can't see where the primary eruption took place. Not so with this one. The main vent will be obvious.

There is no maintained trail; you basically just go up 1.5 miles and then back down when you're ready. There is an old jeep trail you can follow at the start, heading south, but before it starts heading downhill, you'll need to head uphill, straight up on a path of your own choosing. Once you reach the summit, traverse the crater rim to the middle summit, the high point of this trail, and enjoy the views.

Directions: From Weed, take Highway 97 north for 16 miles. Turn right on Deer Mountain Road and drive 4 miles to Deer Mountain Snowmobile Park. Turn right on Forest Road 19 (42N12) and drive south about 3 miles to Forest Road 42N24. Turn right and drive 3 miles to a gate and park. Access is free.

13. Avalanche Gulch Trail

EFFORT: Difficult
LENGTH: 10.0 miles
GEOLOGICAL FEATURE(S): Glaciation, Volcanism
LOCATION: Shasta-Trinity National Forest

Description: Alternately known as the John Muir Route or Sisson Trail, this is a climb to the 14,162-foot summit of magnificent Mt. Shasta, leaving from the 6,900-foot high Bunny Flat trailhead, the most frequently used starting point for Shasta climbers. Avalanche Gulch is considered the easiest route to the summit and is classified as non-technical.

Mt. Shasta, dominating the landscape from all over northern California, is an irresistible challenge to many and an inspiration to many more. Since prehistoric times, its remote grandeur has encouraged fanciful legends in the human mind, and continues to do so in modern times. It has supposedly served, among other things, as the birthplace of humanity, residence of fairies and dwarves, home to Big Foot, and as a popular alien landing site. Harmonic Convergence festivals have been held here, and a race of magical people from the lost continent of Lemuria are said to live inside the mountain [see inset next page].

Although we doubt that you'll get a glimpse of any of the supernatural creatures rumored to be present, we think that the mountain's natural charms are enough of an attraction for anyone. You don't have to climb all the way to the summit. Climbing even a couple of miles up Mt. Shasta is an enchanting experience.

Before we get to the trail description, let's get all the warnings out of the way. Sign in at the registry station before setting out. Hike this route in early summer, and take an ice axe, crampons, insulating layers, and a windproof parka if you're going all the way to the summit. Also, to hike above 10,000 feet in the Mt. Shasta Wilderness area, you must have a permit. The permit requires that you pack out everything, including your fecal matter. Helmets are recommended to protect against falling rocks, a common hazard on this route. Wear sunscreen at all times, and carry lots of water. The weather is highly variable, depending on the wind conditions. Check conditions at a ranger station before setting out. Do not make this trip alone. It is best to go with someone who has already done it and knows the ropes. Finally, for one reason or another, plenty of people turn back, as you should if you are feeling unsure about your abilities. There are guided climbs to the summit offered by local commercial outfitters if you're insecure about trying it on your own. That's a good option for a first timer.

If the rewards of the trail are commensurate with the effort, you know this is going to be a totally awesome experience. The total length of the hike is between five and six miles with an altitude gain of over 7,000 feet. For experienced hikers, it usually takes between eight and ten hours to go up and between four and five hours to come down, depending on how much time you take for sightseeing, photography, etc. and how seriously you're affected by the thin atmosphere. After the first 1.5 miles, you can stop at the Sierra Club's Horse Camp, a cabin built in the 1920's, where there is spring water and sanitation facilities.

Just beyond the cabin, you're above the tree line, walking through talus slopes and pumice.

LEMURIA

The Lemurian-Shasta connection began with the puzzle of how lemurs ended up in India. Lemuria was a term coined to describe a hypothetical continent, which was later submerged, bridging the Indian Ocean and allowing migration of lemurs from Madagascar to India.

One tale inspired by this hypothesis claims that the people of Lemuria were highly advanced and that they escaped their doomed land. Towards the end of the nineteenth century and continuing into the early twentieth, a few articles and books appeared suggesting the Lemurians had settled inside Mount Shasta. The story really gained speed in 1925 when a writer named Selvius published an article in which he claimed that a respected scientist, Edgar Lucian Larkin, had seen a Lemurian village on Shasta through a telescope on several occasions. The legend has been built upon over the years and has persisted into the present day.

From Horse Camp, continue on the trail up Avalanche Gulch to Lake Helen near 10,400 feet. This is a popular campsite for hikers spending the night. Don't be surprised if there are dozens of other tents pitched around you. Melt snow and filter the water here for the next day's ascent, and try to get an early start.

Leaving Lake Helen, the route becomes steeper and heads over the snow-filled Avalanche Gulch. Crampons will be required from this point onward. Later in summer, you can hike up to iron-stained Red Banks without crampons, but the danger from falling rocks is more serious. The rocks along the gulch will provide a sort of staircase when the snow has melted. Along the way, you'll have the Red Banks up above as an enduring landmark.

Veer to the right towards Thumb Rock and climb through one of the passages in the Red Banks. The red pumice here has been dated from a 9,600 to 9,700 year old eruption. If you prefer, you can go around the

Red Banks and over the saddle above Thumb Rock. On the way back, some people slide down the snow, so consider bringing along some waterproof pants. It's much quicker to slide, but this may not be possible after May or early June when the snow is melting and rocks begin to protrude from the snow field.

Once you're past Red Banks and up Misery Hill, you'll be on the summit plateau. Look to your left for stunning views into Shastina, Shasta's second major cone. You can also see Whitney Glacier, named after geologist Josiah Dwight Whitney, and first written about by Clarence King after an 1870 expedition. It is the longest glacier in California and resembles glaciers found in the Alps. Whitney Glacier flows from just below the peak of Shasta in a northwesterly direction through the valley between Mt. Shasta and Shastina. The ice has been measured at 126 feet thick.

Because this volcano is isolated and surrounded by much lower terrain, you can see for vast distances. If the air is clear, all of the Sacramento Valley will be visible to the south. You also get quite an overview of the Modoc Plateau and its expansive lava fields. Look for Mt. Lassen, California's other major Cascade volcano to the east.

Follow Misery Hill to the Summit Ballfield and on up to high point to the north. Evidence of present-day thermal activity exists only in these highest places on the mountain. Just to the west is a cluster of small hot springs. On top of the Hotlum-Bolam Ridge are sulfurous fumaroles where volcanic gases escape from below. Up here, you see firsthand that this volcano is definitely not extinct.

The way back to the trailhead is the same route you used to come up.

Directions: From Mt. Shasta City, drive east on Lake Street. Turn left onto Everitt Memorial Highway and follow it up the flank of Mt. Shasta as it winds toward the trailhead at Bunny Flat about 11 miles from town. The road is open year round to this point. Access is free. Restrooms are available. Permits to climb into the wilderness area are required. They're free and can be obtained at the Mt. Shasta and McCloud Ranger Stations.

14. Brewer Creek Trail

EFFORT: Difficult
LENGTH: 6.0 miles
GEOLOGICAL FEATURE(S): Glaciation, Volcanism
LOCATION: Shasta-Trinity National Forest

Description: There are not many places in California that you can walk on a glacier, but Mount Shasta has seven permanent ice fields. A *glacier* is a mass of ice so large that it flows downhill under its own weight. Glaciers develop in places where some of the snowfall never melts, and eventually the pressure of the new, overlying snow converts the earlier snow into ice. The glacier tears off pieces of the underlying mountain as it moves and grinds up rock beneath it. It's an effective eroding force, carrying tons of rubble where it comes into contact with bedrock, grinding and polishing the rock it passes over. Glaciers also push piles of debris to the side and ahead of themselves, creating ridges called *moraines*. When the glacier is long gone, the moraines remain as evidence of its passage.

The movement of glaciers is not as slow and methodical as it may appear, and there is always a possibility of devastation on and below Mount Shasta. If the ice melts rapidly, lots of water coming down the mountain could turn into a huge debris flow, bringing down rocks and soil and creating danger to the communities below. Avalanches do happen on the mountain as well, and a sufficiently large one could bring massive amounts of debris to the valley. Such a huge debris flow is known to have occurred on Shasta's northern flank in the distant past. Much more recently, in September, 2014, in the midst of California's drought, a large chunk of the Konwakiton Glacier broke off and created a threatening mud slide that rattled some cages in the nearby town of McCloud. Fortunately, the McCloud River was able to contain the flood of water, mud, rocks and ice coming off the mountain.

In places where there were once glaciers that have long since melted, scientists can see the distinctive footprints that remain. Mountain valleys shaped by glacial erosion are U-shaped rather than V-shaped, like those carved by rivers. Other features that are left behind are moraines, cirques, and aretes. On other trails in this guide, we visit many of these features where no ice remains today, but during colder climate cycles vast sheets of ice covered North America. These former glaciers would dwarf those now covering the high valleys of Mount Shasta many times over. Nevertheless, the pockets of ice we'll be visiting are still big and powerful enough to dwarf us.

This trail takes you to Hotlum, Bolam, and Wintun glaciers on the northeast side of the mountain. Hotlum is the largest glacier on Shasta, containing some 1.3 billion cubic feet of ice.

Some people use this as a route to the summit of the mountain, but you don't have to go that far to enjoy the majesty of Shasta. It is 6 miles to the top, with a gain of almost 7,000 feet! For our hike, we will be going as far as the glaciers to get close-up views of them, but will not go to the top of the mountain. On this side of Shasta, above a certain height, it isn't really hiking any more, but mountain climbing.

The trail, a dirt path through the forest, is easy to follow up to the timberline. After the snow melts in summer, rangers mark the trails above that with bamboo wands. Hike the switchbacks up the forested slopes, enjoying the view from on high. For the first two miles, the trail heads south and southwest, and then turns to head west. After 2.5 miles, the trail will be harder to follow.

To get closer to the glaciers, climb higher, up to the saddle between the Wintun and Hotlum Glaciers. From here, you have excellent summit views, as well as intimate views of the ice. To walk on the glacier, you'll need the proper equipment, of course, but you can go this far with ordinary hiking. Make sure you take the time to look at the scoured faces of the rocks along the way, noting how they have been polished and scratched by the movement of ice.

The return route is the same.

Directions: From Mount Shasta City, take Highway 89 east to McCloud. Continue east 3.5 miles and turn left on Pilgrim Creek Road. Proceed 7.1 miles to Sugar Pine Butte Road (Forest Road 19) and turn left. Follow the signs to Brewer Creek Trailhead, turning left on Forest Road 42N02 and then left again on 42N10 to the end. Access is free.

15. Black Butte Trail

EFFORT: Moderate
LENGTH: 5.2 miles
GEOLOGICAL FEATURE(S): Volcanism
LOCATION: Shasta-Trinity National Forest

Description: Black Butte, once known as Muir Peak, is the big, brassy cone sitting beside Mt. Shasta, a prominent landmark visible from several of the other trails in this area and from the major transportation artery in this part of the state, Interstate 5. If you've traveled up and down California at all, you've no doubt passed it by and wondered what it would be like to climb. Time to find out!

Though most people would say that Mt. Shasta is a hundred times more beautiful than Black Butte to look at from a distance, we think the views from this mountain are in some ways superior. For one thing, you get views of Shasta, which you can't get when you're on it. For another thing, its shape and lack of vegetation gives you great views all the way up. On Shasta, which is massive, there are plenty of times you can't see any distance at all if you aren't way up near the top. At any rate, the experience of climbing Black Butte is completely different from hiking on Shasta.

This well-defined trail takes you up about 2,000 feet to the 6,325-foot summit, where you will have fantastic 360-degree views. Black Butte formed about 9,500 years ago through a series of eruptions, leaving this cluster of hornblende dacite plug domes. Compare it to Shastina, Mt. Shasta's second peak, which formed about the same time.

This trail was built by the Civilian Conservation Corps in the late 1930's to access a Forest Service fire lookout at the summit. Pack animals were used to bring supplies to the lookout. You'll see why the site was chosen once you get to the top.

Black Butte from I-5

Head out through a conifer forest, climbing steadily. There are some steep and rocky stretches, and your total climb will be 1,845 feet. Bring plenty of water and a hat, as there is not much shade, but the trail is easy to follow. As the trees thin, views open up before you of the Shasta Valley and surrounding peaks. Mt. Shasta itself looms right there beside you all the way.

The material alongside the trail is classic cinder cone stuff—lots of loose volcanic rock that rained down to form the conical mass around the eruptive center. From a distance, cinder cones often look highly symmetrical, pyramid-shaped, which they are, but as you walk on this mountain, unexpected features will reveal themselves. For instance, there's a canyon you didn't see from below. It's choked with rock and some hardy trees.

The trail swings wide around the mountain, traversing the north flank, then turning east to eventually reach tighter switchbacks up to the summit, sometimes crossing rough, rocky patches. As you near the summit, you'll be able to see the remnants of several eruptive cones, indicating an active volcanic history for Black Butte.

In addition to views, you may notice some pipes and concrete, remnants of the fire lookout tower that was removed in 1975. The base on which that tower stood is the high point of this trail and your ultimate destination. From this narrow perch, you have a total 360-degree view, taking in Mt. Shasta, Mt. Eddy, Shasta Valley, Castle Crags, and the Sacramento River Canyon.

Return the way you came.

Directions: From Interstate 5, take the Central Mt. Shasta exit and head east for 0.7 miles on Lake Street. Go left onto Everitt Memorial Highway. Proceed 2.2 miles, and turn left on a dirt road signed for Black Butte Trail. Stay on the main dirt road for approximately 2.5 miles. Where the dirt road crosses under the overhead power line, take the dirt road to the left. Go approximately 0.5 miles on this road to the trailhead. Parking is very limited. Access is free.

16. Squaw Meadows Trail

EFFORT: Moderate
LENGTH: Up to 8.0 miles
GEOLOGICAL FEATURE(S): Glaciation, Volcanism
LOCATION: Shasta-Trinity National Forest

Description: One of the best things about this hike is that most of the climbing is done in the car before you set out, and you can climb up the mountain a short or long distance and still have an adventure. The trailhead is at 7,800 feet high. Still, it's a steep climb with a gain of nearly 2,000 feet. But the scenery is fabulous and weirdly intriguing, and worth the attempt even if you only go a half mile up. Be prepared for cold temperatures and wind.

In the Ski Bowl parking lot, fill out your wilderness permit and take a moment to examine the map on display. You will see a rock-lined trail leading up the bowl to the right. This trail crosses the saddle above Green Butte and skirts the north side of Red Butte with its strange volcanic landscape. These colorful names are not misnomers. Because you are above the timberline on this trail, you'll have great views along its entire route. Watch for a natural spring along the way.

Wildflowers grow among the rocks, including the western anemone. But there are no trees in this harsh environment. It's cool and windy up here and the rocks are the main inhabitants. There are large boulders all around you, and ahead your view is of the colorful, highly altered green, yellow, red, and purple ridges. The rocks along the trail are colorful too—black, red, light gray, and pink. The vivid colors are a result of alteration of the original rocks by steam. Porous red lava rock like that used for landscaping is abundant. Evidence of the mountain's origin lies at your feet. There is *flow banding* apparent in the rocks—bands of different types and colors of rock indicating liquid flow patterns from when this material was molten.

As the trail winds upward, it becomes rougher, more rocky, and is sometimes indistinct. Even if you are tired, you will want to keep going because the landscape is so strange and wonderful. And just up above you Mud Creek Glacier is calling.

Below Red Butte, enter the natural passage called The Gate, which takes you between Red Butte and Sargents Ridge. Through the Gate, you will drop down into a canyon and an entirely different environment of mountain hemlocks and Shasta red fir. The trail is easier to follow now, taking you less than a mile to the upper meadow with its cool running streams and blooming wildflowers. This sublime, lush meadow is the destination for this hike.

From the meadow, look up for a view of Konwakiton Glacier. Return the way you came when you are rested.

Directions: From Mt. Shasta City, drive east on Lake Street. Turn left onto Everitt Memorial Highway and follow it up the flank of Mt. Shasta as it winds towards the trailhead at the old Ski Bowl parking lot at the end of the road. Access is free.

17. Burney Falls Trail

EFFORT: Minimal
LENGTH: 1.2 miles
GEOLOGICAL FEATURE(S): Volcanism
LOCATION: McArthur-Burney Falls Memorial State Park

Description: Located in the fascinating geological wonderland of northeastern California, a magnificent waterfall, Burney Falls, drops 129 feet in a wide and breathtaking tumult. One hundred million gallons of water fall daily into a deep mist-filled basin below it. The falls, sacred to native peoples, runs year-round, as it is fed from underground springs, so save this one for autumn when the other waterfalls are puny trickles. The waterfall was named after pioneer settler Samuel Burney who lived in the area in the 1850s. The park land, including the falls, was given to the state in the 1920s by another pioneer family named McArthur, hence the name of the park.

A self-guiding loop trail takes you around the falls and past several numbered stops illustrating the park's geology and flora. The trail is paved for a couple hundred yards.

From the parking lot, walk over to the walled overlook for your first look at the magnificent waterfall. Besides its volume, what you'll notice from this vantage point is the fascinating turquoise blue color of the water in the pool. We've never seen water quite this color before. You can also readily see how the two main torrents split around a hard cap of basalt at the top of the cliff. In this area, this volcanic layer lies beneath a layer of Pliocene lake sediments, which the water has eroded at the top of the falls. Under the basalt is a layer of volcanic lakebed sediments of ash and pumice mixed with sand from ancient Lake Britton. Layers of diatomaceous earth or diatomite are sandwiched in the cliff as well. Burney Creek has found several cracks and holes to spring out of along the porous clifftop. Much of the water comes pouring out of the wall below the main falls, seeping down through the basalt before emptying into the pool below. The pool is between 18 and 24 feet deep.

From the overlook, you'll also be able to see darting birds around the falls. The aptly-named black swift nests in the cliff, catching insects on the wing and alighting only in its nest. When you're ready, take the trail downhill to the edge of the pool at the base of the falls.

This is a very civilized trail, switchbacking wide to take you gently downhill. As you descend, approaching the waterfall, notice the drop in temperature. On the last leg of the trail, you'll feel the spray. Once you reach the base of the falls, you have already had the best experience you can have of this waterfall. If you have limited time, you can turn around here and walk back up to the parking lot.

For this hike, follow the trail to the right along the bank of Burney Creek downstream. On your left the creek runs robustly. On the right is a hillside covered with mossy basalt blocks, a talus slope. When you come to a bridge over the creek, turn right onto it. The trail continuing straight is Burney Creek Trail on its way to Lake Britton, another option if you have time. Across the wooden bridge, turn right at the bench, and then turn left to climb up to an overlook. A sign here tells you that you are now level with the top of Burney Falls, which you can see up ahead.

Burney Falls

From here, turn right and climb up a rock stairway away from the falls through a forest of Douglas fir, oak, cedar, and Ponderosa pine. Switchback up a hill with a split-rail fence on the right. A bench has been provided at the high point if you need to catch your breath.

The view from here is across the canyon. Continuing, the trail now turns south to follow the bank of the creek above the falls, leading you to a bridge. Turn left onto it and cross over Burney Creek. A sign on the other bank informs you that a half mile upstream the creek is completely underground. Detour to see that if you wish. To continue with the loop, turn right and then left to go up the paved trail to a road.

Once you gain the road, turn left onto a gravel trail and walk towards the park's entrance station. There are two benches positioned here to allow you a last look at the falls. The trail loops back toward the parking lot. Interpretive panels are positioned along this section of the trail, explaining the geology of the creek and falls.

Directions: From Redding take Highway 299 east to Burney. Go five miles further east to Highway 89, then north 5.8 miles to the park entrance on the left. Restrooms and picnic tables are adjacent to the parking area. There is a small day-use fee.

18. Subway Cave

EFFORT: Minimal
LENGTH: 0.3 miles
GEOLOGICAL FEATURE(S): Volcanism, Caves
LOCATION: Lassen National Forest

Description: If you've never been in a lava tube, this will be a thrilling experience, but be advised that small children may be frightened. This cave is easy to get to and takes only a few minutes to traverse. Bring a flashlight, preferably two, and go through one of the largest lava tubes open to the public. You'll be able to stand upright through the entire length of the tube. At 46 degrees, it's a little chilly, so dress accordingly.

From the parking area, find the trailhead on the northeast side. Walk a short distance on a dirt trail to the cave mouth. The tube is short, but typical, with its smooth walls and ceiling drip features. You can imagine the molten rock surging through this chamber like water through a garden hose. As the flow ebbed, dropping below the ceiling, the heat remelted some sections that then dripped. As the drippy sections cooled, the drip features were preserved.

The floor is rough, so wear sturdy shoes and watch your footing. Near the end of the tube, there's a gas bubble in the floor, an interesting remnant. The loop trail leads you up and over the tube once you've passed through, but we recommend going back through the way you came, as there is nothing of special interest on the overhead path back to the parking lot.

Entrance to Subway Cave

When touring a lava tube or any cave, you have to stop about midway and turn off your flashlight. Total darkness is something we rarely experience above ground, so it does leave an impression on most people.

Directions: Located about a quarter mile north of the junction of Highway 44 and Highway 89 near Old Station, across the road from Cave Campground. Access is free. There are no facilities at the trailhead.

19. Spattercone Nature Trail

EFFORT: Moderate
LENGTH: 3.0 miles
GEOLOGICAL FEATURE(S): Volcanism
LOCATION: Lassen National Forest

Description: This is a sandy, sometimes rocky trail. Wear boots. Lava rocks are rough. This trail is hot and dry and will remind you of the desert. In the summer, hike it early morning or late afternoon. You'll walk through manzanita bushes to observe several different sizes of lava tubes and the main feature of the trail, spatter cones. When lava erupts on the surface, it can emerge through many different vehicles, not only the classic spout from the center of the mountain. Spatter cones were formed from eruptions from secondary vents, often small spouting fountains. As you'll see on this trail, a whole bunch of them can be congregated into a small space and go off simultaneously, creating something like a Las Vegas fountain show except with molten rock instead of water.

Spatter Cone (USGS)

From the parking area, find the trailhead on the south side. The trail signs may seem confusing. Follow the numbered guide available at the trailhead, which helps quite a bit when the signs are pointing you in opposite directions. We saw a snake and a lizard along the way. The snake, although small and harmless, was rather aggressive, lunging out at us when we tried to examine the rocks comprising the threshold of its den. Oh, well, you've seen one lava rock, you've seen them all.

The trail winds through the basalt, taking you from one spatter cone to the next. Observe the melt features preserved in the now solid lava flows, which makes it easy to imagine this rock in its liquid form. Climb up to the spatter cone necks and look inside. This is where the lava came bubbling out. As it cooled, it piled on top of itself to form the cone around the spout. As is typical of spatter cones, the inside is choked with solid rock, so you can't see very far down. As the lava flow loses energy, it settles into the cone and cools there, plugging the opening.

You'll climb gently for much of the first half of the trail, gaining the top of a ridge where the views south, east, and west are breathtaking.

In addition to the cones, you'll also see some collapsed lava tubes. These are much smaller than the Subway Cave tube in the previous hike. Nevertheless, they were formed by the same process. Most of these tubes are discovered only when their ceilings collapse.

The trail makes a wide loop over the volcanic landscape and back to the parking area. The dry vegetation was especially beautiful on our late afternoon hike as the sun rode low in the west on its way to sunset. The sagebrush seemed to be outlined in gold dust.

Directions: The trailhead can be found on Highway 89 at the Sanitary Dump Station across from Hat Creek Campground in Old Station. Access is free. There are no facilities.

Lassen Volcanic National Park

Mt. Lassen, October, 1915 (National Park Service)

Within the Cascade Range lies one of the most intriguing areas of geologic activity in California and is the setting for the remaining hikes in this chapter. Anchored by the other stratovolcano in the state, Mt. Lassen, this national park has just about everything you could ask for from nature, whether you're interested in volcanoes or not. But, really, who isn't? And for those of us who are thoroughly enchanted by volcanoes, this is a must-see, multi-day stop. After all, "volcanic" is part of its name! The volcanic nature of the area is also evidenced in its place names, such as Bumpass Hell and Devil's Kitchen. Volcanic features all over the world, whether they're still active like this one or the result of historic volcanic activity are named after underworld figures, and, indeed, when you observe hot lava flowing over an island or hot water bubbling at your feet, it isn't hard to imagine that the fires of Hell are bursting out of their domain onto the Earth's surface. In fact, it may be just these volcanic features and events that gave rise to the idea of a fiery underworld in the first place, an ancient notion that foretold the later conclusions of science that the interior of the planet is indeed molten.

Hiking is definitely the way to see this park. There is one road going through it north/south, Highway 89, but most of the more interesting features of the park can only be reached on foot. There is also an access road on the southeast side from Chester, but it does not go through the park, nor does it take you to any roadside points of interest. And a short, unpaved road brings you to the extreme northeast corner of the park. To visit all the trailheads in the park will take quite a bit of driving or long-distance hiking.

The fascinating sights you'll visit here are what remains of ancient Mt. Tahama, a volcano that almost completely destroyed itself about 400,000 years ago and again about 200,000 years ago. Evidence of past eruptions and present geothermal activity are all around you, most noticeably in the form of Mt. Lassen at 10,457 feet. Mt. Lassen last erupted in May, 1914, and began as a vent on Tahama. This eruption was recent enough that it was captured on film. Lassen Peak is the world's largest plug dome volcano. That 1914 eruption began a 7-year cycle of outbursts before the mountain settled into its current quieter phase.

But you will have no doubt that there is still plenty of activity just below the ground as you walk past steam shooting up from the earth, boiling water, bubbling mud pots, and warm streams and lakes. Some of these areas are getting hotter, which makes Lassen a likely candidate for future eruptions. This is best place in California for observing geothermal activity by virtue of the variety and number of surface features.

On our first trip to Lassen, it was early October, which is off-season. Most of the campgrounds and services close after Labor Day in preparation for snow season. We were lucky, though, as the first storm of the season arrived the day we were leaving, so we had warm, sunny days to explore with a minimum of company. This park opens as soon as the roads can be cleared of snow, so the window of opportunity varies, but is generally July, August, and September. You can visit the park all year, however, if you want to ski or tromp about in snowshoes.

There are 150 miles of trails in the park leading through pine forests, remnants of lava flows and volcanoes, cinder cones, active geothermal areas, a dwarf forest, and many wonderful and unusual offerings. It is a beautiful park with plenty of opportunity for solitude. There are places here that will make you feel like you're on another planet, where water runs milky gray and soil is yellow and pink. Fortunately, Lassen is easier to get to than another planet. This amazing geological fantasyland awaits just an hour east of Interstate 5 from Red Bluff.

Directions: From Red Bluff, take Highway 36 east to the town of Mineral. Continue past it to the junction with Highway 89, and turn left (north). Proceed to the park entrance. An entrance fee is charged.

20. Cinder Cone Trail

EFFORT: Difficult
LENGTH: 3.0 miles
GEOLOGICAL FEATURE(S): Volcanism
LOCATION: Lassen Volcanic National Park

Description: The best evidence available suggests that this volcano erupted in the 18th century, possibly a little earlier, but within the last 350 years, just a blink of an eye in geologic time. It is a classic cinder cone resembling those we already encountered near Mt. Shasta: The Whaleback and Black Butte. However, this one is younger and more like what you'd see in a cinder cone not long after eruption. Its flanks are covered in loose material which doesn't lend itself to a hospitable environment for plant life. As for humans making the trek to the top, it's not all that hospitable either. The trail, although well established, isn't solid underfoot, and there is no shade. But the view from the top is worth it because it's the only place most visitors can get a good look at the Fantastic Lava Beds (how can you pass that up?) and Painted Dunes. Not to mention that standing on the top of a volcano is a delight in itself.

The trail starts by the boat launch. Take a brochure from the box at the trailhead. Then start out on Nobles Emigrant Trail, a historic pioneer route, past black basalt hills bordering the Fantastic Lava Beds. Note that everything you see, the colorful ash deposits and the young-looking basalt, were deposited here by the erupting volcano we're about to climb. It blew cinders and ash from its central vent while basaltic lava flowed from its base.

At 0.4 miles, bear left at the fork and go another mile and bear left again until you arrive at the base of the imposing mountain.

The climb up 700-foot Cinder Cone can be brutal on a hot day. Your feet will slide with each step on the loose cinders or scoria, the typical ejecta from cinder cones that we've seen before. Two steps forward, one step back.

Cinder Cone

Climbing up this loose rock makes the going tough and slow. But little by little you'll conquer the mountain and arrive at the top where other hikers have thrown themselves on the ground in exhaustion. From this high point, you can look into the crater and walk around the rim to get excellent views of the surrounding landscape, especially the landscape created by this volcano. Its lava flows are responsible for the weird and wonderful Fantastic Lava Beds and the colorful Painted Dunes to the south. You'll also have a great view of Lassen Peak and the domes of Chaos Crags.

The Painted Dunes are not sand but ash deposits, but their hummocky contours and smooth appearance have earned them the nickname "dunes." The brilliant colors of red and gold, even better around sunset, were caused by oxidation of the cinders and ash as they fell on hot lava. Beyond the dunes is a starkly different flow of black basalt. You won't be able to resist taking lots of photos, particularly because of the shifting sun and shadow impacting the colors below.

When you've seen enough of this remarkable landscape, descend the cone and head back the way you came.

Directions: From Highway 44, 11 miles east of its junction with Highway 89, turn right at the sign for Butte Lake. Proceed 6 miles to Butte Lake Campground, and park in the lot by the lake's north shore.

21. Lassen Peak Summit Trail

EFFORT: Moderate
LENGTH: 5.0 miles
GEOLOGICAL FEATURE(S): Volcanism
LOCATION: Lassen Volcanic National Park

Description: In the late afternoon of Memorial Day, May 30, 1914, Lassen Peak erupted, beginning a seven-year period of volcanic outbursts. In 1915, this activity climaxed in a huge explosion of fiery lava that pushed a seven-mile high mushroom cloud into the atmosphere and washed away buildings and timber below. The mountain continued to erupt until 1921, after which it quieted down. This was the most recent eruptive episode in the long history of this mountain, originally a vent on the now extinct, much larger Tahama volcano. Tahama and its progeny are responsible for the unusual landscape of the entire park.

Lassen Peak is visible from all over northeastern California, a major landmark diminished only by its cousin, Mt. Shasta, another of the Cascade Range volcanoes. But Mt. Shasta hasn't erupted for about 200 years, and no other volcano in California can beat Lassen in terms of activity. To find a Cascade volcano more recently active, you have to go to Washington's Mt. St. Helens.

If you want to climb a volcano, this is a good one to choose. The trailhead is at 8,512 feet, culminating at the 10,457-foot peak. Guess what? It's uphill all the way. This sounds daunting, but lots of people manage it, including whole families with young children. Most people make the climb slowly and have to stop frequently to catch their breath in the thin air, but as mountain climbing goes, this is one of the milder adventures.

It's a wide, well-graded trail and easy to follow. Shade is scarce, so wear a hat and sunscreen. Avoid this trail when rain clouds are present, as lightning frequently strikes the summit. From the parking area, the trail will be highly visible. Take plenty of water and be prepared for cooler temperatures as you near the peak. Along the way, you'll encounter ill-prepared hikers in flip-flops, clutching towels around themselves for warmth. The landscape before you is stark. A few pines have gained a foothold on the mountain, but its loose talus slopes are mainly barren.

Other than the thrill of hiking to the top of a big mountain, which is quite a high in several senses, the attraction of this trail is the view. The higher you go, the better it gets. If you're lucky, you'll have a clear day with distant views in all directions. Head out on the trail towards the jagged outcrop you can see from the trailhead.

As you gain altitude, beautiful Lake Helen appears below. The volcanic rocks alongside vary in color from light gray to dark red. Patches of snow remain on the mountain year round. The trail switchbacks up the side of the mountain, sometimes becoming narrow with dramatic drop-offs on either side.

Once you reach the summit, you'll look out over other park landmarks, including Chaos Crags, the Devastated Area, Prospect Peak, Cinder Cone, Butte Lake, and Brokeoff Mountain. Outside the park, you'll be able to see the Sierra Nevada mountains to the southeast, Blue Lake Canyon southwest, the Sacramento Valley and the Coast Range mountains to the west, the Klamath Mountains and the Trinity Alps, as well as Mt. Shasta to the northwest.

Return by the same path, downhill all the way.

Directions: The trailhead is located on the main park road, Highway 89, heading north and climbing from Lake Helen, on the left side of the road.

22. Bumpass Hell Trail

EFFORT: Minimal
LENGTH: 3.0 miles
GEOLOGICAL FEATURE(S): Geothermal Activity
LOCATION: Lassen Volcanic National Park

Description: Poor Mr. Bumpass gave his name to this trail after losing his leg in one of the boiling pools. Make sure you heed the warning signs to avoid the same fate. This trail leads to one of the most popular destinations in the park, and one of the best spots to view the geothermal activity present here. It's a gentle climb to the lookout, and then a steeper descent to the boardwalk area, which winds through the bubbling mud pots and fumaroles. The colors here are gorgeous and otherworldly.

Bumpass Hell (USGS)

Here's a tip if you want to cut the trail shorter: continue past the main trail parking lot and park across from Lake Helen in a pullout. There's another trailhead there that starts you a bit further along on the trail.

Head out through a forested area on a nearly level trail. Through the trees, you get good views of the various peaks in the park. Before long, you come to an overlook of the geothermal area. Look down to see steam rising up from the ground below. The distinctive smell of sulfur will float up and smack you in the nose. From this vantage point, you can observe the soil discoloration caused by the minerals in the water and steam. If anyone in your group is unable to negotiate climbs and descents, this is where you'll leave them. But we hope you're up to it because down below is where the party really rocks.

Follow the trail down steeply to reach an open area beside a creek. Beneath the ground, water is being heated by magma to produce this continuous display of steam wherever the pressure can escape through fissures. These spots are known as *fumaroles*. In some places, the heat source is near enough to the surface to make the ground itself hot. Right beside the trail you'll find a couple of mud pots full of a grayish green ooze heated to a slow boil. As the bubbles of steam escape, the mud issues burbling noises. Between this ongoing sound effect, varying in degree with the size of the bubbles and the hissing of steam, there is quite a little concert going on down here. And the various colors of the surrounding soils (red, orange, yellow, white, and purple) present an artistic backdrop to the music.

The trail, sometimes a boardwalk, winds its way to all of the primary geothermal features and then returns you to the place where the trail heads steeply back up to the overlook. Make the climb and take one last look down at Bumpass Hell before returning the same way you came.

Bumpass Hell boiling mud pot

Directions: From the southwest park entrance, head north past Sulphur Works and continue on the main park road past Emerald Lake to the trailhead parking on the right. There is a restroom.

23. Cold Boiling Lake

EFFORT: Minimal
LENGTH: 1.4 miles
GEOLOGICAL FEATURE(S): Volcanism
LOCATION: Lassen Volcanic National Park

Description: This is an easy walk to the edge of a small lake where you can see bubbles coming up to the water's surface, evidence of underground gases escaping. The lake's name inspired some excitement in us, so we didn't want to pass it up. Having seen hot boiling water at Sulphur Works, we were intrigued by the idea of "cold" boiling water. What could that mean? But the fact is that the name is somewhat of a misnomer and the lake was a bit of a let-down. There is no boiling going on in this lake and the feature for which it's named is underwhelming. We include this destination because the name of the lake will likely pique the curiosity of anybody using this guide, so with this description, you can decide if you want to take the short walk through the woods to check it out for yourself.

From the parking area, walk southwest. After a pleasant walk on a level trail through the pine forest, you emerge at the edge of Cold Boiling Lake. It's a small, shallow body of water edged with forest, a grassy meadow and a muddy shoreline. Find a solid path to get close to the water on the west side of the lake to observe the tiny gas bubbles coming up like fizzing club soda. Admittedly, you would have to be quite the science aficionado to get excited about this, but it is a volcanic phenomenon you won't find elsewhere in this park. The gas bubbles are made by carbon dioxide being released from the cooling magma below ground. These carbon dioxide seeps are common in hydrothermal fields and are one way we know that there's liquid magma fairly close to the surface in this location.

Other than the bubbling gas, you'll see grass, trees, water and dragonflies. It's a tranquil place to sit, and definitely not as crowded as some of the other trail destinations. You might want to spread your picnic lakeside. Alternatively, you can continue on this trail to reach Crumbaugh Lake (1.3 miles) and Mill Creek Falls (3.0 miles).

Return via the same trail.

Directions: From the main park road, drive east past Lake Helen to the Kings Creek picnic area. There are picnic tables and a restroom.

24. Chaos Crags

EFFORT: Moderate
LENGTH: 4.2 miles
GEOLOGICAL FEATURE(S): Volcanism
LOCATION: Lassen Volcanic National Park

Description: The lonely but picturesque Chaos Crags Trail climbs east from Manzanita Lake to Crags Lake on the edge of Chaos Crags, a group of six lava domes north of Lassen Peak, dating from just over a thousand years ago. That makes these volcanoes the youngest formation in the park. Subsequently, about 300 years ago, a series of large avalanches occurred on the northwest slope of the Crags, flattening the forest and leaving a 2.5 square mile debris field called the Chaos Jumbles, through which the park road travels. The avalanches, riding on a cushion of compressed air, traveled at about 100 miles per hour and dammed Manzanita Creek, forming Manzanita Lake.

Chaos Crags can be viewed from several locations in the park. They are an intriguing gray brown dacite formation lying bare-headed, beckoning your boot heels. *Dacite* is a common volcanic rock that looks like a light colored granite. It has a high silica content and is usually light gray in color, but it also comes in red in this park.

The trail begins with a steep uphill, and then levels out somewhat, but continues climbing all the way for a total gain of 700 feet. This one will have you gasping for breath in the thin oxygen if you're a lowlander like us. But if you don't have trouble with altitude, you'll find this an easy trail.

The first half mile parallels Manzanita Creek through a fir and pine forest. Eventually, you'll notice a change of terrain as the trail becomes more rocky, littered with plenty of volcanic rocks and lined with multitudes of manzanita bushes, the creek's namesake plant. The manzanitas, with their smooth red bark, form a lovely ground cover.

Once you reach your destination, a ridge above Chaos Lake, you'll be standing at one of the most prominent points in the park, marveling at the destructive power of the volcano. Rocky protrusions preside over slopes of volcanic ash, some of it stained yellow by sulfur.

If there's water in the lake and you're so inclined, you can descend to it and go for a swim, but late in summer and in dry years, the lake will be merely a small, greenish pond populated by frogs and tadpoles. By September, it will probably be dry, as it was when we visited. There is an optional 1.6-mile trail that circumvents the lake.

The route back is the same, and will likely be just as solitary and peaceful as the hike out. We met no one else on this trail in either direction.

Directions: From Highway 89, turn off at the Manzanita Lake Campground road and park at the small trailhead parking on the left before reaching the campground. There are restrooms and picnic tables at Manzanita Lake, but no facilities at the trailhead.

25. Devils Kitchen

EFFORT: Moderate
LENGTH: 4.0 miles
GEOLOGICAL FEATURE(S): Geothermal Activity
LOCATION: Lassen Volcanic National Park

Description: Devils Kitchen is one of the most beautiful and fascinating sights in the park, especially if you're here for the hot spots. Do people come to Lassen for the fishing? The bad news about this hike is the trip to the trailhead. If you're visiting the main area of the park, you have to leave it, drive all the way to Chester and then back into the park at the Warner Valley entrance, which requires a drive down a rough, unpaved road. If you're staying at Drakesbad Guest Ranch, you have a trailhead of your own and it's a half mile shorter, located behind the ranch house. Otherwise, your trailhead is just before the entrance to the Guest Ranch.

From the parking pullout, take the trail south, crossing over Hot Springs Creek and heading southwest. This route follows the Pacific Crest Trail for a short distance. At the junction with Boiling Springs Lake Trail, turn right, leaving the PCT.

The trail traverses a meadow north of Dream Lake and then enters a tranquil forest, following a wide, dusty path frequented by horses. We saw woodpeckers and deer along the trail, a serene forest walk leading to a place of unexpected volatility. After a short climb, you'll come to a ridgetop and look down into Devils Kitchen, its swirling mists rising up to meet you. It reminded us of a scene out of *MacBeth*, so if you see three old women with a big cauldron down there, you'd better make tracks.

Drop down from the ridge on a steep trail into the "kitchen." This spot is similar to Bumpass Hell, but, being off the beaten path, much less crowded. We were alone the entire time we were here. That made the place stranger yet and only added to its allure.

Like Bumpass Hell, this area is a place where magma is close to the surface. Water seeps down to contact the magma or hot rocks and returns as steam. Surface water is heated to boiling temperatures and volcanic gases escape to deposit minerals on the soil.

Once you reach the bottom of the descent, you'll follow a half-mile loop trail through the fumaroles and warm streams. Mineral deposits have turned the landscape pink, yellow, and orange. Sulfide crystals line the paths. Heat emanates from small dark fissures all around you. Be very careful, as these hot openings are sometimes tiny and not immediately apparent. Jockeying for a good place to snap a picture, one of us stepped nearly on top of one of these fissures, immediately felt the heat and rapidly moved away. You'll be okay if you stay on the path, but some of these vents are within inches of the trail and are not marked or barricaded in any way. In 2010, a visitor was severely burned when he traveled off trail in this area.

When we were there in fall, the ferns were turning yellow, and the brilliance of the colors of soils and plants was inspiring. From the stream, follow the trail up to the most active part of the area where the large fumaroles are belching steam near the trail's high point. From here, you look down and across to where you entered the kitchen. The colors there are particularly appealing from this vantage point. It's a good place to get an overview. The trail descends from here and starts winding back to the loop junction.

Climb back up the slope out of the kitchen, return to the forest trail, and retrace your steps to the trailhead.

Directions: From Chester, drive north on Warner Valley Road for 17 miles. The road turns to dirt just before you enter the park, and then leads to Warner Valley Campground and to Drakesbad Guest Ranch at the end of the road. The road is rough, but is passable for a passenger car. Just before you get to the ranch, there is a pullout for trailhead parking on the left side of the road. There are no facilities.

26. Boiling Springs Lake

EFFORT: Minimal
LENGTH: 3.0 miles
GEOLOGICAL FEATURE(S): Geothermal Activity
LOCATION: Lassen Volcanic National Park

Description: After the rather grand promise of Cold Boiling Lake, which turned out to be a bust, you might be a little skeptical about this one. But there is no comparison. This is a fantastic destination of unexpected colors and impressive geothermal features. The area bordering the lake features fumaroles and boiling mud pots, and the lake itself, the largest hot lake in the world, maintains an impressively high 125° Fahrenheit. You will see nothing like this anywhere else in California. Another bonus—there are very few people on the trails in this section of the park. Like our hike at Devil's Kitchen (previous trail), we met nobody on this fascinating trek.

Starting from the main trailhead in the Warner Valley section of the park, this hike is some trouble to get to, but is an easy trail that climbs gradually about 200 feet through the forest to the lake.

From the road, take the trail south, crossing over Hot Springs Creek and heading southwest. This route follows a section of the Pacific Crest Trail. Head uphill to the junction with Devils Kitchen Trail in less than half a mile, then turn left and continue to stay on the PCT toward Boiling Springs Lake. At the next fork, bear left to stay on the PCT. The trail is rocky and dusty, traveling uphill through a forest with little understory and littered with tree branches and fallen trees.

Boiling Springs Lake

When you reach a junction where the sign points ahead to Terminal Geyser and right for Boiling Springs Lake Circuit, go right. The trail is more level from here to the lake. You'll come up over a rise of reddish sediment and white rocks hydrothermally altered by the minerals in the hot water. Then you're standing on the north shore of Boiling Springs Lake. It's quite a sight, murky greenish water surrounded by gray and white mud. From here, you can go either way around the lake, a 0.7 mile trip. Do not leave the trail and attempt to get down to the water. It's very dangerous and the ground isn't solid.

Most of the action is on the south side of the lake: bubbling mud pots, boiling water, and steam vents. There will be more mud action early in summer than later in the season when the mud dries.

The smell of sulfur is heavy in the air around the steam vents. The unusual coloring of the lake is the result of the heavy mineral content of the hot springs. Like the other features in this park, below the lake, relatively close to the surface, a magma chamber heats groundwater and the surrounding rock to create the fascinating sights at this location.

The loop around the lake is worth the extra time. It gives you different views, including a magnificent view from the east shore of Lassen Peak, a sight not otherwise visible on this hike.

If you continue past the lake on the PCT, and then take a short side trail left, you will reach Terminal Geyser (Hike #27). When you're ready, return on the same trail.

Directions: From Chester, drive north on Warner Valley Road. The road turns to dirt just before you enter the park, and then leads to Warner Valley Campground and to Drakesbad Guest Ranch at the end of the road. Before you get to the ranch, there is a pullout for trailhead parking on the left side of the road.

27. Terminal Geyser

EFFORT: Minimal
LENGTH: 4.4 miles
GEOLOGICAL FEATURE(S): Geothermal Activity
LOCATION: Lassen National Forest

Description: After a peaceful forest hike, you'll arrive at a steaming fumarole and two warm pools, about 100 degrees Fahrenheit, in an active geothermal area. Don't expect to see Old Faithful spouting here. Despite its name, this is not really a geyser. These are hot springs arising out of vents in the ground, spouting with plenty of force into a steam cloud. You can approach this destination either from the north within Lassen Volcanic National Park or from the south. Directions to both trailheads are given below. The start of the trail within the park follows the same course as Hike #26 for Boiling Springs Lake. Described here is the alternate trail originating from Willow Lake.

Willow Lake is a unique ecosystem, a floating sphagnum bog hosting rare plants and buzzing with dragonflies. Mats of moss grow on the water's surface and so much grass grows in the water that it at first appears to be a meadow. There too you may find the interesting carnivorous sundew plant. It is reddish-tinged and ensnares insects with sticky "dew" on its tentacles. We wish it happy mosquito hunting.

After leaving the lake, you'll enter meadows where wildflowers will be blooming in season. Continuing, you'll walk through Lassen National Forest and then into the national park. The trail continues, wending its way through the conifers rather uneventfully until you approach the geyser area. In some places, you may find the trail chewed up from horse traffic. Before you reach your destination, you'll smell sulfur and hear the steam hissing.

When you reach the fumarole, you're greeted by hot steam rising up from fissures in a rocky crevasse. The steam shoots in a continuous spray to up to 40 feet high. The soils around the geyser are colorfully stained from minerals within the water. The water at the source is boiling. Be careful to stay safely away from the steam vents, as the steam can cause serious burns. There are many holes where the water emerges, some very tiny, creating billowing clouds of steam. The water issuing from the fumarole runs as a small stream down to pools enclosed in rocks.

The pools are shallow, only a couple of feet deep, and about five to six feet in diameter with muddy bottoms. They are the perfect size and temperature, though, to create inviting personal hot tubs. Because the pools require a hike to reach, they are usually not crowded. As you would expect, the pool closest to the fumarole is the warmest. People have arranged rocks to create several such pools, each successively cooler as the stream moves away from the hot water source.

A cool fall day or night would be perfect for this trek if you intend to soak in the pools. In early morning before the sun hits the ground, the pools are especially peaceful, and the woods are intriguingly veiled with rising steam. In winter, snow covers the trail. In early summer, the stream will be full and vigorous with snowmelt. By autumn, the fumarole may be the only source of water. Mosquitoes can be a serious problem on this trail, so bring insect repellent.

Directions: This trail departs from Willow Lake. From Chester, go on Feather River Drive and turn right at the sign to Willow Creek. The last several miles to the lake are on a very rough road. The trailhead is at the east side of the lake, where you will also find a toilet.

For the longer route (5.4 miles round-trip) originating in Lassen Volcanic National Park and picking up Boiling Springs Lake along the way, from Chester, go northwest on Feather River Drive to Warner Valley Road and go 17 miles to the Drakesbad Guest Ranch on a dirt road. Your trailhead is just before the entrance to the Guest Ranch.

SECTION 3
THE MODOC PLATEAU

The Modoc Plateau is a high plain of accumulated lava flows in a lightly populated corner of California with abundant wildlife and beautiful forests. Here, most notably in Lava Beds National Monument, evidence of geologic activity abounds. There are over 400 lava tubes in the monument, many of them open to visitors. So bring your flashlights, hardhats, and camera, for you are about to see some of the most fascinating geology California has to offer, from massive craters to icy caverns and all manner of delights in between.

In contrast to the dramatic stratovolcanoes that make up the Cascades, the Modoc Plateau consists primarily of wide-ranging lava flows and one broad shield volcano known as the Medicine Lake volcano, which extends throughout the region and encompasses Lava Beds National Monument.

As defined in the introduction to the Cascades, a stratovolcano is a volcano made of alternating layers of lava and pyroclastic debris. In contrast, a *shield volcano* is made from successive lava flows across the landscape rather than an explosive eruption. Shield volcanoes are typically broad and much less steep than stratovolcanoes. Because this volcano is not a tall mountain like Lassen and Shasta, it's easy to miss it, even when you're driving on top of it. But the Medicine Lake volcanic complex has been in the making for over a million years and is actually larger in volume than Mt Shasta, exceeding 200 square miles. It's named for what is now a peaceful and beautiful lake sitting in a crater that was created about 100,000 years ago when a series of massive eruptions occurred.

Although the Modoc Plateau is a distinct geologic province within the state of California, it is actually the southernmost tip of a much larger geologic province known as the Columbia Plateau. The Columbia Plateau consists of a series of Miocene flows of fluidic basaltic lava that simply poured over the land instead of erupting as a volcano. The resulting *flood basalts* or *plateau basalts* of the Columbia Plateau have an estimated volume of 25,000 cubic miles!

As you drive along the Modoc Volcanic Scenic Byway, you'll begin to glimpse blocky black rocks through the trees, and as the trees thin, you'll see youthful looking basalt all around you. There are many visible remnants of the Medicine Lake eruptions, including lava tube collapses, pumice deposits, craters, cinder cones, obsidian flows, and, of course, the lake itself sitting within the old caldera.

As you might anticipate from this description, the hikes in this province are all about volcanism, but they are by no means all alike. There's nearly infinite variety to be seen in the differing ways magma emerges onto the landscape and hardens into surface material, and all of them have a story to tell about our turbulent past.

Lava tube entrance (NPS)

Trails of the Modoc Plateau:

28. Mammoth Crater
29. Valentine Cave
30. Big Painted Cave and Symbol Bridge Trail
31. Black Crater Trail
32. Fleener Chimneys
33. Schonchin Butte Trail
34. Heppe Ice Cave
35. Captain Jack's Stronghold Trail
36. Whitney Butte Trail
37. Cave Loop Road
38. Burnt Lava Flow
39. Medicine Lake Glass Flow
40. Spatter Cone Loop

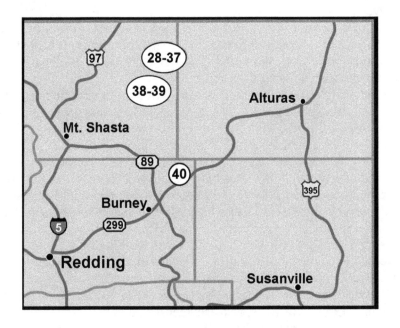

Lava Beds National Monument

Tucked into the northeastern corner of the state, Lava Beds National Monument is in the high desert at 4,000 to 5,000 feet and is so isolated that it is going to take some effort for most of us to get there. Because of that, it is usually not crowded. The closest town of any size is Tulelake, "the horseradish growing capital of the world."

It's worth noting that because it's in the rain shadow, this section of California is extremely dry, a desert environment, while the northwest corner, on the same longitude and less than 200 miles away, is the wettest area of the state, containing California's rain forests.

Because Lava Beds National Monument is rife with volcanism, we're going to spend some time describing its history and features before listing the trails. The trails in the monument are just a few of the fantastic attractions you'll want to visit on this trip. For geology buffs, even the roads leading to the monument are full of amazing sights.

Over the last 500,000 years, repeated eruptions from the Medicine Lake shield volcano have created a rugged landscape of cinder cones, lava flows, spatter cones, lava tube caves and volcanic craters. Medicine Lake is the largest volcano in the Cascades and Lava Beds contains only about ten percent of its surface area.

The lava from this volcano had a low viscosity, a term that describes how easily a substance flows. Maple syrup and ketchup are examples of highly viscous liquids, while water and milk have a low viscosity. It's the amount of gas contained within that determines the viscosity of lava. Close to the vent, the lava contains a higher amount of gas and is therefore fairly fluid. The resulting basalt will have a smooth, ropy surface and is called *pahoehoe* (pronounced pah-ho-ee-ho-ee). Further from the vent, some of the gases have escaped and the lava is less fluid. The resulting rock is more angular and sharp, and is known as *aa* lava (pronounced ah-ah). The volcanic rock types resulting from the Medicine Lake volcano are basalt, andesite, dacite, and rhyolite. Most of the surface rocks in Lava Beds National Monument are basalt.

Due to the harsh volcanic landscape, there is sparse vegetation through most of Lava Beds, primarily consisting of sagebrush and grass. Towards the southern boundary, some juniper trees spring up, and as you leave the monument to the south, you enter a pine forest among the fascinating volcanic landscape of the Medicine Lake Highlands (definitely worth driving through).

The biggest attraction here is the multitude of lava tubes, over 400 of them, two dozen of which have been developed for public exploration. Development generally consists of clearing of floor debris and installing stairs and ladders, as well as the occasional bridge. The monument contains the largest concentration of lava tube caves in North America.

Pahoehoe Lava

Lava tubes are created during an eruption of low viscosity lava flowing downhill. As the lava comes into contact with air, it begins to cool and forms a crust on the outside of the still-fluid lava inside, insulating it from the cool air. You've probably observed this process when a bowl of hot pudding is left sitting long enough to form a top skin. When you peel the skin off, the pudding beneath is still hot. The outer walls of the lava tube continue to solidify, becoming permanent rock, but the flow inside tapers off when the eruption is over and the molten lava drains out of the interior of the tube. Most of the tubes in the monument are from the Mammoth Crater flow and are approximately 30,000 years old.

There are all kinds of caves in the monument, developed and "wild," some where you walk in standing up, and some where you must crawl around through crevices. There are smooth tubes and rough tubes, straight and curving tubes. There is a cave containing a fern grotto and Native American pictographs. There are caves containing permanent ice. You can choose your level of difficulty. It's easy to lose your sense of direction underground, but in most of the tubes, you can't be lost for long, with the notable exception of the Catacombs (discussed below). Find out all the details at the Visitor Center, including information about ranger-guided tours. If you stick to the caves on Cave Loop Road, you'll probably have company and won't get into too much trouble. If you're more experienced at caving, you can opt for some of the less developed options. In any case, never go caving alone.

You can get lanterns for free at the Visitor Center, but we found that our flashlights were more powerful and also allowed for beam adjustment. Helmets are not necessary, but it's hard to avoid hitting your head on the low ceilings when you're looking down, up, ahead, and behind yourself. Since the floors are often rough, you'll find yourself concentrating on footing rather than how close your noggin is to the ceiling. Temperatures are much cooler in the caves, so bring a sweatshirt. Wear sturdy boots for caving and for hiking over lava rocks. Surfaces are uneven and some lava is quite jagged.

If you're planning on exploring any of the wilderness caves in the monument, register at the Visitor Center so someone will know where you are in the case of an accident.

Collapsed lava tube at Lava Beds NM (NPS)

In addition to non-stop geological intrigue, the monument is also historically important. It has been occupied by various Native Americans for hundreds, perhaps thousands, of years. Rock art can be seen in several locations in the park, including Painted Cave, Fern Cave, and Petroglyph Point.

More recently, this is the site of the major battles of the Modoc Indian War of 1872 and 1873. Before the arrival of European settlers to the area, the Modoc Indians lived here, hunting, fishing, and fashioning boats and homes from the tules around Tule Lake, now much smaller than it once was. With the arrival of settlers in the 1850s, the lifestyle of the Modoc was changed forever. Numerous confrontations ensued, culminating in a standoff between the Modocs and the U.S. Army when the Modocs left the reservation they had been assigned to and returned to this land.

The Modocs fought numerous battles with the Army in an effort to resist being returned to the reservation. They were greatly outnumbered, however, and ultimately succumbed. The Modocs were then removed to a reservation in Oklahoma, and their leader, Captain Jack, was hanged. Details of the war will be revealed on the trail through Captain Jack's Stronghold (Hike #35) and is also described in detail in the nonfiction book *Bury My Heart at Wounded Knee*.

About 45 years after the Modoc Indian War, a mill worker named Judson D. Howard began exploring the Lava Beds area intensely. He discovered and named many of the caves, sometimes revealing their entrances by pulling away rocks. He discovered the most complex cave in the monument, The Catacombs, explored it, named it and many of its features, and mapped it. Howard is also largely responsible for obtaining federal protection for these lands.

Although the land looks stark and forbidding, many animals do live here. There are raptors living in the monument year round, feasting on numerous rodents. Bald eagles spend the winter here in great numbers. Other birds that call this place home are various species of hawks, falcons, and owls. Other wildlife in the park include mule deer, rattlesnakes, squirrels, kangaroo rats, yellow-bellied marmots, jackrabbits, California quail, and the rare sage grouse. Avoid rodents, which may harbor diseases, and be aware that snakes can be lying in crevices in the rocks.

The Klamath Basin bordering the monument to the northeast is an important stop on the Pacific Flyway for migrating birds, and perhaps you'll have an opportunity to stop there as you head out north from the monument on Hill Road and Highway 161. When we drove by the wildlife refuge, we were entranced by a large flock of white pelicans. In fall, this area is teeming with millions of migratory geese and ducks, plus grebes, herons, cormorants, gulls, coots, terns, avocets, and many others.

Plan on at least two days to visit the monument. If you're intending to explore the lava tubes in depth, more time will be required. There is a campground, visitor center, and restrooms, but no food services or gas stations in the monument.

Directions: From Interstate 5, take Highway 97 north at Weed to Highway 161. Travel east on Highway 161 to Hill Road, turning south (right) and following the Monument signs. From Tulelake, travel north on Highway 139 to Highway 161, turning west to reach Hill Road. Travel south on Hill Road to the north entrance of the Monument. From here, turn right and follow the main park road to the Visitor Center. Or, if you turn left, you can visit Captain Jack's Stronghold and continue on out to Petroglyph Point. A self-registering fee station is available in the parking lot of the Visitor Center.

There are other routes into the monument, but no others with good paved roads. From the south, however, you can plan a rewarding trip along the Modoc Volcanic Scenic Byway (closed in winter) from Bartle on Highway 89. From there, you can take the gravel side roads to the Burnt Lava Flow (stupendous) and Glass Mountain. Medicine Lake has picnic tables, restrooms, and is a fine swimming spot in summer (and it's free).

Time to go for a walk.

28. Mammoth Crater

EFFORT: Minimal
LENGTH: 0.4 miles
GEOLOGICAL FEATURE(S): Volcanism
LOCATION: Lava Beds National Monument

Description: This is where it all began, so this stop makes a good springboard for your exploration of Lava Beds National Monument. Mammoth Crater is one of the most impressive features in the monument and is the source of almost all of the lava tubes you will explore. This crater is a remnant of a huge eruption from about 30,000 years ago, an impressively deep pit in the earth. Because of the crater left behind, it may look like this volcano erupted in a mighty explosion, but that isn't the case. You can think of this volcano as an immense lava lake that overflowed and poured out its contents over the landscape. The outpouring of lava was so great that it covered the monument from here to Tule Lake to the northeast. Although numerous eruptions have contributed to the lava beds in this park, the Mammoth Crater eruption covers about 70% of it. The resulting rock type is primarily basalt.

The paved trail climbs steeply up to the rim to an overlook into the depths of the crater below. This is an awesome view. There's an interpretive sign here explaining the volcanic event that created this spectacle. When you're ready, continue on the trail down to a lower overlook inside the crater where you'll feel miniscule, and then climb back out.

Directions: Entering the monument from the south, traveling north on Highway 49, just after the paved road ends, locate the parking area for Mammoth Crater and Hidden Valley on the left. Alternatively, from the Visitor Center, turn left on the main park road and drive about a mile to the graded gravel road leading off to the left. Take it for about 2 miles to the Mammoth Crater/Hidden Valley parking area.

29. Valentine Cave

EFFORT: Minimal
LENGTH: Varies
GEOLOGICAL FEATURE(S): Volcanism, Caves
LOCATION: Lava Beds National Monument

Valentine Cave (NPS)

Description: This cave has smooth floors and high ceilings, making it easy to navigate, at least in the beginning. It also has some especially notable features. If you're choosing just a few of the lava tubes, make this one of your choices.

Just inside the mouth of the cave, you'll see extraordinary lava shelves along the walls and around the huge column in the center of the cave (left side in accompanying photo). The technical term for these features is *benches*, and you can easily see why. The benches are about three feet off the floor, six inches wide, and have well-defined lips. They are the remains of small streams of lava flowing after the main chamber emptied out.

The column right in front of you is remarkable. Go around either side of it deeper into the cave. This is an unusually wide cave, navigable for some distance. There is a second column after the first. After passing this, the cave splits and goes two directions, and then tunnels head off along several paths. Continue if you wish, though the unusual features of this tube are right at the start.

Directions: Valentine Cave is located along the road to the southeast entrance to the park, just north of Caldwell Butte. Heading south, turn left onto the access road.

The Center of the World

Lava Beds National Monument houses a magical underground place that does not appear on the park map. The Modoc Indians believed it was the center of the spiritual and physical world. Is it a myth? No, it's really there, and you can visit it to experience your own spiritual journey. It is Fern Cave, a collapsed lava tube with a dense mat of ferns growing in its mouth. Many artifacts have been discovered here, dating back thousands of years to the ancient ancestors of the Modocs. How strange to see ferns in this semi-arid high desert place. But inside the cave it is cool and moist. The continual condensation of water on the ceiling and walls creates a kind of rain forest inside, simulating annual rainfall of 100 inches.

The interior of the cave is heavily decorated with rock art. The pictographs are black and white, made with charcoal and a chalk-like substance. There are trails of white dots, circles, man and animal-like figures, and zigzag patterns. There is one unprecedented drawing, a crescent with circles on its top and bottom left side. Some researchers have proposed that this unique drawing is a representation of the Crab Nebula supernova that occurred in July, 1054 AD when the crescent moon was close to Jupiter and the supernova.

For reservations for a ranger-led tour (your only option), call Lava Beds Visitor Center.

30. Big Painted Cave & Symbol Bridge Trail

EFFORT: Minimal
LENGTH: 1.5 miles
GEOLOGICAL FEATURE(S): Volcanism, Caves
LOCATION: Lava Beds National Monument

Description: This trail passes many large collapsed lava tubes and other volcanic features as it leads you to a Native American rock art site. Bring flashlights to light up dim recesses in the caves, but they are not necessary to visit these two sites.

The gently ascending trail leads northwest through the open volcanic landscape, heading toward Schonchin Butte. The trail is rocky in places, so watch your footing. It is also hot, so wear a hat and carry water.

Symbol Bridge Pictographs

Soon after starting out, you can take a short spur trail on the right to a huge tube collapse. You may recall that lava tubes often remain hidden underground until a portion of their ceiling collapses. That's what you're seeing here. Shortly after the first one, the trail crosses another such collapse, a ravine choked with immense chunks of basalt.

After a half mile, you reach a signed junction. The left arm takes you down to Big Painted Cave, a huge chamber accessible as the result of a collapse similar to those you've seen earlier on the trail. Make your way carefully down to the mouth amid the boulders. You'll notice as you descend into the cave that the temperature drops dramatically. Take a break in this cool, shady spot before returning to the junction and continuing straight on to the destination of this hike, Symbol Bridge, at 0.8 miles. A narrow path leads down into the entrance to the cave.

Around the entrance, the basalt walls contain Modoc pictographs painted over thousands of years. On the left side of the opening are some very clear symbols resembling cogwheels. The trail continues just inside the cave, where you'll see more pictographs of animals, human figures, and geometric shapes. Unfortunately, there is also some more modern graffiti here. This cave is called a bridge because of another collapse deeper inside that allows the sun to shine in like a skylight or back door.

When you're ready, retrace your steps to the trailhead.

Directions: Take Skull Cave Road east off the main park road to the parking area and trailhead on the left.

31. Black Crater Trail

EFFORT: Minimal
LENGTH: 1.0 miles
GEOLOGICAL FEATURE(S): Volcanism
LOCATION: Lava Beds National Monument

Description: This trail has a lot to offer. It's short, it has great views, and it takes you to what we believe to be the most beautiful spatter cones in the park. Geologically, it's an amazing place.

A *spatter cone* is a volcanic feature where hot gases mixed with molten lava escaped through a fissure in the earth's crust. In a way, they're miniature volcanoes. Contrast this sort of eruptive feature with the large cinder cone, Schonchin Butte, and the overflowing Mammoth Crater, all very different ways that magma emerged onto the surface.

You'll hike on a flat gravel trail for a short distance and then turn right towards the cones. The trail continues ahead toward the Thomas-Wright Battlefield if you want to check that out.

Ascending over rough black lava, you reach the rim of a large crater at about 0.3 miles. The trail continues inside on a cinder path around the crater's center. Take some time to look closely at the material. The flow patterns are lovely and obvious. You can easily imagine what it looked like in liquid form. Though the rocks are generally black, if you look close, you'll see a wide range of colors from bright red to jet-black.

Black Crater

If you can tear your gaze away from the rocks, you'll notice that you have a great view of the Klamath Basin to the northeast and the rest of the monument around you, including the chunky Devils Homestead Lava Flow. Off to the west Mt. Shasta rises up to meet the sky.

On the far side of the cone, the trail leads out over the back of it and down. Perhaps the most interesting part of this hike is found on the backside of the cone. Right away, there is a fine example of *pahoehoe*, the smooth, ropy type of lava, which is less characteristic of this flow than the sharp and jagged type known as *aa*. As you look closely at the lava, you'll notice metallic colors shimmering there—shades of gold, silver, copper, and bronze. We doubt that lava can get any more beautiful than this. Take some time to enjoy it.

As you continue on the trail, you'll see that there are at least four distinct spatter cones here. You can climb up and look into the craters of each one. The trail makes a loop around the entire complex, with short spurs through the rocks where people have found interesting views.

Coming back around the front of the formation, you follow the trail through a gully and then back to the flat trail you came out on. Retrace your steps back to the trailhead.

Directions: The trailhead and parking area are on the east side of the main park road north of the Visitor Center.

32. Fleener Chimneys

EFFORT: Minimal
LENGTH: 0.25 miles
GEOLOGICAL FEATURE(S): Volcanism
LOCATION: Lava Beds National Monument

Description: This short trail takes you to two large spatter cones, similar to Black Crater (Hike #31), but not quite as attractive. The main difference here is that the central crater is deep. The cones were created by thick, pasty molten lava burbling up and piling on top of itself. A hole is left in the center where the lava emerged, giving it a chimney-like appearance. The hole inside one of the chimneys is fifty feet deep. The chimneys are the source of the tremendous aa lava flow called The Devil's Homestead, an eruption that occurred between 2,000 and 8,000 years ago. You'll pass over this black, blocky lava field on the main park road. There is a pullout, and it's worth a stop.

There is a picnic area here shaded by western juniper trees. The picnic tables were constructed by members of the CCC; the logs were obtained at Oregon Caves and the rocks were gathered locally. A wheelchair-accessible toilet is also available here and the trail is paved up to the point where it begins to ascend the flanks of the cones. Beyond this, you must walk, but the trail is easy, rising gently to the rim of the craters. They have metal bars placed over them to prevent people from falling in (or climbing down inside).

From the top of the northern chimney, if you look to the north, you'll see a perfectly-shaped dome nearby, the remains of a collapsed lava tube. You can walk down and examine it more closely if you want, but if you've already done the cave loop, you may be a little hard to impress at this point.

The trail makes a circuit around the chimneys and then back to the parking lot.

Wildflowers, such as Indian paintbrush, phacelia, and mariposa lilies can be seen in the area in season. Coyotes, pronghorn, and deer have also been spotted crossing the road at various times.

Directions: On the main park road, from the Visitor Center, go north past the turnoff for Merrill Cave. The access road is on the left before you reach the Black Crater trailhead.

33. Schonchin Butte Trail

EFFORT: Difficult
LENGTH: 1.8 miles
GEOLOGICAL FEATURE(S): Volcanism
LOCATION: Lava Beds National Monument

Description: If you want to climb to a high point at Lava Beds, Schonchin Butte is your best bet. It's the only cinder cone in the park with a formal trail to the top. It's a steep climb, rising 600 feet, that will leave most people breathless. From just about anywhere in the monument (above ground, that is), you'll be able to gauge your position by locating this prominent landmark. It has been said that the entire world of the Modocs can be seen from atop this peak.

Schonchin Butte, named for Old Schonchin, a chief of the Modoc people, is a cinder cone like those we've already encountered, an eruption that occurred more than 60,000 years ago, emplacing andesite with a high silica content and blocky basalt that piled up on top of itself up to 100 feet high. Today this volcano is a fire lookout staffed by rangers from May to September. The trail and lookout tower were built by the Civilian Conservation Corps between 1939 and 1942.

If you climb this trail in late spring or summer, you'll be rewarded with abundant wildflower blooms of penstemon, Mariposa lilies, and sulfur flowers.

Starting at the northeast side of the cone, the trail is signed "Schonchin Butte Trail: Foot Traffic Only." The trail switchbacks up the mountain, making the climb a little easier. There's not much variation as you climb through sagebrush and bunch grass over volcanic soils. As you come around to the north side of the cone, the environment is a little less barren with juniper trees and some grass. When you come upon a bench in the shade of a juniper, you may want to rest a bit. The trees are old, twisted, and stunted, testifying to the severity of life here.

Walking in open sun, you come to a fork. You can go either way here to reach the summit and lookout. Notice that the trail is now covered with red cinders, the typical ejecta of cinder cones.

Once you make it to the lookout, you'll see that the tower is built on a pile of splattered lava from the main vent of the cone. You'll find an inscription in the cement telling you that you're at 5,293 feet in elevation, over a mile high, and that the cement was poured on 8/26/1942.

Take a seat and take in the view. To the north, you'll be looking into Oregon, perhaps as far as Crater Lake. To the east, look into Nevada and the Warner Mountains. West, snow-capped Mt. Shasta rises up to dominate the landscape, and south you look out over the Medicine Lake Highlands with its pine forest cover. Closer in, you can see Tule Lake, and between that body of water and the base of this cinder cone, a bare, black lava flow of blocky basalt. Most of Lava Beds was covered over by the eruption of Mammoth Crater (Hike #28) about 30,000 years ago. But this flow was more viscous, building up into impassable walls of rock, so the more fluid lava of Mammoth flowed around rather than over it. If you could get a close up view of the two lava flows side by side, you'd be able to see the difference between them—the ropy lava of Mammoth vs. the blocky lava of Schonchin.

Rest a while, enjoy your perch and then descend via the same route.

Directions: Heading north from the Visitor Center on the main park road, just after the turnoff for Merrill Ice Cave on the left, you'll reach the road for Schonchin Butte on the right (east).

34. Heppe Ice Cave

EFFORT: Minimal
LENGTH: 0.8 miles
GEOLOGICAL FEATURE(S): Volcanism, Caves
LOCATION: Lava Beds National Monument

Description: This trail takes you to a large collapsed lava tube that is easily explored and contains frozen pools of water. Begin by walking out under pine trees with bitterbrush, yarrow, and buckwheat alongside. Red-tailed hawks, ravens, and turkey vultures can often be seen riding the air currents above.

At the end of this short trail, you'll come upon an enormous collapse. Heppe's Bridge is visible at the far end. Continuing along the trail, you pass Heppe's Chimney, a fine example of a *hornito*. A hornito is similar to a spatter cone. It's often formed when lava pushes up out of the roof of a lava tube under pressure, splattering up and over itself, creating this feature. Another name for a hornito is a *driplet cone*.

Follow the trail into Heppe Cave. It has large openings at either end where the ceiling collapsed. At the cave entrance, where it is cooler than the trail you just left, ferns have found a niche to dwell in. Lichen also grows on the inside of the cave. Swallows nest here in spring, and other animals use this cave as a reliable source of water. At the bottom of the trail is a pool of water on a base of ice.

This isn't the only ice cave in Lava Beds. There's Merrill Ice Cave, which you can visit, as well as the extraordinary and beautiful frozen display in Crystal Cave. To protect this special cave, visitors have access only on small guided tours during the winter.

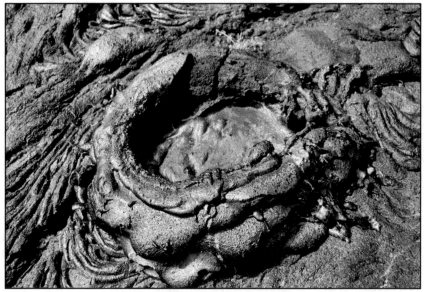

Hornito (NOAA)

In a park visited by few, Heppe Ice Cave is a spot visited by even fewer. So take a few moments to sit and enjoy the solitude before retracing your steps. It will probably be just you and the chipmunks.

Directions: From the Visitor Center, go north to the gravel road for Mammoth Crater, and turn left on that. Pass Mammoth Crater heading south out of the monument. You will see a sign to Heppe Ice Cave. Turn left and proceed to the parking area.

35. Captain Jack's Stronghold Trail

EFFORT: Minimal
LENGTH: 0.5 or 1.5 miles
GEOLOGICAL FEATURE(S): Volcanism
LOCATION: Lava Beds National Monument

Description: There are two self-guiding interpretive trails into this historic site. Take the shorter or longer one, as you please. Both are fairly level and include representative volcanic features.

During the Modoc War of 1872-1873, the Modoc Indians used these tortuous lava flows to their advantage. Under the leadership of Captain Jack, son of a Modoc chief, the Modocs took refuge here in a natural lava fortress in November, 1872. Their grievance was based on the refusal of the U. S. government to give them a reservation of their own near their ancestral home on the Lost River. They were forced, instead, to share the Klamath reservation with the Klamath and Pit River Indians. The Klamath people were their long-time enemies, and they were not well treated on that reservation.

From this base, a group of 52 Modoc men held off U. S. Army forces numbering up to twenty times their strength for five months. In the end, however, Captain Jack and his followers were vastly outnumbered and were taken into custody. During the war, Captain Jack shot and killed General Edward Canby during peace negotiations. For that act, he and three of his men were hanged on October 3, 1873.

As you walk the trail, you will soon see how defensible this spot would be in a gun battle. There are plenty of places to hide. You'll visit two caves along the trail, temporary homes to the first and second in command on the Modoc side. You'll also see examples of how the Indians and the U. S. Army built fortified walls to enhance their defenses.

Climb around on the rocks and ambush your hiking buddies. Also, climbing to lookout points, you'll notice what fine views you have of the entire area. This was not only advantageous to the Modocs, but is currently of benefit to the many raptors that live in the monument. Nesting in the rough cliffs roundabout, they have a keen view of anything going on below in the monument and around Tule Lake.

Directions: From the Visitor Center, drive north on the park road and follow it as it turns to head east. After passing the junction with Hill Road, proceed about three miles further to the parking area and trailhead on the right. Restrooms and picnic tables are available.

36. Whitney Butte Trail

EFFORT: Minimal
LENGTH: 6.6 miles
GEOLOGICAL FEATURE(S): Volcanism
LOCATION: Lava Beds National Monument

Description: The trail takes you past collapsed lava tubes and 5,010-foot Whitney Butte to the western park boundary and the edge of the Black Lava Flow (aka Callahan Lava Flow), the youngest lava flow in the park, where you can get up close and personal with a vast field of jagged basalt.

Before setting out for Whitney Butte, take the short trail to Merrill Ice Cave with its permanently frozen floor and natural air conditioning. There was once a lot more ice in this cave. At one time it even played host to ice skating parties!

This flat trail will take you across the wilderness through low-lying desert type vegetation of bunchgrass, sagebrush, and wildflowers with no shade. As you go, you'll see Mt. Shasta on the horizon ahead.

At 2.2 miles, the trail forks. Bear left, walking along the northern flank of Whitney Butte. By its shape, you can easily identify it as a cinder cone. Continuing on the trail, you'll curve around to the western side of Whitney Butte.

At 3.3 miles you'll reach the vast Black Lava Flow, a thick basaltic andesite field forming a wall of jagged rock that marks the end of the trail. This lava erupted from 250-foot high Cinder Butte just outside the park boundary only 1,120 years ago. You can see why this spot became a boundary, as the lava field acts as a natural barrier to just about any type of land use.

Just prior to reaching this point, you may have noticed an informal spur trail leading up Whitney Butte. If you want to climb it, that's your route. You'll see the collapsed center of the volcano and have even better views than those from the trail below.

Return along the same trail.

Directions: From the Visitor Center, proceed north 1.2 miles, then turn left for Merrill Ice Cave and proceed to the trailhead parking area.

37. Cave Loop Road

We're going to conclude our Lava Beds section with the most popular spot in the park, Cave Loop Road. Beginning at the Visitor Center, this one-way road takes you to most of the explorable caves in the monument, so we're lumping them together for the sake of expediency. You can try them all, of course, if you have the time. If not, we've chosen a few we don't want you to miss. It's worth remembering that lava tubes are generally hidden under and within a lava flow, as they couldn't have been created without lava hardening above them. They're discovered when erosion causes a partial collapse of the ceiling, revealing the cave. No doubt there are many other lava tubes at Lava Beds that have not yet been discovered.

Lava Tube Entrance

We won't describe the trails through the caves in too much detail, since the route you take and the distance you travel can vary so much. But we will mention the most unique features of each cave. Remember to stop along the way and shine your light on the ceilings and the walls.

Because of the unusual nature of these trails, we're deviating from our customary format and provided the length of the caves in feet rather than miles. This distance represents the total length of the caves in one direction. You will probably make your own route inside the tubes, so time and distance will vary with each spelunker. Also, because Cave Loop Road is so short, directions are not given to each trailhead, but the caves are listed in the order you'll encounter them on the one-way road.

Mushpot Cave

EFFORT: Minimal
LENGTH: 770 feet
GEOLOGICAL FEATURE(S): Volcanism, Caves
LOCATION: Lava Beds National Monument

Description: This cave is perfect for beginning spelunkers. It is lighted and has information along the path about various lava formations. The entrance is in the middle of the visitor center parking lot. Don't skip

Mushpot because you're looking for a more adventurous encounter. This cave is quite interesting and worth the few minutes it takes to walk through it, especially if you're unfamiliar with the features found in lava tubes. This cave has quite a few of these, so you'll learn the jargon here before going out to the unlit and unsigned tubes.

Climb down the stairs into a tube tall enough to walk through upright. The cave will remind you of modern museum displays. The signs along the way have blue buttons to push that light up the features being explained. Even though the tube is lit, take your flashlights to get a better view of the drip patterns on the walls and ceiling. Drips that hang down from the ceilings are called *lavacicles*. Depending on how fluid the lava was that formed them, they can be little nubs or thin needle-like features.

The trail ends after a third of a mile where the tube runs out. Turn around and return.

Golden Dome

EFFORT: Minimal
LENGTH: 2,229 feet
GEOLOGICAL FEATURE(S): Volcanism, Caves
LOCATION: Lava Beds National Monument

Description: The most formidable part of this cave is the ladder leading down into it. It's straight down with a narrow passage near the top, so watch your head.

The unusual feature of the cave is the yellowish bacteria coating the ceiling. When these are wet, they glimmer with a golden luster in the beam of your light, hence the name of the cave.

Look for the pahoehoe floors as you go, another interesting feature of this tube not often seen elsewhere.

Blue Grotto

EFFORT: Minimal
LENGTH: 1,541 feet
GEOLOGICAL FEATURE(S): Volcanism, Caves
LOCATION: Lava Beds National Monument

Description: This is a fairly easy cave to explore. Its name comes from the colors of the ceiling that looks like it's been coated with black, light blue, and white frosting. In the main chamber below the ladder, you can go either direction. Behind the ladder the cave branches into several tunnels, some of which have ceiling collapses to the outside, providing some welcome natural light.

Catacombs

EFFORT: Difficult
LENGTH: 6,903 feet
GEOLOGICAL FEATURE(S): Volcanism, Caves
LOCATION: Lava Beds National Monument

Description: This one is for the thrill-seekers. It's the longest lava tube in California and one of the longest in the country. There are multi-tiered tunnels and interconnected passageways that remind us of the "twisty passages" maze of that classic adventure game, Colossal Cave. In the game, you never wanted to be there. But plenty of people do want to be here, and it can be a lot of fun in a scary kind of way. If you venture far enough, you'll have to crawl and squeeze through the passages and should be prepared for rough going. The first 800 feet are high enough to walk through. After that, the ceiling ranges from a mere 12 inches to 3 feet high.

People do sometimes get lost in this cave, but are usually safely recovered. Despite its many tunnels, this system has only one entrance.

Don't attempt this cave if you don't have caving experience. Bring a compass, study the map ahead of time, and carry a small backpack, as many passages are tight.

Sunshine Cave

EFFORT: Minimal
LENGTH: 466 feet
GEOLOGICAL FEATURE(S): Volcanism, Caves
LOCATION: Lava Beds National Monument

Description: This one is short, so you can easily travel the entire length without scaring yourself.

Just within the entrance, notice some interesting flow patterns. Large chunks of the ceiling have fallen to the floor—you'll be walking over them. As you go, you'll encounter two collapses in the ceiling where the sun shines in, giving this cave its name. At one of the openings, plants have grown around the hole and hang down into the cave.

There is a wooden walkway in this cave to make it easier yet, but in a couple of places you will need to duck.

Sentinel Cave

EFFORT: Minimal
LENGTH: 3,280 feet
GEOLOGICAL FEATURE(S): Volcanism, Caves
LOCATION: Lava Beds National Monument

Description: This cave is easily walked and large enough to stand upright through the main tube if you don't venture into the side tubes. The most unusual feature here is a tube within a tube, and that's why we're including it.

End of Lava Beds National Monument

38. Burnt Lava Flow

EFFORT: Minimal
LENGTH: Varies
GEOLOGICAL FEATURE(S): Volcanism
LOCATION: Modoc National Forest

Description: This is a weird and wonderful place worth a side trip on good gravel forest roads. Located southeast of Medicine Lake and south of Glass Mountain, Burnt Lava Flow is one of the youngest flows in the area, estimated to be only 200 years old, and is one of many flows originating from the vast Medicine Lake volcano complex. The source of this flow is the High Hole Crater cinder cone, which stands prominently above the field. It provides a dramatic focal point and possible destination for your adventure.

The landscape is black and blocky for miles around. The lava comes right up to the road on the west side where a smoothed spot near a pullout allows you entry into the field. You can stop at any spot where it's safe to pull off the road. There's not much traffic to contend with.

The only vegetation within the lava field is contained in "islands" that the lava spared.

There is no trail over the flow. You just put on some sturdy boots and climb up onto it. It's very rough and difficult to walk on. Gloves will be a tremendous help here since you'll need your hands to steady yourself on the uneven surface.

A few things to look for while you're traversing the once-fluid lava are flow structures and bubble holes (vesicles).

Burnt Lava Flow

Directions: From McCloud, go east on Highway 89 to Harris Spring Road and turn north (left). After a little over 4 miles, you reach a fork. Bear right on Forest Road 49 and proceed about 30 miles. Turn right onto Forest Road 56 and continue on the gravel road 4 miles to the edge of the flow. Access is free. There are no facilities.

39. Medicine Lake Glass Flow

EFFORT: Minimal
LENGTH: Varies
GEOLOGICAL FEATURE(S): Volcanism
LOCATION: Modoc National Forest

Description: A visit to the Glass Mountain Geologic Area is a truly unique and fascinating experience. Plan your trip somewhere from July to October, as snow closes the area throughout winter and spring. The "glass" is actually gray dacite and rhyolitic obsidian, a vast 4,000-acre lava flow from the Medicine Lake volcano. Like the Burnt Lava Flow (Hike #38), this volcanic event is quite young, about 300 years old, and remains in pristine condition. Visiting these companion lava flows, along with a picnic stop at Medicine Lake in the volcanic crater, would make a terrific day trip. Though the two flows originated from the same magma chamber, the conditions of the eruptions were significantly different, resulting in different types of rocks being formed.

Obsidian forms when the lava cools very quickly, too quickly to allow for the formation of crystals that are present in other volcanic rocks (even in basalt, though they are too small to see). It is called a glass because it is amorphous and therefore has the same non-crystalline structure as window glass.

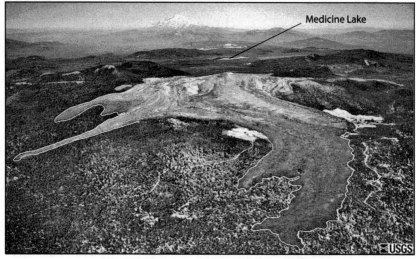

Glass Mountain obsidian field (USGS)

There are several glass flows in the highlands, including Grasshopper Flat, Little Glass Mountain, Glass Mountain, and Sugar Hill. These flows were used as prime obsidian quarries by native peoples to make arrow heads and spear points. Obsidian from the Highlands was traded throughout Northern California. If you know what you're looking for, you'll see evidence of those prehistoric mining efforts, as the most highly favored pieces were below the surface.

You can explore the glass flow at will, enjoying the unusual landscape. Wear gloves to avoid being cut. And avoid walking on the glass, sticking instead to informal pathways among the friendlier rock that appears here, gray dacite.

Directions: From Interstate 5 north of Redding, take Highway 89 east for about 30 miles. Just past Bartle, turn left on Forest Road 49. Proceed to Forest Road 97. Turn right and go 6 miles north to Forest Road 43N99. Turn left (north) and proceed to the southern edge of the Glass Mountain Geologic Area. Park alongside the road. The glass flow is directly off the road. Access is free. There are no facilities.

40. Spatter Cone Loop

EFFORT: Moderate
LENGTH: 4.8 miles
GEOLOGICAL FEATURE(S): Volcanism
LOCATION: Ahjumawi Lava Springs State Park

Description: If you're looking for a place to satisfy your thirst for adventure, this is it. Ahjumawi is remote and visited by fewer than 2,000 people a year. This park, a wilderness of forest primeval surrounded by water, is unusual in that you cannot drive to it. You have to take a boat. Make this an all-day adventure or even an overnight adventure and you will be amply rewarded. There are a few primitive campsites lakeside. If you fish, be sure to bring your tackle along. And because of the remoteness of this location, make sure you don't go alone and let someone know your schedule.

Ahjumawi means "where the waters come together" in the native tongue of the Pit River Indians. A series of lakes, rivers, and creeks come together here, forming a huge freshwater system through and around the volcanic island. The park trails explore lava fields, lava tubes, a spatter cone, cold springs, ponderosa pine forests, marshland, bedrock mortars, prehistoric fish traps, and wildflowers.

Over two-thirds of the park is covered by recent (three to five thousand years) lava flows from the Medicine Lake Highlands, so much of the land is rough black basalt. Flowing up through the basalt near the shoreline are cold freshwater springs. The source of these springs may be Tule Lake, fifty miles to the north, or it may be precipitation and snow melt. The abundant groundwater in the area moves through the subsurface through fractures in the basalt.

Once you arrive at the island on the shore of Horr Pond, take the trail away from the water. You can take the loop in either direction. We're going counter-clockwise.

You'll soon leave the shade of trees as you cross over the lava field through rabbit brush and sagebrush. On your walk to the volcanic features, keep an eye out for bald eagles, great blue herons, and mule deer.

When you come to a junction with the Osprey Trail to the right, continue straight. There's almost immediately a spur trail to the left. Pass it by and continue north. The end of the loop and the main destination for this trail is the spatter cone, a 5,000-year old lava vent. Examine its steep sides and imagine the lava shooting up through the center. When you're ready, head south on the return leg of the trail. You'll shortly reach some lava tubes which by now may be old hat, but are still of interest to the volcano aficionado.

Heading back to the trailhead, you'll be graced with the imposing figures of Mt. Shasta and Mt. Lassen, the two mighty Cascade Range volcanoes that we visited in the previous chapter. When you come to a junction with Lava Springs Trail and the shore of the lake, turn left to return to the boat dock.

Directions: From Highway 299 in McArthur, turn north on Main Street and pass the Intermountain Fairgrounds. Continue north on a graded dirt road for three miles. Launch from the P.G. & E. boat launch known as "Rat Farm." This trip is ideal for kayaks, but small power boats are allowed to access Ahjumawi. Larger power boats are not recommended due to shallow access points to the park. Cross Big Lake, veering left to reach the Horr Pond boat dock. There is a restroom.

SECTION 4
COAST RANGES

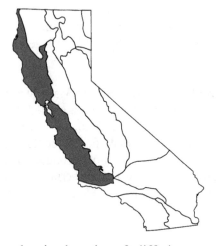

The extensive ranges of coastal mountains that border the western edge of California reveal the dynamic nature of the earth's surface and tell a fascinating story of what happens in the violent zone where tectonic plates meet. The mountains were largely formed by the Pacific and North American Plates bumping up against each other and by the shearing action of the San Andreas Fault. These ranges are a complex amalgam of sedimentary, metamorphic, and volcanic deposits of differing ages. The hiking trails through these mountains are varied, offering many types of pleasures, including unusual erosional patterns, evidence of powerful earthquakes, rare mineral deposits, abandoned mining operations, marine fossils, and loads of beautiful non-geology stuff as well.

The Coast Ranges, like the Klamath Mountains, played an active role in formulating the theory of plate tectonics. At first, geologists couldn't understand why so many different rock types representative of completely different depositional environments occurred in juxtaposition. In frustration, geologists coined a term for the whole mess, and the rocks were referred to as "The Franciscan Mélange," named after San Francisco.

Since this province showcases such an important tectonic plate boundary, it seems appropriate to take this opportunity to briefly review plate tectonic theory. When two plates interact at a boundary, there are a limited number of responses available. One possibility is that the two plates collide head-on, which is referred to as a *convergent boundary*. If the plates are made out of similar material (that is, two oceanic plates or two continental plates), both plates will crinkle up. The wrinkles are perceived on the earth's surface as mountain chains, such as the Himalayas in India, which came about when the Indian subcontinent crashed into Eurasia between 40 and 60 million years ago. It's also possible to have a convergent boundary where one plate over-rides another. This happens when two dissimilar plates collide, an oceanic plate with a continental plate. In that case, the less buoyant, more dense oceanic plate slides down underneath (is *subducted* under) the continental plate.

A second type of collision results when the plates slide past each other in opposite directions, forming a *strike-slip* or *transform fault* boundary. This is the type of boundary that forms the present-day San Andreas Fault running north/south through California.

A third type of boundary interaction, termed a *divergent boundary*, results when two plates are moving away from each other in opposite directions. In the Atlantic Ocean, new oceanic material is being created at the mid-oceanic ridge, which is the divergent boundary between the North American Plate and the African Plate. An example of a well-known divergent boundary on land is the Great African Rift Valley.

Around 30 million years ago, the North American Plate and the oceanic Farallon Plate were colliding at the edge of the continent where California now resides. As the more dense Farallon Plate dove under the buoyant continental plate, parts of the plate heated up, and the resulting melt gradually made its way back to the surface, where it eventually cooled and became basalt. On the journey to the surface, some of this material encountered continental crust, melting it as well, resulting in a mixture chemically somewhere between the two, typically forming the light-colored plutonic rocks diorite and granodiorite. This process continued until most of the oceanic plate was consumed and the violent collision between the plates rumpled up the land, beginning the formation of the mountain ranges we see today. Bits and pieces of the oceanic plate that were not consumed ended up stuck on the North American Plate as described in the Klamath Mountains chapter.

MAJOR CALIFORNIA FAULTS

1. S. San Andreas
2. Hayward-Rodgers Creek
3. San Jacinto
4. N. San Andreas
5. Elsinore
6. Calaveras
7. Garlock

The subduction of the Farallon Plate brought another, different oceanic plate smack dab up against the North American Plate. This is the Pacific Plate, which is still there today. The meeting place between the Pacific Plate and the North American Plate is California's infamous San Andreas Fault. At 750 miles long, San Andreas is the longest fault in California, with movement along the fault of approximately two inches a year. Of course, that movement is averaged over geologic time and actually occurs in fits and starts. In human time, there may be no observable movement at all. Additionally, the fault is not a single fault but rather a system of faults. There may be steady movement along one portion of the fault while there is no movement at all along a different portion.

Sign in Parkfield, CA

Although geologists talk about plates sliding past each other as if it's a smooth, continuous movement, in reality, the plates do not slide easily past each other at all. Different portions of the plates will be stuck in place, unable to overcome friction and move past each other. This results in the buildup of a tremendous stress. The stress builds until there is a sudden release of energy, revealed on the surface as offset and resulting in an earthquake. You can see evidence of this sort of offset on the Earthquake Trail (#44) at Point Reyes National Seashore and The San Andreas Fault Trail (#53) at Los Trancos Open Space Preserve.

As an example of how this works, we can refer to a fairly recent event, the Loma Prieta earthquake, that was observed, investigated, and measured with all of the modern equipment and knowledge then available. The 6.9 magnitude earthquake shook the San Francisco Bay area on October 17, 1989. It was centered on the San Andreas Fault in the Santa Cruz mountains and ruptured along a 25-mile segment of the fault at a depth of between 3 and 11 miles underground. The resulting surveys concluded that the Santa Cruz mountains had moved four feet to the north and six feet higher during that event. This is something to keep in mind when we talk about the continental plate moving at an average rate of one or two inches per year. While that is true, the average is a misleading description of what actually takes place.

The rocks that make up the Coast Ranges reflect their tectonic boundary origin. The largest group of rocks, the Franciscan assemblage (or Franciscan Mélange), consists of alternating layers of sandstone, shale and siltstone, with occasional limestone. The layers formed when underwater sediments violently cascaded down into submarine canyons in a sort of underwater landslide. Eventually, the energy carrying the sediments decreased, and the sediments ended up deposited at the base of the canyons. Over time, the sediments hardened into rock. They were later scraped off the oceanic plate and carried down into the oceanic trench as the Farallon Plate collided with the North American Plate. Later, after most of the Farallon Plate was consumed and the oceanic trench destroyed, compressive stresses brought about by the collision of the Pacific and North American Plates caused the buoyant rocks to be raised up and tilted. No longer underwater, they began to erode, with the silt and clay layers eroding faster than the sand layers. We'll see some of these upturned rocks on the trails with their sea shell fossils intact.

In addition to sandstone, you'll encounter erosion-resistant chert in the Coast Ranges. *Chert* is a fine-grained rock formed in the deep ocean from the accumulation of microscopic skeletons of tiny one-celled animals called radiolarians.

In the Coast Ranges, whenever you see tilted, layered rocks unevenly eroded with some layers sticking out and some layers eroded back, you're seeing an ancient sea bottom of sand, silt, mud, and muddy ooze.

Metamorphic rocks can also be found in the Coast Ranges. As you can imagine, when the Farallon Plate was subducting under the North American Plate, the existing rocks were subjected to intense pressure. One of the most common of the resulting metamorphic rocks is serpentine. Although serpentine is fairly widespread in California, it's rare in the rest of the United States. It's only because of the unique plate boundary system that rocks like serpentine are found here. Serpentine forms from hydrothermal metamorphism of peridotite, dunite, and other ultramafic rocks. Serpentine is weak and is responsible for many of the frequent and sometimes disastrous landslides that occur along the coast.

The coastal province is extremely large, extending from the top of the state in the north all the way down below San Luis Obispo into the Sierra Madre Mountains in the south. It continues inland from the coast over the Santa Cruz Mountains, incorporating the Mount Diablo Range, and then tapering off as it descends into the Great Valley to the east.

Mount Diablo, Mount Tamalpais (known locally as Mt. Tam), and the Santa Cruz Mountains offer extensive developed trail systems within the Coast Ranges. The East Bay Regional Park District has been extremely active in acquiring parklands, and they are much appreciated by Bay Area residents. The Point Reyes National Seashore and Pinnacles National Monument are two geologically important sites we'll visit to glimpse the wonders wrought along the uneasy San Andreas Fault zone. There are so many interesting day hikes in the coastal mountains that it's difficult to choose a handful, but we've tried to present a diverse few with representative geology to get you started. After that, you're on your own, but we hope that hiking in the gorgeous coastal mountains will be extra special once you have the geological experience to recognize what's going on underneath your boots.

Northern California Sea Stacks (U. S. Fish and Wildlife Service)

Trails of the Coast Ranges:

41. Ecological Staircase Nature Trail
42. Petrified Forest Trail
43. Kortum Trail
44. Earthquake Trail
45. Black Diamond Mines
46. Trail Through Time
47. Donner Creek Canyon and Falls Loop
48. Fossil Ridge Trail
49. Rock City
50. Castle Rock Trail
51. Round Top Loop
52. San Andreas Fault Trail
53. Stevens Creek Nature Trail
54. Mine Hill Trail
55. Senador Mine Loop
56. Tafoni Trail
57. Castle Rock and Goat Rock Loop
58. Moses Spring Trail
59. Balconies Cliffs and Caves
60. Old Cove Landing Trail
61. Limekiln Trail
62. Nipomo Dunes

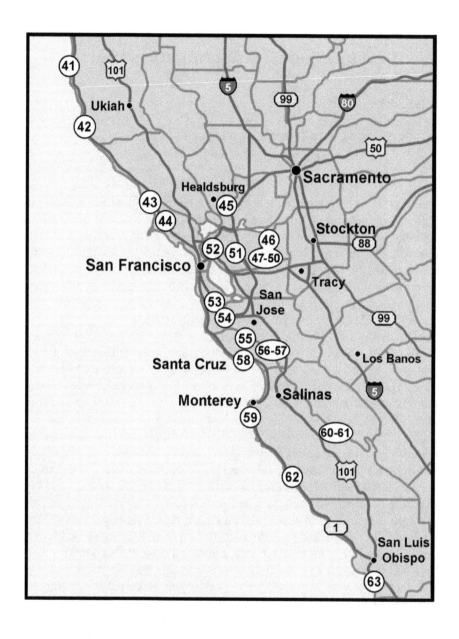

41. Ecological Staircase Nature Trail

EFFORT: Moderate
LENGTH: 5.0 miles
GEOLOGICAL FEATURE(S): Erosional Features
LOCATION: Jughandle State Reserve

Description: There are plenty of stairs on the Ecological Staircase Trail, both ecological and manufactured. Jughandle State Reserve is the site of an interesting and important geological process, the creation of marine terraces. There are five distinct terraces here supporting different ecosystems, the youngest located at the beach and the oldest in Jackson State Forest. Each "stair" climbs about 100 feet and 100,000 years backward in time, proceeding inland for a distance of three miles. Two and a half miles of that trip are covered by this trail.

The reserve is a natural scientific laboratory in which to observe landscape evolution. A *terrace* is a topographically flat area of ground that was created when a body of water resided for a prolonged period of time at that elevation. Terraces can often be observed carved out in mountains surrounding a valley that used to be filled with a much-larger lake (such as Lake Bonneville in Utah or Lake Lahonton in Nevada).

The terraces at Jughandle State Park were created by wave action against *graywacke* (pronounced "gray-wacky") sandstone cliffs and subsequent uplift caused by the meeting of tectonic plates. The terraces are unusually well preserved and distinct, making this one of the best places in the world to study terrace formation.

With that said, we have to insert a caveat regarding how "visible" that geologically significant process is to the hiker. Along most of the trail you'll be walking through a pretty forest with no visible geology. The trail brochure describes the flora along the way, but not much geology, and that's because the geology is subtle and is detected through the differing plant communities. As you walk over an ancient sand dune, for instance, you may not be aware of it. On the headlands loop portion of the trail and later in the pygmy forest, however, you will have a chance to see something of what lies beneath.

At the trailhead, grab a pamphlet to guide you through 40 numbered stops along the way. Note that some of the numbers are missing, but the post is usually still intact. Also take a moment to study the interpretive panel showing the layout of the terraces.

The trail starts by heading west towards the ocean and Jughandle Cove. At the grassy coast you are on terrace #1, and, if it is spring, you are likely to be treated to blooming poppies, Indian paintbrush, baby blue eyes, wild strawberry, and seaside daisies.

A new terrace is gradually being formed here under water. Each terrace is flat and was once the beach before a period of uplift raised it above sea level.

As you come around the headlands and turn inland, you'll notice that the trees near the coast—fir, pine, and spruce—are bent and twisted by the furious coastal winds. Up ahead you can see the bridge that supports Highway 1 over Jughandle Creek. We'll be passing under that bridge shortly and heading uphill through the forest.

Across the cove, the soil layers are exposed in the cliff face. Down below is a beach where the creek runs into the sea. From the parking area, there is a trail and steep staircase down to that beach if you want to visit it later.

For now, continue inland, into the coastal scrub where you may very well startle a brush rabbit. At stop #6, you'll find a fir tree lying on its side and creating a sort of tree cave with its roots and branches. It's fun to duck into this space, especially for the kids.

Soon you're routed back near the parking area where a trail goes right to it or ahead to continue the nature trail. Continue straight to walk under the Highway 1 bridge to the top of a tall staircase. This takes you down to the edge of the creek where willows grow thickly. The post for Stop #10 is at the base of the staircase, but the number is missing.

Cross the bridge to continue the trail on the other side of the creek, climbing out of the ravine. The narrow trail is hemmed in by vegetation on both sides. Be careful that the leaves brushing your legs aren't poison oak. You'll enter a forest of Bishop pine, flowering currant, red alder, and wax myrtle. The dark currants hang in brilliant pink blossoms all along the trail. Tall trees tower high overhead and sway in the breeze. Their creaking and the occasional woodpecker's drumming are the only sounds in the forest.

Finally, after stop #18, you reach the second terrace. The only evidence of this is the changing plant community. Now the forest is dominated by Sitka spruce and Grand fir. Douglas fir, western hemlock, tanbark oak, hairy manzanita, rhododendron, huckleberry, salal, and sword ferns are also present.

As you head further inland, noting that you're walking on historical sea bottom, redwoods begin to appear in numbers. The understory is typical of coastal redwood forests, consisting of shade-loving plants like sword fern, deer fern, red huckleberry, redwood sorrel, and mushrooms.

Once you reach the 300,000-year old third terrace at stop #30, you're walking on ancient soil indeed. As you proceed, you'll notice a change in the surrounding vegetation as you approach the fascinating pygmy forest where highly-acidic topsoil and near-surface hardpan prevent deep root growth, resulting in extremely stunted plants. The pygmy forest was the main impetus for preserving this land. It was first studied in 1936 by Swiss soil scientist Dr. Hans Jenny, and was set aside as the Pygmy Forest Reserve in 1968. In 1969, it was declared a National Natural Landmark. Today, it's part of Jughandle State Reserve.

Leaving the state park, you enter Jackson State Forest where a boardwalk transports you over the lichen-covered ground to avoid damage to the delicate ecosystem. The lichens help to prevent erosion. Don't leave the trail, as this is a truly unique environment that is extremely sensitive to intrusion. True pygmy forests occur only in isolated patches in northern California where wave-cut terraces have remained flat over hundreds of thousands of years of uplift. Over time, the minerals in the soil leach down to a depth of about 18 inches where the iron particles collect and form a hard, impenetrable layer. The top layer is eventually nearly white, having lost its mineral content. No new soil is created and there is no higher terrace to provide nutrient run-off. This is the environment that these plants struggle with, adapting by growing slowly and compactly, practicing a sort of extreme energy conservation.

The trees appear even more stunted as you continue. A hundred year old tree will be just a few inches in diameter and reach only a couple of feet tall. Pygmy cypress, Bolander pine, Bishop pine, rhododendron, salal, huckleberry, and manzanita grow here. Notice how all of the plants in the pygmy forest are less robust than the same plants we saw earlier on the trail.

The trail loops around at the end, after which you will retrace your steps to the trailhead, now traveling mainly downhill back to the coast.

Directions: On Highway 1, five miles south of Fort Bragg and five miles north of Mendocino, turn west into the Reserve parking lot. Note: Those who want to skip the hike can still visit the pygmy forest in Van Damme State Park. This alternate trailhead can be found on the left on Airport Road three miles off of Highway 1 just south of the main entrance to Van Damme State Park.

42. Bowling Ball Beach

EFFORT: Minimal
LENGTH: 1.5 miles
GEOLOGICAL FEATURE(S): Erosional Features
LOCATION: Schooner Gulch State Beach

Description: In addition to an interesting geological oddity, Bowling Ball Beach is a beautiful spot to watch the sun set or spend some time beach combing and picnicking. It's imperative that you come at low tide or you won't see the "bowling balls."

Bowling Ball Beach

The short trail leads out into a thicket of vegetation and may be muddy at certain times of year, then through a grassy bluff to a climb down slippery steps, logs and rocks where a ladder used to be. There's still a rope you can hang on to. Getting down to the beach here requires a little effort and care, but most people will be able to do it. Once you hit the beach, turn right to walk about 0.2 miles, at which point you'll start to see the rocks that make this place geologically interesting. They're large round boulders in the surf, strangely lined up in rows atop a hard wave-cut platform as if somebody arranged them here. But that isn't the case. This is a natural phenomenon. The lanes of boulders are best observed if you go out into the water to get parallel with them, and the cool photographs you may have seen are best taken low to the ground.

So what are these things and how did they get here? After you've had an eyeful of the boulders in the surf, turn around and go up to the sandstone cliff at the top of the beach. This cliff is composed of the Miocene Galloway Formation. Notice that there are similar boulders sitting at the base of the cliff and some still embedded in the cliff, as well as lots of indentations where boulders used to be. These boulders are called *concretions* and are much harder than the surrounding material in which they are embedded. Concretions are formed by the tendency of like minerals to precipitate around a common center.

As the cliff erodes over time, the concretions remain intact and are deposited at the base of the cliff. Gradually, the shoreline recedes, leaving these sandstone nodules behind. By observing the lanes in which the bowling balls line up, you can picture where the edge of the cliff used to be.

Back to the bowling balls in the surf—some of these are loose, but some are still eroding out of their parent rock, which you can observe around the base of some of the boulders.

When you're ready, the way out of here is the way you came in. Scrambling up to the bluff is actually easier than coming down and should pose no problem.

Directions: The state beach is located three miles south of Point Arena where Schooner Gulch Road intersects State Highway 1. There is a small parking area on the west side of the highway. There are two trails here. The southern one leads to Schooner Gulch beach. You want the northern one to Bowling Ball Beach. Access is free.

43. Salt Point Trail

EFFORT: Minimal
LENGTH: 2.5 miles
GEOLOGICAL FEATURE(S): Erosional Features
LOCATION: Salt Point State Park

Description: Beginning at Gerstle Cove, this gorgeous coastal trail, named for the salt that accumulates in rock crevices, will give you access to ocean vistas, a rugged shoreline, and some fascinating geology. Meanwhile, gulls, cormorants, pelicans, and other marine birds will keep you company. This is also a haul-out spot for several types of marine mammals, and harbor seals are nearly always sighted on the rocks just offshore.

Geologically, there are several things going on here—rare erosional patterns, historic quarrying activity, and a tectonic plate boundary. The lands of this park straddle the San Andreas Fault. On the west side of the fault, you're standing on the Pacific Plate. On the east side, you'd be on the North American Plate. Therefore, the rocks on the bluff trail are quite different in age and composition from those in the forested slopes further inland where the primary rock type is the Franciscan Mélange. Along this trail, the rocks we'll visit belong to the German Rancho Formation, a tilted sequence of sedimentary rocks consisting of Paleocene and Eocene sandstone, conglomerates, and mudstone. Although we'll talk in more depth about the plate movement in subsequent sections, it's worth remembering here that while you're walking on the Pacific Plate on this trail, you and the land under your feet are moving northward relative to the land on the east side of the fault. This has been ongoing for a long time, so the rocks at the beach originated somewhere down south and are just passing by on their journey northward.

The parking area and the beginning of the trail are located on the flat marine terrace that used to be the beach in Pleistocene time. The flatness of the bluff is evidence that it was once a beach and was subsequently uplifted above the level of the sea. Today, this flat surface makes a pretty good parking lot. Down below, the waves are carving yet another such terrace. These terraces are formed in a stairstep fashion because marine sediments accumulate at sea level during stable periods and then, during times of change, the land rises and a new beach forms. Several of these terraces are preserved along the Ecological Staircase Nature Trail (Hike #41).

As you explore the area, you may see evidence of past quarrying efforts like cut slabs of sandstone and drill holes. In the mid-1800s, this site was mined for sandstone that was used to build streets and buildings in San Francisco. Before that, it was an important salt collecting site for native peoples.

The first segment of the trail is flat gravel and wheelchair accessible. As soon as you get to the bluff over the ocean, you'll notice some interesting erosional patterns in the rocks below.

At 0.25 miles, cross Warren Creek. If you want to take a side trip, take the spur trail here down to the cove at the mouth of Warren Creek. Then return to the trail and continue north past some remarkable pitted sandstone called *tafoni*, an Italian word meaning "cavern." The name comes from Sicily where impressive honeycomb structures have formed in the coastal granite.

You'll want to spend some time here because the rocks are delightful and unusual. We've seen similar tafoni at Rock City (Hike #49) on Mt. Diablo and other coastal trails like the Tafoni Trail (Hike #53), but this is a massive feast of tafoni, so not to be taken for granted.

Although there are various hypotheses regarding the formation of tafoni, we think the explanation provided for Mount Diablo's Rock City applies best here. At Rock City, it has been suggested that percolating groundwater dissolved the cementing minerals in the sandstone and then deposited the material on the outer layers, creating a sort of shell. When water penetrates through the shell, it encounters the easily eroded sandstone under it and carves out a smooth, circular cavity, leading to these interesting formations. This process is sometimes referred to as *cavernous weathering.*

Poke around the rocks at your leisure, making sure you take time to look at the salt crystals that have accumulated inside some of the hollows. Even the rocks that don't exhibit tafoni have interesting patterns of weathering, some of them showing off a colorful tortoise shell design.

Salt Point Tafoni

When you reach Stump Beach Cove at just over a mile, take the road steeply down to the beach to a picnic area. This is the end of our described route, but you can extend your hike by picking up the coastal trail to the north of the Stump Beach parking area and walking another two miles to Fisk Mill Cove. If you press on, you will cross Miller Gulch, then Phillips Gulch, and eventually Chinese Gulch. Both Chinese Gulch Creek and Phillips Creek fall over the steep bluff in thin waterfalls stretching down to the beach below.

The Fisk family ran a ranch here for many years and their family cemetery is situated along the coastal trail just to the north. When you're ready to turn around, return by the same route. As you make your way back, reflect upon everything you've observed on this trail. Although it seems quite peaceful here now with only the gulls and the waves in motion, everywhere you look is evidence of movement and change on a massive scale. There are rocks that originated far out to sea and rode in. There are sea stacks that used to be surrounded by a softer matrix, now gone. There is the terrace you're walking on, which used to be at sea level. Some of the rocks now on the Sonoma Coast came from somewhere much further south. The more you think about the history of the landscape in sight, the more you can appreciate that nothing is static after all. Like a crime scene investigator, the geologist must observe all of this evidence and put together the sequence of events that came before. In this spot, the story being revealed is one of the most challenging. Pieces of this puzzle are yet to be found.

Directions: From Jenner on Highway 1, proceed north 16 miles, then turn west into the park's main entrance at Gerstle Cove and follow the signs to Marine Terrace Parking Area. There is a fee, picnic tables, and restrooms. Salt Point has a small visitors center open from April to November on weekends and holidays.

44. Earthquake Trail

EFFORT: Minimal
LENGTH: 0.6 miles
GEOLOGICAL FEATURE(S): Fault Activity
LOCATION: Point Reyes National Seashore

Description: Although the lighthouse and beaches get a lot more attention in this beautiful coastal park, it is well worth walking the little geology trail if you are visiting Point Reyes. It won't take much time and you'll get to see visible evidence that the ground moves. Interpretive signs along this short, paved loop describe the plate tectonics, the 1906 earthquake, and related geology that are at work at this tempestuous plate boundary. Looking at any map of the area, you can see where the fault runs, as Tomales Bay, a long, narrow body of water, marks the plate boundary in a thoroughly visible way.

From the visitor center parking lot, locate the trailhead between the picnic area and restrooms. Walk out on the trail a short distance to a fork, then bear left to begin the loop. If you're here in spring, a gorgeous blanket of poppies will be blooming trailside. During the 15 minutes we were on this trail, we saw swallowtail butterflies, barn swallows, and a garter snake.

The first stop is a sign telling you that the San Andreas Fault is just in front of you, marked by a string of blue posts. If you look carefully at the hillside along the line made by the posts, you'll be able to make out a hint of the offset still visible. Following the posts, you'll come to the highlight of this trail. It's an old wooden fence, a rare bit of readily observable evidence of movement produced during a major earthquake. In this case, we're referring to the great 1906 San Francisco earthquake, estimated to have been about 7.9 magnitude. It occurred along the San Andreas Fault and broke ground for 270 miles. The shifting land moved two sections of this fence away from one another, marking the exact location of the boundary between the two plates. The fence on the west side moved north with the Pacific Plate. The fence on the east side moved south with the North American Plate, creating a remarkable 16-foot offset.

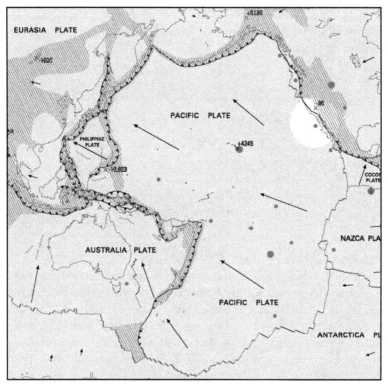

Pacific Plate size and direction of movement (USGS)

The relative movement for stike-slip faults, such as the San Andreas, is named according to which direction the opposite side seems to move to the viewer. The fence seems to have moved to the right; therefore, this is called a "right lateral" fault. If you walked over the fault, turned around, and looked at it again, you would see the same result: that is, the fence would appear to have moved to the right. So it doesn't matter which side of the fault the viewer is standing on; the result (and hence the name) is the same.

As the two plates grind in opposite directions alongside one another, stress begins to build up at the plate boundaries. Although the plates overall are moving at a fairly steady pace of one to three inches per year, the boundaries, which are rock against rock, can't really slide past each other. They are basically stuck. The boundaries "bend" and stress builds up. Eventually the stress overcomes the resistance to sliding and there is a release of energy, sudden movement along the fault, and a resulting earthquake.

Besides this dramatic evidence of plate tectonics in action, Point Reyes offers another clue that it is situated on a plate boundary. The rocks on the west side are quite different from those on the east side of the San Andreas Fault. The best match that has been found so far are rocks found in the Tehachapi Mountains 300 miles to the south! The same story has been reconstructed for Bodega Head just to the north of Point Reyes. On one side of the fault the rock type is granitic. On the other, it is the Franciscan complex, consisting of sandstone, greenstone, and serpentine. The differing rock types offer valuable clues to scientists trying to decipher geologic history. By matching the rock type here to its southern origin, they are able to deduce the path of the plate movement.

If you stand here and consider that this piece of land was once 300 miles to the south, you get a pretty good mental demonstration of the entire plate tectonic process.

After marveling at the disjointed fence, continue around through a meadow to close the loop and return to the parking area.

Directions: From Highway 1 in Olema, take Bear Valley Road west into the park and then turn left toward Bear Valley Visitor Center. Access is free. There are restrooms and a picnic area. There are two parking lots. Park in either one, but the upper lot is closest to the trailhead. Make sure you allow time to visit the superb visitor center before or after your walk.

45. Petrified Forest Trail

EFFORT: Minimal
LENGTH: 0.5 miles
GEOLOGICAL FEATURE(S): Fossils
LOCATION: 4100 Petrified Forest Road, Calistoga, CA

Description: A level, self-guiding interpretive trail winds through a grove of petrified trees that were felled and buried by debris from a major Pleistocene volcanic explosion. This is a privately owned attraction with a museum and gift shop. It was established in 1910 by Ollie Bockee and her family.

On this site, large redwood trees hundreds of feet high, up to 8 feet in diameter and 3,000 years old, were blown down in the path of a massive volcanic blast coming from the northeast. They were buried in volcanic ash and, over time, as groundwater flowed over and through the buried trees, the organic material in the wood was replaced by silica that was dissolved in the groundwater. Silica is the name given to the combination of the rock-forming molecules silicon and oxygen. Quartz is made up of pure silica, and minerals for which silica is a major component are known collectively as silicates. Check the redwoods beside the trail for sparkling quartz crystals. Some of the quartz may appear reddish from iron staining (rust).

Gradual soil erosion has brought these petrified trees into view, although many remain buried. Also, some of the fallen trees have been partly excavated and sprayed with water to display their crystalline composition more clearly. The signs along the way help to direct you to points of interest and explain the process of petrifaction.

Start the trail from behind the gift shop with a sampling of petrified logs, mostly light-colored in the characteristic style of the fossilized redwoods here. Head uphill to the left through a shady grove, noting the exposed *tuff* (rock formed from volcanic ash) among the manzanita bushes. This is the material that fell upon the area, burying and preserving the trees. Examine the rock along the trail for bits of volcanic glass, more evidence of the ancient blast that brought havoc to the forest.

The first petrified tree you come to is a pine. It's called the Pit Tree because it is located in a 15-foot deep pit with light-colored ash walls.

Next you come to the Gulley Tree, which has broken into blocky chunks. Continue on through a meadow.

A plaque dedicated to Petrified Forest Charlie and his mule is located along the trail. He was a sheep rancher who originally owned this land and was friends with local writers Jack London and Robert Louis Stevenson. Charlie discovered the petrified forest in 1870 and generously showed it off to the public.

Visit the Giant Tree and the Queen Tree, checking out their root balls, knots and growth rings. One reason this spot is so interesting is the exceptional size and age of some of these downed redwoods. It's hard to imagine the force that knocked them over. The Queen Tree was about 2,000 years old when the volcanic blast took it out. The Monarch Tree has the distinction of being the largest intact petrified tree in the world. It's 105 feet long and six feet in diameter. The Robert Louis Stevenson Tree is a good spot to look more closely at how the finer features of the original living tree were preserved in stone.

Complete your stroll by visiting the museum and gift shop.

Directions: From Calistoga on Highway 29/128, take Petrified Forest Road west for four miles to the entrance to the park on the right. Or, from the Redwood Highway (101) in Santa Rosa, go north to Mark West Springs Road. Proceed east to Mark West Springs where the road becomes Porter Creek Road. Continue east to where the road splits. Bear left on Petrified Forest Road and then turn left into the parking area. A fee is charged.

46. Black Diamond Mines

EFFORT: Moderate
LENGTH: 5.5 miles
GEOLOGICAL FEATURE(S): Mining
LOCATION: Black Diamond Mines Regional Preserve

Description: On this trip, we'll explore the site of historic coal and sand mining operations, visit a pioneer cemetery, and maybe do a little wildlife watching. In the 1850s, coal was discovered here in the foothills of the Diablo Range and several mines were set into operation. Five separate towns sprung up around the mines, occupied primarily, but not exclusively, by Welsh immigrants. This was the largest coal mining operation ever in California, producing nearly four million tons.

By the turn of the century, the coal mining stopped and the people left or turned to cattle ranching. But mining of a different sort was to resume in the next century. In the 1920s until 1949, underground activity resumed as 1.8 million tons of sand were mined here. The Somersville-area mine produced sand used by the Hazel-Atlas Glass Company in Oakland. The Nortonville-area mine supplied sand to the Columbia Steel Works in nearby Pittsburg. Mine shafts, tailing piles, an old cemetery, and some other remnants of the past are scattered in these now peaceful hills in this 3,700-acre park.

In spring, wildflower displays here are among the best in the East Bay, decorating the open grassy hillsides and cool canyons with swaths of purple, yellow, white, and red. There's an extensive list of wildflowers available in the Visitor Center. Among the many flowers we saw in April were California buttercup, Indian paintbrush, California poppy, blue dick, California mustard, and lupine.

Birdwatching opportunities are also good. On our trip, we did see several birds, including an aggressive turkey vulture that buzzed us and plenty of slowly circling red-tailed hawks. We did not see any other animals, but there are reportedly raccoons, skunks, opossums, bobcats, foxes, coyotes, deer, and mountain lions in the area.

As is the case in all of the Diablo foothill parks, summer can be brutally hot and dry. The best time to visit is winter or spring.

Get a trail map at the entrance kiosk, as there are many trails crossing each other in the area we're going to explore, and it can be confusing even if you have the map. This hike was planned by stringing together several trails to take you to a majority of the mining history sites, including the interesting Rose Hill Cemetery. But there are certainly much shorter routes if you prefer. In fact, on a short loop of the park's heart, you can see most of the sites of interest and take a mine tour. We would suggest signing up for a tour as soon as you arrive if you plan on doing it. The tours are popular and often fill up, so you may have to wait a while. It's worth it, though, to see the extensive tunnel system built through the sandstone.

From the parking area, walk uphill on an old road to a fork. The Nortonville Trail goes straight toward the picnic area and the Stewartville Trail goes left. Head straight through the picnic area, past a tailing pile on the left, to the Greathouse Visitor Center. This is a really cool stop, so don't miss it. The Visitor Center and Mining Museum is housed in a large underground chamber at the end of a mining tunnel. Artifacts from the mining operations and towns are on display there, including a couple of Chinese coins and children's toys. Also, the four types of coal (anthracite, bituminous, subbituminous, and lignite) are displayed, with a short description of how coal is formed.

Most of the coal found in the U. S. occurs in the Appalachian Mountains and is much older than the Eocene-age coal found here. Coal is made by the compression of masses of plant material that once grew in a swampy environment. Over time, the plants are buried and, through pressure and heat, the non-carbonaceous material is driven out of the deposit. With increased pressure and time, the coal becomes more and more pure carbon material. Lignite, the least pure type of coal, is made of barely decomposed plant matter, just one stage past peat. Lignite is the type of coal that was mined here. Anthracite, at the other end of the scale, is made of almost pure carbon. This purity results in anthracite being the cleanest burning coal and therefore the most highly prized of the four types. Coal was deposited so abundantly in the Eastern United States that the time of deposition, the Pennsylvanian and Mississippian periods, are often lumped together and referred to as the Carboniferous. The Carboniferous period occurred between 360 and 286 million years ago. To find coal in Northern California that was deposited 50 million years ago is exciting because it provides evidence that a swamp-like environment existed here at that time.

You'll also see a model of a mine and a description of the method used to get the sand out. In "room and pillar" mining the sandstone is blasted out to form "rooms," and the sandstone left intact between them form natural support pillars.

After leaving the Visitor Center, facing its entrance, climb up the railroad tie staircase to the right. This will lead you up to the Greathouse Portal, the original opening to the sand mine, now barred. Peer inside to see the tunnel disappearing into the distance. Step onto the Lower Chaparral Trail on your left and follow it to another junction. In addition to the mining remains, evidence of the human settlements include exotic plant species still growing here today, including the black locust, pepper tree, almond, eucalyptus, and tree of heaven.

Just ahead and to the left is a large pile of sand. Go over and check it out. This is the sand that was mined here to produce glass. You'll be struck by how white and pure it is. The rock from which the sand was derived is called "quartz arenite," which is the name given to very pure sandstone where the grains are all the same size. Throughout the park you will find such sandy spots alternating with light-colored sandstone, crumbly shale outcroppings, and very black, loose soils that are decomposed dark shales, all sedimentary layers once on a sea floor. Return to the trail and continue south on Chaparral Loop.

To the left of the trail you'll see train tracks and a mine opening. Above the tunnel is the date "1930." This is the Hazel-Atlas sand mine that operated from the 1920s until 1949. Samples of the glass made from sand mined here are on display in the museum.

Return to the trail and retrace your steps to the previous junction next to the sand pile. The Lower Chaparral Trail is to the left. Go straight to return to the picnic area on the eastern side of the Chaparral Loop. Return to the Nortonville Trail and go left towards the cemetery, which is visible as the cluster of trees on a hilltop to the west.

At this point, you have probably wandered around for about 0.8 miles.

Go through a gate and pass a muddy pond on the right. There will likely be cattle lounging around it. At a fork, bear right. This wide dirt road is open and hot, and it is uphill to the cemetery, so this is one of the least pleasant stretches of our route. Rose Hill sits at 1,506 feet. Puff up to the cemetery gate and past a huge old willow tree to explore the grave markers. Take time to read some of them. You'll notice that a large percentage of the graves here contain young children and infants. Many more contain people who died as young adults, including women who died in childbirth. When you consider how small these towns were and how short a time this area was occupied, it seems like these Jones and Richards families were trudging up that hill on a far too regular basis.

Exit the cemetery out the back gate and follow a footpath down to the Nortonville Trail. Turn right on it and continue through the green hills to a junction with Black Diamond Trail under high-voltage power lines. This is Nortonville Pass.

A large loop can be made by taking Black Diamond Trail all the way around a rocky ridge and back up to this point. Looking ahead down Nortonville Trail, you'll see that we're about to go steeply down for a half mile. On this out-and-back route, that means that coming back is going to be a monstrous endurance test. By taking the big loop route, you can avoid that, but the trail is longer. There is yet a third option that we'll detail shortly.

For now, continue on Nortonville steeply down the open slope for a half mile. At the bottom you'll reach a junction with Black Diamond Trail. Turn left on it and go through a gate.

At the next junction with Coal Canyon Trail, bear right to follow Black Diamond Trail. After 0.7 miles on Black Diamond Trail, you will join paved Black Diamond Way. Continue 0.14 miles to a junction with the top end of Coal Canyon Trail on the left.

Continue on pavement for 0.2 miles to a junction with Cumberland Trail on the right. Take it a short distance to visit an adit and an air shaft. Stooping, you can walk into the opening of the air shaft and look up to see a grate and light above. This shaft was used to vent harmful gases from the mine. Retrace your steps to get back on Black Diamond Way.

This is where you make your decision regarding the way back. If you continue on Black Diamond Way, you'll make a wide loop and come back out on Nortonville Trail just above the long downhill slope, avoiding that torturous half-mile climb. So why would we want to hike up that horrible dusty half mile to Nortonville Pass if we don't have to? The answer is Coal Canyon. It is a charming little adventure that we're grateful to have stumbled upon. In a park with so many hot open roads to hike, this hikers-only trail is a completely welcome diversion. And now that you're done with your history lesson, why not treat yourself? Be advised, however, that Coal Canyon Trail is steep and uneven, and may be strenuous for some.

For our chosen route, backtrack on Black Diamond Trail to the junction with Coal Canyon Trail. Turn right onto it and explore Jim's Place, a hollowed out room in the sandstone with a chimney and "shelves" carved into the walls where someone named Jim presumably lived for a while. Then duck into the shade of pine trees on this narrow trail. Notice the huge pine cones and scan the trail for pine nuts. They're black or dark brown and oval-shaped, about the size of sunflower seeds, and were an important source of nutrition for the native Bay Mi-Wuk tribes.

The trail goes steadily downhill into the narrow canyon. It is a rocky and rough single-track, but all the more fun for that. The trail is 0.88 miles long, and you'll be sorry when it's over. It soon joins up with a deep creek bed, usually dry. If you're lucky enough to catch the water running, you'll have a perfect adventure in this canyon, walking beside water splashing down the steep grade towards the canyon bottom. When we were here in April, the creek bed was dry, but the flowers were vigorously in bloom all around us.

Cross the creek bed a couple of times on the way down, no problem when it's dry. We walked through some of that fine white sand along the way, and then walked across one of those black shale slopes, the rock crunching like cinders underfoot. The smooth sandstone was there as well. Look out for loose pieces of coal along the trail. They will be generally rectangular in shape and look sort of like burnt wood. If you find one, notice how easily it falls apart between your fingers. The coal found here is extremely friable and of generally poor quality.

At the bottom of the canyon, the trail spills out into a wide flat area where you walk forward to exit the canyon and join up with Black Diamond. Proceed on Black Diamond Trail back to the gate and junction with Nortonville.

Turn right and trudge up that punishing half-mile climb. Let's hope you didn't come here on a hot day. At the top, congratulate yourself, catch your breath, and continue past the cemetery and back to the parking lot.

Directions: Take Highway 4 to the Somersville Road exit in Antioch. Go south on Somersville Road to the Preserve entrance. Park in the lot at the end of the road. There are toilets and picnic areas here. On weekends, an entrance fee is charged.

47. Donner Creek Canyon and Falls Loop

EFFORT: Difficult
LENGTH: 6.0 miles
GEOLOGICAL FEATURE(S): Erosional Features
LOCATION: Mount Diablo State Park

Description: This steep loop takes you up one side of Donner Canyon and back on the other, with a seasonal waterfall at the back of the canyon. For the best waterfall action, take the hike in winter, but be aware that the trails can be muddy and even harder to negotiate. We went in mid-April and couldn't imagine a better time. The astounding variety of wildflowers blooming from one end of the hike to the other was more than sufficient reward for the effort. The trails were dry but the creeks were still flowing, and the waterfall, though modest, was running. Avoid this trail in summer, however, as it will kill you.

Among the flowers you may see blooming in spring are California poppy, lupine, birds eye gilia, blue dick, blue-eyed grass, fiddleneck, globe gilia, California buttercup, goldfield, brodiaea, bush monkeyflower, hound's tongue, Indian paintbrush, Indian warrior, Ithuriel's spear, Chinese house, cow parsnip, miner's lettuce, mules ear, and cream cup. Of course, these flowers will be receiving visitations from numerous types of butterflies and bees.

This is a trail that can introduce you to the geology of the mountain, from the sedimentary mudstone at the trailhead, through metamorphic serpentine, and then igneous basalt at the falls. Wow, this trail has it all!

From Regency Drive, step past the gate on the left and walk down to the trail. Turn left and go past the gate marking the state park boundary. The park's trails are well signed, so if you pay attention to the signposts, you'll easily find your way.

Head south on Donner Canyon Road, walking along Donner Creek, passing through stately blue oaks, California buckeye, and gray pines. Looking back, you have a good view of the large diabase rock quarry nearby.

The road is wide, running across the 140-million year old Knoxville Formation, a Mesozoic clayey mudstone. If it has rained recently, this material creates sticky mud and an uncomfortable hike. You'll share the road with equestrians and bicyclists. Various trails take off from this road, but resist them for now. Near the start of the hike, watch for ground squirrels in the grass at the edge of the trail. In some spots along the creek, the calls of cicadas are boisterous. The road will climb gently for the first mile, a deceptive beginning.

After almost a mile, you'll reach the Donner Cabin site on your left. It was once a park residence, but burned down several years ago. When you reach a junction with Hetherington Loop Trail, you may choose to take it, as it parallels the road. We recommend it for several reasons. It's cooler and a little less steep than the road, and is more scenic. It's also a hikers-only path. Otherwise, continue straight on Donner Canyon Road. The rest of us will turn left onto the narrow Hetherington Loop Trail.

As the trail climbs, you'll enter a chaparral habitat, characterized by toyon, sage, manzanita, yerba santa, and buckbrush. This section climbs steeply, dipping in and out of dense shrubbery, producing wildflowers in earnest. The trail joins back up with Donner Canyon Road eventually. Turn left onto it. Proceed to the junction with Meridian Ridge Trail, where you turn right. This is the beginning of the loop section of our trip.

It is on the Meridian Ridge Trail that you'll first notice some serpentine, California's state rock. Serpentine forms from the reaction of hot seawater with peridotite, a material derived from the upper mantle. The seawater is heated by the extrusion of mantle material (as magma) onto the ocean floor. Later, after millions of years, the serpentinized periodotite creates an unusual soil that hosts a distinctive plant community dominated by manzanita, digger pine, and scrub oak.

You've reached enough elevation by now to see down to the valley below and the town of Clayton. Look back occasionally for these views.

Climb a short distance to the junction with Middle Trail, a tiny opening to your left. This narrow trail switchbacks uphill mercilessly through a jungle of shrubbery and a huge variety of wildflowers. It's a beautiful trail, mostly encased in brush, but sometimes emerging into tiny flower-filled meadows. Watch your step as you go; the fall down into the canyon is a long one. When the view opens up for brief stretches, you'll see a fascinating geologic formation across the canyon. Don't worry, you'll be over there soon, up close and personal.

At the junction with Falls Trail, turn left. Climb about a quarter mile until you come to a creek where you will find a good spot to sit down and catch your breath. Shortly after this, the trail crosses a shallow creek and heads uphill again. Near the creek is where ladybugs hang out in winter, covering the rocks and tree branches in semi-hibernation. As warmer weather comes, the beetles will mate and leave for the coastal valleys.

Emerging onto a ledge overlooking the canyon before you, you'll see the waterfall falling down the back of the canyon over a mossy backdrop.

The prevailing rock will change again, this time to dark basalt, or greenstone, created from volcanic eruptions on the ancient sea floor at a divergent boundary. These are the same volcanic eruptions that resulted in the serpentinized periodotites described earlier. This rock has been dated at 190 million years old. It was brought here when the Farallon Plate was subducted under the North American Plate.

You come near the falls about a half-mile beyond the creek crossing. The waterfall flows over and through the basalt. Just a few feet further on the trail is a nice place to stop for a break. When you're ready, continue on the single-track trail as it traverses the back of the canyon and turns to head north on the other side. In some spots, this trail is scary, extremely narrow with steep drops on the left. Finding a place to allow people to pass you can be difficult. But this segment of the hike is one of the best, and is perfectly safe if you watch where you're stepping and keep the children close. The flowers on the slope to your right are gorgeous with the brilliant colors of red Indian paintbrush, golden poppies, purple lupine, and Chinese houses. Down below you the creek tumbles along.

At last you reach the outcrop that was so tantalizing a sight from across the way. Fractured beds of reddish-brown Franciscan chert reveal their structure, alternating with bands of shale between each layer. Chert, which also goes by the common name flint, is a sedimentary rock from deep oceans, composed of the recrystallized skeletons of radiolarians, tiny single-celled creatures that lived millions of years ago in the open oceans. The radiolarian skeletons are made primarily of silica.

Franciscan Formation Chert at Mt. Diablo

A few steps along, you'll come to a wall of rock exhibiting fine chevron folds, contortions created by high pressure and temperature deep underground. Chevron folds are near and dear to geologists and never fail to ratchet up their pulse rate. As you continue on this trail, a waterfall will come into view quite some distance below you. Happily, nature has placed a couple of boulders beside the trail here for a strategic perch. Sit here with a view of the canyon and waterfall below and the rocky flower-covered hill above. This spot will also put you eye level with some turkey vultures as they swoop through the canyon.

When you're rested, continue over a bump of a hill and descend steeply to Cardinet Oaks Road. Turn left and walk the road steeply downhill. Make your way down the canyon until you reach a junction with Donner Canyon Road in another half mile. Turn right and continue your descent for 1.5 miles to the trailhead.

Directions: From Concord, drive through Clayton to Regency Woods. From Marsh Creek Road, turn right on Regency Drive and go to the end of the road. Park on the street beyond the last houses. There is no restroom or water here. There are also no picnic tables. Pack up your snacks and take them along to enjoy on the trail. Access is free.

48. Fossil Ridge Trail

EFFORT: Minimal
LENGTH: 1.5 mile
GEOLOGICAL FEATURE(S): Fossils, Erosional Features
LOCATION: Mount Diablo State Park

Description: This is a trek up to the top of Fossil Ridge, an interesting feature called a "hogback" with exposed marine fossils.

The trail leads through grassland and oak woodland. Like most trails on this mountain, the best time to visit is in early spring when the wildflowers are blooming, new green grass covers the hills, and the heat is tolerable. Mt. Diablo (Devil Mountain) is aptly named because in summertime, it's as hot as Hades on the mountain flanks. We hiked this trail in early March when a few blooms were already out and the green of the grass and trees was clean and fresh. This is not an exceptionally pretty trail, but it has good views and intriguing geology. We suggest combining this trail with a trip to nearby Rock City (following hike).

Find the signed trailhead on the south edge of the parking area. Start climbing steeply uphill on a partially paved service road. As you gain elevation, you'll come into good views of the surrounding ridges and the mountain summit to the east.

After about five minutes of walking, the trail becomes easier as it levels out. The paved section of the road will end, but the trail will still be a wide, easy dirt road with some up and downhill stretches. The trees thin out on top as you climb gradually into a fully exposed segment of the road. On your left, the hillside drops off steeply. On your right, in the distance, you have views of the Coast Ranges. On a clear day, this will be a little sugarcoating for this walk.

At a half mile, you come to the end of the road and a turnaround. A trail sign reads "End of Trail." This is deceptive because this is really where the real trail begins. Look to the right of the turnaround and locate a single-track trail up to the top of the ridge just ahead of you. Climb up to a wooded area with exposed rocks. Once you reach the top, you have some more good views toward the coast. Turn left to follow the ridgetop.

Marine fossil hash

Examine pieces of the exposed rock periodically to discover the fossils. The most recognizable are bone-white clam shells. They're embedded in what at first appears to be a boring rock (as if!) of gray and brown. But look closer. Much of the matrix in which the recognizable clam shells are located is composed of shells as well, lots of smaller pieces. In fact, this matrix may have almost no other components but fragments of shells. This type of deposit is called a *fossil hash*, which is indicative of a turbulent depositional environment. Think of the bits and pieces of shell you find on a beach. Because of the powerful motion of the waves crashing against the shore, it's rare to find a whole, undisturbed shell in the sand. In keeping with the geologic theme of "the present is the key to the past," the broken up fossil hash suggests that the depositional environment of this sandstone was a shoreline, such as a beach. Over time, while the tectonic plates at the coast kept grinding against one another, the coastal mountains were formed and the sandstone that used to be at sea level ended up here.

Fossils like these help scientists piece together the natural history of a region. With just a casual observation, we've already concluded two things about this rock—it was once the sandy bottom of a sea and it was located in a place where the wave action was substantial. With more in depth analysis, scientists can tease out a wealth of information about not only how the rock was formed, but when and under what conditions, drawing conclusions about environment, climate, and biota.

Continue across the ridgetop for a short distance until you emerge onto a grassy knoll overlooking a canyon. Look across the canyon to the hillside directly in front of you. There you will see the exposed rock running up the hill in two distinct linear outcrops. Also notice that the vegetation patterns are different on one side of the outcrop than the other. On one side you have brush and trees. On the other there is mainly grass.

This is a good place to discuss the formation and structure of a *hogback* because you've got an excellent view of one over yonder. A hogback is a steep-sided, narrow-crested outcrop that results from severe, vertical or nearly vertical tilting of rock strata. The formation was named for Hog's Back of North Downs in Surrey, England, which in turn was named for its resemblance to—that's right—a hog's back. The ridge you're standing on and its partner across the way are composed of alternating beds of sandstone and shale, marine layers that were once on the bottom of the sea. During the natural process of orogeny (mountain-building), they were lifted and tilted to a nearly vertical plane. During subsequent periods of erosion, the softer shale layers have weathered more readily than the harder sandstone, creating gaps between the sandstone layers. Much of the shale is gone, eroded into soil. The vegetation differences result from different soil types. Certain plants prefer shale soils, others sandstone.

This is the end of the trail. When you're ready, return the way you came.

Directions: From Interstate 680 in Danville, take the Diablo Road exit. Go east as the road becomes Mount Diablo Scenic Drive and then South Gate Road. Follow South Gate Road to the Uplands Picnic Area which is across from Lower Rock City picnic area and just before you reach Rock City. Park here. There are restrooms nearby and a couple of picnic tables and water fountain here.

49. Rock City

EFFORT: Minimal
LENGTH: Varies
GEOLOGICAL FEATURE(S): Erosional Features
LOCATION: Mount Diablo State Park

Description: The name of this place beckons, doesn't it? Before we visited for the first time, it brought to mind images of the Flintstones' Bedrock. Interestingly enough, while we were there, it did the same. And we were not alone. Children clambering through the wind caves spoke of their "bedrooms."

Rock City is a massive playground of boulders, wind sculptures, and depressions created in fine-grained sandstone by wind and water erosion. There are paths leading to and among different groupings of the rocks, but this is not a formal trail or even a hike. It is a meander. Walk among the rocks and crawl into the shallow caves and have fun.

Near the beginning of the trail is a trio of interconnected depressions called wind caves, wildly entertaining to the youngsters as they move freely among the three rooms. On your right is the sandstone wall and on the left is a fine view of the lower flanks of the mountain.

The sandstone here is made of quartz and feldspar that were originally part of the ancestral Sierra Nevada mountains. The particles eroded from those mountains were carried down by streams to the ancient sea that covered this area 50 million years ago. The sediment on the bottom of the sea eventually became sandstone and then, much later, that sea bottom was pushed up and tilted as part of California's coastal mountain range.

The hollows and caves you see here are formed through natural erosion in which rain water mixed with carbon dioxide from the air forms a weak acid that dissolves calcite in the rock, weakening the bonds that hold it together. The paths of the dripping, running water determine the areas where the rock is dissolved, leaving these interesting patterns. This process is ongoing.

The primary trail through Rock City has now become part of the much longer Trail Through Time and is signed as such. Shortly after the Flintstone wall, you'll reach a junction where the main trail turns right. For our route, continue straight.

You'll head down a rough section of trail through a narrow channel to see a lovely little cave that has openings on both sides, forming a kind of miniature Utah-style arch that you can pass through. You can continue further on this trail if you want, but when you're ready, return to the Trail Through Time and go left. You'll pass some more sandstone boulders containing hollows and some side trails that you can explore at will. Watch your step, as there are quite a few roots waiting to catch your feet and trip you.

The trail continues to a steep section down over rocks to get to Sentinel Rock, a monolith that you can climb with the aid of stairs and railings installed by the Civilian Conservation Corps between 1933 and 1942. It's a steep climb of 200 feet to the viewing platform, but it's worth the effort because it gives you a good overview of the boulder playground. Spend as much or as little time as you want before heading back the same way.

If you have time, combine this stop with Fossil Ridge Trail (previous hike). Together, they make for two easy adventures and a very pleasant day trip.

Directions: From Interstate 680 in Danville, take the Diablo Road exit. Go east as the road becomes Mount Diablo Scenic Drive and then South Gate Road. Follow South Gate Road to Rock City, reaching shortly after passing through the entrance station. Parking may be difficult to find on weekends, but you can park alongside the road if necessary.

Rock City wind caves

The Trail Through Time

The Trail Through Time...what an intriguing name. It conjures up images of worm holes and psychedelic vortices— time travel, the stuff of science fiction. But this is not science fiction. It's science fact. The trail does take you through time, geological time, millions of years, in fact, not in the blink of an eye, but in a strenuous mountain trek.

The trail goes from the base of the mountain to the summit, from the Miocene (from 24 to 5 million years ago) to the Jurassic (208 to 144 million years ago), covering 150 million years, traversing the geologic story of Mount Diablo a step at a time. That story is like an undisciplined work of fiction, jumping back and forth in time and abruptly from place to place. The topography of this mountain is upside down. Normally, the oldest rocks are on the bottom and each successive layer is younger, the surface layer being the most recent. But here, the highs are low and the lows are high, a geologic condition called *topographic inversion*.

The original rocks found on this mountain were deposited in the right order, with oldest rocks on the bottom, and then tilted up. After the rocks were tilted, the softer Miocene rocks eroded away, while the harder Jurassic Franciscan Formation rocks resisted erosion and remained topographically high. So the trail proceeds up the mountain and back in time.

The trail begins on Blackhawk Road at 750 feet in elevation. It takes you past Blackhawk Quarry, a very rich deposit of Miocene mammal fossils. As you go through Sycamore Canyon, you pass through sandstone and mudstone deposits containing numerous marine fossils. Continuing, the trail reaches Rock City at 1,300 feet, a 50 million year old Eocene sandstone outcrop. The path crosses the Mount Diablo Thrust Fault on its travels through the Cretaceous Period. At 2,300 feet, it reaches the Sunset Picnic Area. On the last climb of the trail, you enter the Jurassic Period characterized by the ancient sea floor deposits of basalt, shale, chert, and greywacke. At 2,900 feet, the trail reaches Juniper Campground and then continues paralleling the Summit Road to end at the Summit at 3,849 feet.

50. Castle Rock Trail

EFFORT: Minimal
LENGTH: 3.0 miles
GEOLOGICAL FEATURE(S): Erosional Features, Fossils
LOCATION: Diablo Foothills Regional Park

Description: This nearly level, wide road is popular with equestrians and bicyclists, as well as local residents out for a weekend stroll. For us, it's a visit to stunning sandstone outcrops and marine fossils.

From the parking area, you'll notice the equestrian and cyclist trailhead across the road. The hikers' route is past the gate on the paved road into Castle Rock Park. You can take either. The trail above skirts around the main park area and also allows you to avoid climbing a gate, but the gate is easy, so don't worry about it.

Walk up the paved road into the park past the picnic area, swimming pool, and park buildings. This is a private park, but hikers are allowed trail access through it. The road turns to gravel past the restrooms. You'll be walking through Pine Canyon alongside Pine Creek all the way with moderate shade. The landscape is primarily rolling grass-covered foothills of Mount Diablo with oak trees providing contrast. The trail is an old wagon road called Stage Road (and signed that way as well).

Leaving Castle Rock Park behind, you'll pass a gate and continue to a fork. Bear right to stay on Stage Road. Before long you arrive at a sandstone wall on the right that clearly exhibits bedding. The rock wall is tilted to almost vertical and several distinct layers are revealed, showing how sediments were deposited when this was a sea floor.

A short distance further you arrive at a rock on the right with a hole bored through it by water erosion. You won't be the first person to climb up into the round room inside the rock. It's a cozy little den with two windows, big enough to sit in.

The creek is on the left, and beyond that is the beginning of the intriguing series of sandstone crags known as Castle Rock, so named for their resemblance to castle turrets. Notice the many caves and holes in the cliff face. If you have your binoculars, you'll be able to see that the holes are used by nesting birds. The white streaks beneath the holes are a giveaway. Hawks, including red-shoulders and Coopers, are often seen in the oak trees near the trail. You may also see golden eagles.

There are many creek crossings on this trail, seven of them, and it may not be much fun from December to March, depending on rainfall and horse traffic. In fall, the first several of them will be dry, but during rainy season, you'll get wet fording them. There are also a couple of gates you may have to climb over when locked.

After the first stream crossing, you'll spot a narrow footpath leading to the right through the grass. In spring when the grass is growing, this path may not be apparent. If you come to the second creek crossing, you missed it, but by turning right and following the edge of the creek a short distance, you'll be there. Take the footpath past a grape arbor of sorts to a slide in a cliff above the creek bed. There's a rich layer of marine fossils in this cliff. Some of them wash down to the creek bed each year. If you look carefully for whitish rocks, you'll find pieces of this exposure. Thick clusterings of mollusk shell fragments can be seen. This sort of rock, composed mainly of shells with some sandstone is known as a "hash" for obvious reasons. Shell hashes in the Diablo foothills are generally of the Briones Formation. You can see these on Rocky Ridge in Las Trampas Regional Park, Fossil Ridge on Mt. Diablo (Hike #48), and various other locations in the area. If you look closely at the shell pieces, you may find some that are large enough to recognize as a clam, the dominant type of fossil. Pectens, the bivalve mollusk made famous as the symbol for Shell Oil Company, also occur, but are less common.

Why are the shells so completely shattered? Deposited in a shallow marine environment, the shells were slammed about by waves, turbulent storm currents, smashed on rocks, and generally abused until finally coming to rest and being buried.

It was at this detour to the fossil site that we came upon a bobcat and got within twenty-five feet of it before it sauntered off along the creek bed. It was also very near here that we saw a clutch of about twenty quail in the underbrush. Mountain lions have reportedly been spotted in Pine Canyon over the years, but it will be quite unusual if you see one.

Returning to the main trail, continue to the second creek crossing. Good views on the left of Castle Rock are still with us as we ford the stream for the third and then fourth time, keeping Pine Creek and the Mount Diablo State Park boundary to the left. After the fourth crossing, you'll be surprised to find a couple of picnic tables for a rest or snack.

Streams following the fourth crossing contain a small amount of running water, but it's easy to step across on rocks.

Eventually you'll come to Pine Pond, a reed-choked body of water frequented by ducks. This is the turnaround point.

On the way back, after passing the picnic tables, you may want to descend to the creek below to the right. There are several footpaths down to the trail there that edges right up to the state park boundary fence. This detour will keep you away from speeding bicycles and horses.

Directions: In Walnut Creek on Interstate 680, take Ygnacio Valley Road east to Oak Grove Road. Turn right (south) and continue as this road becomes Castle Rock Road. Proceed to the end of the road where it is blocked by a gate and there is parking on the left. Access is free. There are no facilities.

51. Round Top Loop

EFFORT: Minimal
LENGTH: 1.7 miles
GEOLOGICAL FEATURE(S): Volcanism
LOCATION: Robert Sibley Volcanic Regional Preserve

Description: It's a little funny to think of a volcano in the middle of the heavily-populated Oakland area, but this one no longer poses any threat and hasn't for a long time. Round Top is one of the highest peaks in the Oakland Hills and is what's left of a 10-million year old volcano. The evidence of this past shows up in several types of volcanics, including basalt and tuff (volcanic ash). There are exposed dikes and ancient mudflows. However, the volcanism on display here is not very dramatic, so we wouldn't recommend it to anyone who has to travel any distance. For locals, though, it's well worth a visit to learn about the volcano in your back yard.

You'll find the trailhead on the left of the exhibit building. Or you can start on a paved fire road on the right side. We prefer the foot trail. There is a map behind glass at the exhibit building that you can study before setting out, since we found no brochure to take with us. Also, lots of different trails and fire roads cut through the preserve, so if you get your trail set in your mind, you'll be better able to follow it.

Be prepared to share your time here with dogs. This is a very popular dog walking area with the local residents. And if you bring your own dog, plastic bags are provided at the fire road entrance.

During the first leg of the trail, Round Top will be on the right. The road is unshaded and hot in many seasons. At Marker 2, you'll see an exposed volcanic conglomerate with *paleosol* (literally, "ancient soil"). Iron rusting gives it a reddish color. The road is rocky, cutting through a chaparral-like landscape. We were there in October, yet a few resilient poppies were blooming. Also in color were some pyracantha bushes with their bright red berries.

When you come to the split between the Volcanic Trail and Round Top Loop, detour onto the Volcanic Trail to pick up some interesting volcanic outcrops. At Marker 8, you'll see a contact place between the Orinda sedimentary deposits and the igneous rocks from this volcano, broken by a near vertical chert bed.

At marker 9, there is a massive basaltic outcrop separated from weathered conglomerate by a fault. A *conglomerate* is a consolidation of gravel and may appear pebbly. Even if you're not a geology buff to the degree that you want to stop and peer at conglomerate, you'll still find the little canyon past the gate enjoyable. Suddenly you're facing a wall of multicolored rock, pinks and reds. The colors came about from hydrothermal alteration associated with steam and gases released from the volcano. Depending on the time of day, there is shade in this curve formed by the walls around you.

Turn around here and head back to the split with Round Top Loop to continue.

If the day is a clear one, you'll have occasional views of the San Francisco Bay and Golden Gate Bridge in the distance.

After climbing a bit, you'll come upon a spot where someone has arranged concentric circles of rock into a labyrinth. If you follow the path around and around, you end up at the center. Look closely and you'll see that those visiting before you have left offerings, as though they have made a symbolic journey into themselves. The day we were there, there was an acorn, a bead, and a nickel. If stumbling on this geometric construction surprised you, more surprises await.

Further along the trail you'll come to the edge of a cliff. Look down into the canyon. It has a marshy bottom and contains a labyrinth like the one you just passed, but bigger. The canyon also has a smaller rock circle on a ledge and a rock outline of a human hand. Use any of the several spur trails to find a good spot at the top of the canyon to take a picture from on high before following the path around and eventually down to the canyon bottom.

Round Top rock circle

The rock circles appeared in 1972; their builder is unknown to park officials who periodically clean out the offerings left at their centers, a painted rock here, a marble there. Once you emerge from the canyon, the trail changes quite a bit and the geology portion of the hike is over. You'll go over a ridge on a gravel road between two pine trees, and then descend a narrow, rocky footpath into a burned-out eucalyptus grove. The dead branches clattering in the wind sound like dry bones. This is a somewhat steep downhill walk. After this, you'll be walking among trees on the shady last leg of your hike back to the exhibit building and parking lot.

Although there is one picnic table near the front gate, it's not very inviting. You can carry your lunch on the trail and spread a blanket at the bottom of the rock circle canyon. Or you can take advantage of your location and find another park to picnic in. There are several parks along Skyline Boulevard, including Tilden Regional Park and Redwood Regional Park.

Directions: From Highway 24 just east of the Caldecott Tunnel in Oakland, take the Fish Ranch Road exit west to Grizzly Peak Boulevard. Stop at a turnout for a gorgeous view of the Bay. It will astound you. Turn left and drive to Skyline Boulevard, proceeding on Skyline to the park entrance. While you're driving on Skyline, you can contemplate the fact that the road follows the trace of the 74-mile long Hayward fault, the East Bay cousin of the San Andreas. Access is free.

52. Marin Headlands Trails

EFFORT: Minimal
LENGTH: 3.5 miles
GEOLOGICAL FEATURE(S): Erosional Features
LOCATION: Golden Gate National Recreation Area

Description: The Marin Headlands occupies the north shore of the entrance to the San Francisco Bay, the fabled Golden Gate. It's a historically and geographically important site and a treacherous waterway for ships to navigate. Often fog-bound, this entrance required three lighthouses to guide vessels safely into the Bay. Point Bonita lighthouse was the third of that trio, built in 1855 and still in operation by the U. S. Coast Guard. You can visit the lighthouse if you're here on a Saturday, Sunday, or Monday afternoon and want to add some history to your geology. As a promontory at the entrance to the Bay, this was also a highly defensible location during war time. Fort Barry and Fort Cronkhite were built here and military bunkers are still on site. This was also the site of a Nike Missile base during the Cold War. Today, the site is a museum and the only fully restored Nike Missile site in the country.

In addition to history and geology, this is an incredibly beautiful spot to spend a few hours enjoying green hills, wildflowers, and ecstatic views of the Bay, Golden Gate Bridge, and San Francisco.

Geologically speaking, the Marin Headlands is an ideal place to see the world famous Franciscan Complex. As we've mentioned before, understanding the formation of the Franciscan was critical to the development of plate tectonic theory and the workings of a tectonic subduction zone. The rocks we'll see here were created by that process of plate subduction. In particular, the assemblage of rock types here is known as the Marin Headlands terrane, a subset of the Franciscan that has been intensively studied by geologists. A *terrane* is a well-defined area of land and the closely-related rocks that make it up. You'll be able to observe some of these rocks in road cuts as you drive along Conzelman Road. One of the most distinctive is the swirly, reddish-brown *ribbon chert*, so called because of its extremely thin bedding layers. Recall that chert is a microcrystalline rock from the deep sea floor composed of radiolarian shells. With the naked eye, the radiolarians look like grains of sand, indistinguishable from the rest of the rock, but the microscope reveals the strange beauty of these one-celled animals. These fossils have been dated to between 100 to 200 million years old, indicating that the chert was deposited over a whopping 100 million year time period, and their type shows that they lived in a tropical or sub-tropical environment, obviously not what we have here today.

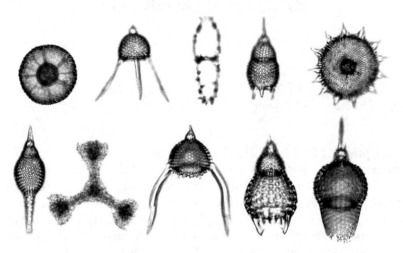

Radiolarian shells (USGS)

The other two primary rock types we'll see here are a Jurassic-age basalt and greenish-gray greywacke sandstone. In lesser amounts, there is also limestone and serpentine. These once discrete layers of rock have all been lifted up, ground down, pushed, folded and crunched into the mixture we see today by the long-term stresses of residing at a plate tectonic boundary. Studies of the Headlands have determined that the terrane originated in the central Pacific near the equator. It then moved northeast with the oceanic plate, colliding with the North American Plate at Mexico and subsequently moving northward on the continental boundary.

As for that gorgeous bay, it was formed about 8,000 years ago at the end of the last ice age when the glaciers melted and the seas rose to flood what had been a large valley with a river running through it. The bay is actually a drowned river valley.

If you have time and you're here when the lighthouse is open, before or after your hike, park at the end of Conzelman Road and walk the trail to the end where the lighthouse stands at the point. Look down below at the shoreline to see a spectacular example of jagged black *pillow basalt*. This volcanic rock takes its name from its resemblance to pillows and was created when an eruption of lava occurred on the sea floor, deep underwater. As the lava flowed from the fissure, it was cooled and rolled around by sea water, creating a distinctive looking rock with rounded edges.

For your hike, park in the Battery Alexander lot off of Field Road. From the south end of the parking lot, locate the long, sloping trail toward the beach. Head out on this trail, taking note of a footpath to the right about two-thirds of the way along, and make your way downhill to a wide beach with a long island just offshore. That's Bird Island, a greenstone (basalt) sea stack where you'll no doubt see shorebirds roosting or flying.

The beach is composed of dark, extremely coarse sand weathered out of the chert. Take a handful and look at it closely to see that it contains a variety of colorful pebbles, some translucent and some opaque. The red and green specimens are the chert. A hand lens here will be of some help to see the wide-ranging variation in the material.

To continue hiking, you have a choice, depending on the tides. If it's low tide, you can walk north along the beach, which will give you up close views of the cliff faces and the rocks. But if the tide is in, you'll have to walk back up the trail to the afore-mentioned path and turn left (north) onto it and then turn left again at the next junction, continuing north. Note that this trail is not on the official trail map, but people have made informal trails between this beach and Rodeo Cove to the north. That's where we're headed.

Either hiking over the grassy bluffs or on the beach sand, you'll end up in no time at Rodeo Beach. At the south end of the beach, you'll see an outcrop of pillow basalt that has been slightly altered into greenstone. Any cream or pink layers of rock you see here are limestone, and the reddish brown stuff is chert. The bedding layers of the chert are easy to see. Note where they are twisted and turned up at vertical angles. As you can see, these rocks, once laid down in discrete horizontal sequences, are now jumbled together and mashed up.

Ribbon Chert of the Marin Headlands terrane

As soon as you step onto Rodeo Beach, observe an outcrop of chert with highly distinctive layers, lying on the diagonal. This is the ribbon chert we mentioned earlier.

Continue north on the beach, noticing the same coarse sand encountered earlier. To your right is a high natural sand dam between the ocean and Rodeo Lagoon. During storms, the sea sometimes washes over that barrier. A trail circles the lagoon if you want to take a side trip. Altogether, it's about 1.8 miles.

At the north end of Rodeo Beach you can see some of the sandstone that makes up the Marin Headlands terrane.

From here, climb up on the Coastal Trail to walk atop the sandstone of the Franciscan mélange dramatically close to the intensely eroded Hawk Tail Beach. Stay on the narrow trail that hugs the shoreline for the best views. You'll dip down into and out of a ravine before reaching Tennessee Point, our turn around place for this hike. Return the way you came.

Directions: From Highway 101 heading south, exit on Alexander Road and turn left (Marin Headlands – Coastal Route). Just before Alexander Road takes you onto Highway 101, turn right on Conzelman Road. Stay on Conzelman as it loops around the headlands, giving you incredible views of the Golden Gate Bridge. There are a couple of pullout vista points along the way that you may be able to stop in, though they are notoriously crowded. Also, the traffic here is often challenging. You can avoid it by taking Bunker Road (Tunnel Route) into the park, but then you miss out on these world-class views. When you come to a roundabout, circle around to the other side and continue on Conzelman past more lookout points and more views. Head toward Point Bonita until you get almost to the end of the road. Turn right on Field Road, then right again, past Battery Wallace to Battery Alexander. Park here.

53. Tafoni Trail

EFFORT: Minimal
LENGTH: 2.6 miles
GEOLOGICAL FEATURE(S): Erosional Features
LOCATION: El Corte de Madera Open Space Preserve

Description: The reward on this hike is the intriguing weathered sandstone formation at trail's end. It appears out of place and oddly fascinating, sculpted by water over time. You and the kids will not be able to resist climbing on and in the smooth hollows.

After walking through a shady forest on a wide, level road, you reach a junction. Follow the sign to the right, and shortly you are there. This section of the trail is open to hikers only, but the rest of the trail is popular with mountain bikers, so expect them. We saw several on a Saturday trip.

The sandstone sculptures are tucked in among the trees, undulating tawny boulders with smooth surfaces. Cast off your daypack and scramble among them to find a good spot to relax. Although there were plenty of people out on the trails, we had these rocks to ourselves when we arrived.

"Tafoni" is a term that is applied to any rock that has weathered so that it has a honeycomb structure. See Hike #43 for an explanation of how it forms.

After exploring the tafoni formations and their many pockets and crevices, head back to the junction. At this point, you can return the way you came, or you can proceed ahead on a quarter mile spur trail to a perfect picnic spot with a view of the Pacific Ocean.

Directions: Head west on Highway 92 towards Half Moon Bay. Turn south on Highway 35/Skyline Boulevard and proceed 8.5 miles to Skeggs Vista Point parking area on the east side of the highway. This parking lot must be entered from the other direction, so drive further along and turn around. Once you've parked, cross the highway on foot and walk north a few feet to the trailhead. Access is free. There are no facilities.

54. San Andreas Fault Trail

EFFORT: Minimal
LENGTH: 1.5 miles
GEOLOGICAL FEATURE(S): Fault Activity
LOCATION: Los Trancos Open Space Preserve

Description: The 1.5 mile San Andreas Fault Trail is a self-guiding interpretive loop with nine numbered stops keyed to a brochure. Definitely pick up the brochure at the interpretive panel at the edge of the parking area, as it explains fault movement and earthquake mechanics and it has a useful map of the trail. The trail was built in 1977 to increase public awareness of our geologic environment. Here you'll learn about sag ponds, benches, and other earthquake phenomena, and recognize evidence of fault activity on the landscape.

You can walk the fault trail loop and leave it at that, or you can make a longer loop to explore the other offerings of this small preserve. The San Andreas Fault cuts the park in two, marking the boundary of the North American and Pacific Plates. As we have discussed before, the two plates are grinding against one another as the Pacific Plate moves northwestward. Friction prevents the smooth movement of the plates against one another, causing a tremendous build-up of stress. When enough stress builds, the rocks at this boundary will snap into new positions, releasing all of that pent-up energy in the form of an earthquake. In this area, the movement along the fault averages ¾ inch per year.

From the west side of the parking lot, go through the fence, find the narrow hikers-only path, and climb to a viewpoint and the first stop. From this vantage point, you can see Loma Prieta peak 23 miles to the southeast on the North American Plate. That mountain gave its name to the disastrous 1989 earthquake along this fault.

You're standing on the eastern edge of the Pacific Plate. Stevens Creek Canyon marks the boundary between the two plates. Seems a bit eerie to be standing at such a temperamental spot on the Earth's crust, doesn't it?

Continuing on the trail, at the second stop you'll see Mount Diablo rising up to the east, San Francisco in the distance to the north, and Mount Tamalpais just beyond it. Closer, you can see Crystal Springs Reservoir and the San Andreas Lake in the valley defined by the San Andreas Fault.

As you walk this trail, take a moment to examine some of the boulders along the way. Many of these are coarse conglomerates, a sedimentary rock composed of different types of pebbles cemented together. The source of these rocks is Loma Prieta Peak to the south. They were washed down by streams, and those that ended up on the Pacific Plate moved northward away from the source mountain to their eventual present-day positions, providing a concrete demonstration of movement along a plate boundary.

Throughout this hike, you'll pass posts with either yellow or white tops. The yellow-topped posts mark the location of the major fault. The white ones indicate minor faults.

After stop #2, turn right and then immediately right again to resume the trail. You'll arrive at a junction. Go straight and then at the next junction, go straight again.

Next, the trail takes you through a meadow where you'll find wildflowers blooming in spring. You'll be walking among madrone,

California bay, oak, coyote brush, poison oak, and ferns. Many of the magnificent old oak trees are covered with moss and various types of lichens, and the bays perfume the air. In the shady, damp areas, watch for mushrooms. When leaf litter is high, the trail may become indistinct in spots.

You'll walk generally eastward for 0.3 miles before reaching stop #3. A wooden bench is positioned here, as well as the fault markers. To your right is the grassy slope leading up to Page Mill Road, and to your left is a somewhat flat area, after which the slope continues down to the creek. The flat spot is called a *bench*. It's created by the continual activity of the fault. As the ground ruptures in an earthquake, the sides of the rupture pull apart. In time, these fill in with dirt. The area where this occurs tends to be flat, creating this fault indicator. The trail goes past the bench to the left here.

At station 4, you'll see the reproduction of a fence that moved as much as three feet to the northwest during the great 1906 earthquake. Part of the original fence is still standing, but the section showing the offset is a reproduction. Although this is pretty impressive, it's a fraction of the offset observable at Point Reyes National Seashore (see Hike #44). If you look down the line of yellow posts, you'll see that the fault runs right through the fence offset.

This is a fun place to separate from your hiking partner for a moment, each of you standing beside one of the fence sections. Standing on either side of the fault, wave at each other knowing that if you stood there long enough, you would eventually lose sight of one another as you rode your plate on its continuing journey.

However, we don't have millions of years to fritter away, so continue walking, heading west to stop #5. Just after this stop, the trail splits. The trail coming in on the right is the return of the loop. Bear left here to start the 0.7-mile loop portion of the hike.

Stop #6 offers another remnant of the 1906 earthquake, a sag pond. A *sag pond* is a place where the fault has created a depression, or sag, in the overlying rock. If you come after rains, as we did, there will be an actual pond here. Otherwise, it will be a dry depression.

After this stop, you'll walk parallel to a minor fault marked by white-capped posts and then loop back to head east again and walk through thick and fragrant vegetation to close the loop. Retrace your steps from here back to the parking area.

Directions: From Interstate 280 in Palo Alto, turn west on Page Mill Road and drive seven miles to the parking area on the right. You can also reach the trailhead by driving one mile east off of Skyline Boulevard. If the lot is full, park across the street in the Monte Bello OSP lot. Access is free. There is an outhouse on the Monte Bello side.

55. Castle Rock and Goat Rock Loop

EFFORT: Moderate
LENGTH: 3.4 miles
GEOLOGICAL FEATURE(S): Erosional Features
LOCATION: Castle Rock State Park

Description: This loop will take you to three of the main attractions of the park, two weathered sandstone outcrops and a waterfall, and will route you along Ridge Trail for spectacular views. Note that you can shorten the trip by turning around at either Castle Rock or Castle Rock Falls.

Take the shady Castle Rock Trail among madrone, Douglas fir, black oak, coast live oak, and tanoak trees. After 0.2 miles, take a right onto a dirt road. At 0.3 miles, you'll reach 40-foot Castle Rock, a huge sandstone formation and namesake of the park. You may see rock climbers training here. Explore the sandstone caves at your leisure on the 0.6 mile loop around the sandstone formation. Keep a lookout for tafoni (see Hike #43).

Descend to join Saratoga Gap Trail and walk along the creek through a second-growth redwood, Douglas fir, and madrone forest. Enjoy the tumbling creek and the mossy rocks and branches, as well as several types of ferns thriving here. Depending on the season, look for mushrooms or wildflowers in the lush landscape. Wildflowers you may see include coral-bells, Ithuriel's spear, miner's lettuce, and woodland madia. Cross the creek over a bridge and continue on the other side.

Notice that the creek will pick up some speed as you approach the waterfall. At just over one mile, you reach an observation deck framed by madrone providing views of Castle Rock Falls and the surrounding area. The waterfall tumbles over a cliff face into the canyon below. On the opposite cliff, look for rock climbers inching their way up.

Leaving the creek and the forest canopy, the path continues along a steep hillside through chaparral, ascending with some rough spots, but generally easily. It will be hotter here among the manzanita and toyon, as well as more rocky. Look for blooming bush monkeyflower, Indian paintbrush, lupine, winecup clarkia, madia, Chinese houses, sun rose, mariposa lilies, and chamise.

At 1.8 miles, cross a bridge and come to a signed junction 0.2 miles further. Turn right and cross on the east side of Varian Peak.

Your views across ridges and deep valleys out to Monterey Bay and beyond will be wonderful as you climb this steep, narrow trail. In places, you'll scramble over rocks. In one place, you'll cling to a handhold to help you negotiate some narrow steps carved into the cliff. Don't worry; the trail will get easier soon. At the Ridge Trail junction, turn right.

At the next junction, go left and soon arrive at the interpretive exhibit. Find Goat Rock Trail and follow it to Goat Rock, another sandstone formation with interesting weathering patterns. Chances are good that someone will be climbing here. Take the trail around to explore the other side of the formation.

Return to the Ridge Trail, turn right, and head back to the Saratoga Gap Trail, where you will turn left to hike the final 0.4 miles back to the trailhead.

Directions: From Highway 92, take Highway 35 south. Pass the junction with Highway 9, heading south on Highway 35 for 2.6 miles further to the Castle Rock State Park parking lot on the right. There is an entrance fee.

56. Mine Hill Trail

EFFORT: Moderate
LENGTH: 6.0 miles
GEOLOGICAL FEATURE(S): Mining
LOCATION: Almaden Quicksilver County Park

Description: Almaden Quicksilver County Park preserves the remains of historic and prehistoric mining activity. Native Californians mined cinnabar, a beautiful red mineral composed of mercury and sulfur, at this site. They dug a tunnel and removed the mineral using stone tools. The cinnabar was valuable for use as a pigment and widely traded.

Later, the cinnabar was mined for the mercury it contained, commonly referred to as quicksilver. Mercury mining began in the 1840s and was used as an amalgamating material for gold. The mercury was of paramount importance to the California gold rush, for without mercury the gold could not be refined. This site, along with the New Idria mine near Hollister, were the primary sources of mercury at the time. Prior to these two mining operations, mercury was imported from Europe.

In addition to gold refining, mercury was heavily used in the 19th century in the hat-making industry, particularly in making beaver pelt hats. The mercury caused the hats to be stiff enough to stand straight up. Mercury is extremely damaging to the central nervous system and is thought to be the chemical responsible for the term "mad as a hatter."

Cinnabar continued to be mined until 1972 when the Environmental Protection Agency banned the use of mercury to refine gold. By then, it was seldom used any more anyway, having largely been replaced by safer cyanide techniques. Mercury is still used in developing countries, however, despite the danger.

The New Almaden Mine was the most productive mercury mine in North America, spawning a busy town where, by 1865, 1,800 people resided. Large-scale mining ceased by 1927, and the population eventually dispersed, as is typical of mining communities.

The southeast section of Almaden Quicksilver Park has a wide variety of terrain and a large number of mining remains. The Mine Hill Trail, an old mining road, starts at the Hacienda entrance and runs the entire length of the park for 7 miles to the park's northwest entrance at McAbee Road. Many trails branch off from Mine Hill Trail leading to old mines, camps, and a cemetery. The landscape is primarily grass-covered hills with some oak woodland. The park is well used by local residents on foot, horseback, and bicycles.

At the Hacienda Entrance, check out the mining museum before hitting the trail. Also, consult a trail map. There are lots of route options here, and you may want to string together your own combination of trails to best meet your interests. We've put together a rough figure-eight style route designed to hit as many of the historical sites as possible without covering too many miles. There is one major mine on the other side of the park, which you can walk to on the Mine Hill Trail, but we've listed that site as a separate hike starting from the McAbee Road entrance (Hike #57).

Walk around the gate at the trailhead and start on wide Mine Hill Trail through an oak woodland environment. To the west you'll see the Hacienda Reduction Works site with its fenced in collection of old mining machinery. Also note the Almaden Quicksilver Chimney on a hill. Built in the 1870s, the chimney vented sulfur fumes from the reduction works.

At 0.4 miles, you will reach a junction with Hacienda Trail to the right and English Camp Trail to the left. Continue straight on Mine Hill Trail.

Climb steadily but gradually up switchbacks to 1,000 feet at Capehorn Pass, reached after a little over a mile. As you go higher, the landscape will be dominated with a chaparral environment of manzanita, madrone, and broom. In season, wildflowers include blue dicks, buttercups, saxifrage, Indian warrior, padre's shooting star, Johnny jump-ups, baby blue eyes, lupine, and poppies. At the pass, you'll be rewarded with a great view of San Francisco Bay.

The Hacienda Trail heads off to the right here at the pass, leading to the Mockingbird Hill park entrance. Ahead, the trail forks. The right fork is the Randol Trail. Go left to stay on Mine Hill. If you're hiking in morning or evening, keep a lookout for deer. They are often seen along the trail. Also be aware of the blue-green serpentine outcrops as you go. The same hydrothermal fluids that resulted in the deposition of the cinnabar vein altered the surrounding country rock to serpentine.

Continue another 0.65 miles to a junction with Day Tunnel Trail, right. The mine entrance is sealed, so there isn't much to see, but it is a good spot for a picnic with a table and a view, if you're ready for that. Otherwise, continue on Mine Hill Trail another quarter mile to English Camp, an old mining encampment.

From here follow Mine Hill Trail for 0.3 miles. You'll come to April Trail which goes right for 0.2 miles to the April Tunnel. Continue on the Mine Hill Trail past the old Powder House for another 0.4 miles. A short (0.1 miles) spur trail goes left here to visit the San Cristobal Mine site on 1,740-foot high Mine Hill. Go ahead and take this little detour where you can walk into the mine tunnel up to a point where you encounter a locked gate.

Return to the Mine Hill Trail and continue 0.3 miles to the trail's high point at Bull Run. Here, a side trail goes a short distance to the Catherine Tunnel on the right. Mine Hill continues ahead along the open ridge on its way to the far side of the park, but it will continue without us.

After your long climb, take advantage of the picnic area here before turning left onto the Castillero Trail and passing through a gate. Now we will be heading back west, rounding the south side of Mine Hill. After 0.6 miles, you'll encounter Hidalgo Cemetery Trail. If you want to visit the cemetery, it is a half mile from this junction. This side trip will add a mile to the length of our route.

The Castillero Trail continues 0.4 miles to a complex junction where the Yellow Kid Tunnel Trail and the English Camp Trail come in from behind and right, and Church Hill is ahead and right. English Camp is on our left, and directly ahead, the Castillero Trail crosses through another gate and then joins up with Mine Hill Trail. For a change of pace and a slightly shorter route than Mine Hill, let's take English Camp Trail back. It will head generally west.

Shortly, you come to the Main Tunnel site. From here, it's almost a mile to the junction with Mine Hill Trail, downhill. When you reach it, turn right, go around the trailhead gate, and head back to the parking area.

Directions: From Highway 101 in San Jose, exit on Highway 85 east. Exit on the Almaden Expressway heading south. Proceed 4.2 miles to Almaden Road. Pass through New Almaden on Almaden Road to the Almaden Quicksilver County Park Staging Area on the right, next to the Ranger Station and museum. Access is free.

Patrick Daniel Tillman

On the way to Hike #56 or #57, keep your eyes out for the memorial to Pat Tillman at Almaden Way and Bertram Road next to the New Almaden Mine California Historical Landmark plaque. Tillman was a local boy who became a football star and later a war hero.

After graduating from Arizona State, he became a professional football player with the Arizona Cardinals. In the wake of the 9/11 tragedy, Tillman gave up his NFL career to join the Army, becoming a local hero and a national symbol of patriotism. On April 22, 2004, he was killed in Afghanistan by friendly fire, an incident that his unit originally attempted to cover up and that is still surrounded by controversy. Tillman was posthumously promoted from specialist to corporal. He also received posthumous Silver Star and Purple Heart medals.

The memorial, which contains a granite block from the New Almaden mine, was designed and built by locals who knew Tillman personally. It was dedicated in 2008.

---

57. Senador Mine Loop

EFFORT: Minimal
LENGTH: 2.0 miles
GEOLOGICAL FEATURE(S): Mining
LOCATION: Almaden Quicksilver County Park

Description: There is one major mine located near the McAbee entrance to this park, the Senador (Senator). See the previous hike for background information on the mercury mining history to be found here.

Walk past the gate at the end of the road and the restrooms and begin hiking on the Senador Mine Trail. It heads through grass-covered hills, passing a junction with the New Almaden Trail on the left. That will be our return route. Continue to the mine site on a fairly level course.

Three huge concrete structures are the remains of the mine's 40-ton Herreschoff Furnace. The Senador Mine opened in 1863 and was worked until 1926. The reduction plant was built in 1915. Its multi-hearth furnace and electric dust precipitator were the first ever used in the quicksilver industry. The mine produced 20,000 flasks of mercury. Large piles of mine tailings (waste rock) can be seen nearby. There's a picnic table and horse trough here.

From the mine site, the trail climbs up to a high point and then curves around to the south with views of the Almaden Valley and Santa Teresa Hills. Mount Umunhum (Ohlone for "hummingbird") is the highest peak at 3,486 feet. To the south, Guadalupe Creek runs below Guadalupe Reservoir and its dam. The fish in the reservoir are unsafe to eat due to mercury poisoning as a result of the mining operations. Mercury runoff from these mines continues to contaminate San Francisco Bay to this day.

At the end of the Senador Mine Trail, you come to the Guadalupe Trail. Hop onto it and go left. To the right, Guadalupe Trail goes down to the creek to run parallel to it and on past the dam and reservoir. There is a picnic table down by the creek about a half a mile from here if you want to extend your hike a little by going down to the shade of the oak trees by the creek. You'll need to come back up to this junction to continue, adding a mile to the route.

From here, the Guadalupe Trail will continue for 0.6 miles to a junction with Mine Hill Trail and New Almaden Trail. You can take either one back to the trailhead. The New Almaden route is slightly shorter. Turn left on New Almaden Trail and proceed 0.3 miles to the junction with Senador Mine Trail. Turn right and continue a short distance to the trailhead.

Directions: From Highway 101 in San Jose, exit on Highway 85 heading east. Exit south on the Almaden Expressway and then turn right on Camden Avenue. Turn left on Leyland Park Drive, and then right on McAbee Road. Proceed to the end of the road and park along the street. Access is free.

58. Old Cove Landing Trail

EFFORT: Minimal
LENGTH: 3.0 miles
GEOLOGICAL FEATURE(S): Erosional Features
LOCATION: Wilder Ranch State Historic Park

Description: This beautiful former dairy land became a state park in 1974, and is now 7,000 acres, 900 of which are under cultivation. While you're here for hiking, you may want to explore the park's history as well. When Mission Santa Cruz was established in 1791, the area became part of the mission pasture lands. When the lands were divided into large land grants called "ranchos," Wilder Ranch became part of Rancho Refugio, a Mexican land grant of 1839. Historic buildings include the adobe rancho house built by rancho grantee Jose Bolcoff. A dairyman, Delos D. Wilder, acquired part of the land in 1871. His restored 1897 Victorian house and another farmhouse are open for tours. The Wilder family operated the dairy until 1969.

The park also contains a preserve for nesting snowy plovers, a threatened species, at Wilder Beach.

Our trail is an excellent coastal walk with views of a seal rookery, interesting pocket beaches, and the historic cove. We found ourselves stopping often to admire our surroundings, so allow more time than you might usually for a 3-mile walk. Even if you aren't interested in the geology (nah!), you'll find plenty to recommend on this trail.

Begin on an old ranch road at the edge of the parking lot. It's signed "Nature Trail" in some places. Be advised that this is a popular bicycle path, so be aware of oncoming two-wheelers. Cross over some railroad tracks and head toward the ocean on a wide, easy trail. On your left is a marsh area that is off limits to visiting humans. On the right is a field sometimes planted with Brussels sprouts. As we've seen before, these relatively flat areas along the bluffs were once marine terraces carved out by the waves, just as the beach below is being carved today.

At 0.6 miles you'll walk past Wilder Beach to the left where there are numerous wading birds poking about for a meal. There's a viewing deck here and a bench. This will be your first good view of the ocean.

It was here that we encountered a bobcat on the trail. It didn't seem afraid of us and let us take its picture. In addition to the bobcat, we saw several squirrels, brown pelicans, seagulls, and red-winged blackbirds.

At 0.7 miles out, you come to a spur trail to the left that leads out onto a narrow stretch of land that drops off steeply on either side. Unless you suffer from vertigo, take this path and stand at the end looking back at the eroded cliff faces of the coast. This vantage point offers a good view of the vertical mudstone and sandstone beds and their blocky joint patterns. And this gives us a good stopping point to discuss the composition of the local bedrock.

You're standing on a formation known as the Santa Cruz Mudstone, a Miocene sedimentary deposit. It's composed of fine-grained silts and clays washed into the sea by streams as well as the shells (frustules) of diatoms, common one-celled marine plants. You may be familiar with diatoms in the form of diatomaceous earth, but the tiny organisms are also used for make-up (blusher) and in some tooth-whitening products. The shells are made of silica, which forms a sort of glass when subjected to heat and pressure during the rock-forming process. This "melted" silica becomes the cement that binds the particles of the stone together. This makes a fairly strong and hard sedimentary rock. But this formation is highly fractured and faulted. The various layers were deposited at different times and differ in composition, which affects the weathering process, as some layers are more resistant than others and erode at a slower pace.

Return to the trail and continue until you get to another footpath leading toward the beach. If you want to get away momentarily from the bicycle traffic and get closer to the beach, you can take this alternate trail and make your way parallel to the main trail but closer to the edge of the cliff.

View from Old Cove Landing Trail

Among the interesting geologic sights along this trail are the numerous rocky shelves, or shore platforms that jut out into the waves. They're nearly flat on top, so that when the waves crash over them, they leave a foamy runoff that looks like a carpet of snow at first, and then like a lovely waterfall as the water runs off the flat surface back to the ocean. One of the best places to view these platforms is at the end of our trail between Fern Grotto Beach and Sand Plant Beach. These black surfaces are the more resistant layers of chert, above which the softer siltstone layers have been eroded away by wave action. Watching the water run off these shelves can be mesmerizing

As you follow the main path again, you'll have vegetables growing on your right. When we were there, red and green Swiss chard were flourishing. At 1.2 miles, you'll come to Fern Grotto Beach. A steep dirt trail leads down to it beside a small rivulet running in a rocky channel. At the bottom, duck under or climb over the fallen tree and you are on the beach. To your right is the fern grotto, a sea cave where ferns grow from the ceiling and sides, and water drips through the joints in the sandstone.

Notice that you're standing in a deep recess in the sea cliff. One of the things that creates such interest along a coastline is the lack of homogenous weathering. Wherever the waves hit the land, the rock is broken down, but at varying rates. Right here, the land weathered further in than the cliffs on either side of us. Where there are faults and fractures in the bedrock, areas of weakness occur. A surge channel then forms where the waves attack that area, and, eventually, the channels deepen and widen, carving out a little inlet or grotto.

The beach here is perfect for a picnic. And if you want to make this the end of your hike, the total trip is 2.5 miles. We suggest pushing on just a short distance, however, for some gorgeous views of the surf. Climb back up to the main trail and continue just up and around the next bend. There you will come upon Sand Plant Beach, which you can recognize by the marshy looking area at its back. Descend to the beach if you wish. The trail has now become the Ohlone Bluff Trail as it continues north.

The path back is the same you came in by. If you want to go further, you can continue on the Ohlone Bluff Trail for as long as you like before turning back. Who could blame you? The ocean is majestic and the rocks are spectacular.

Directions: Heading north on Highway 1 from Santa Cruz, go four miles to the Wilder Ranch State Park turnoff on the ocean side of the highway. Go to the end of the road and park in the lot. You'll see the trailhead with a sign reading "Nature Trail" on the southwest side of the lot. To avoid the day-use fee, you can also park along Highway 1 just before the park entrance. Restrooms are available.

59. Point Lobos Trails

EFFORT: Minimal
LENGTH: 0.75 to 2.75 miles
GEOLOGICAL FEATURE(S): Erosional Features
LOCATION: Point Lobos State Reserve

Description: Point Lobos is beloved as one of the most scenic spots on the California coast. The Reserve is here in part to showcase one of two remaining native stands of the Monterey cypress in the world, the other being at Cypress Point across Carmel Bay. Climate change is the primary reason the trees have gone from vast Pleistocene forests along the coast to these two small damp headland areas. Human history has also been preserved in this park. In days gone by, Whalers Cove was a whaling base for Chinese and Japanese immigrants. The Whaling museum there has an abundance of information about that period in Point Lobos history. In addition to photogenic trees and history, this park boasts beautiful rocks and important geology.

There are three main types of rocks at Point Lobos. The oldest is the Santa Lucia granodiorite formed from ancient underground volcanos. *Granodiorite* is a rock similar to granite, but containing more plagioclase feldspar (dark colored) than orthoclase feldspar (white or pink colored). It's highly resistant to erosion and is the rock that provides the hard bedrock of Point Lobos. On top of this is the 60 million year old Carmelo Formation, a mixture of sandstone, mudstone and conglomerates. The top layer is composed of sedimentary rock of marine terraces. The beautiful white sand beaches we see today are composed of quartz weathered out of the granodiorite formation while the pebble beaches contain rocks washed out of the Carmelo conglomerates. The granodiorite is exposed at Whalers Cove near the park entrance and again at the southern extremity of the park at China Cove. Otherwise, you'll be walking over sedimentary rock.

Along the bluff trails, look for wildflowers in season, including purple irises, seaside daisy, sticky monkey flower, and brilliant orange-red Indian paintbrush. Almost any time of year will offer some type of floral bloom, including wild lilacs in winter.

The Cypress Grove Trail is a 0.75-mile loop starting at Sea Lion Point parking area and leading through Allan Memorial Grove where you will see the oddly-shaped Monterey cypress trees as they employ their curious but effective defense against the battering winds. The trees sprout gnarled and contorted branches and walnut-sized cones. They cannot be cultivated away from the moist sea breeze since they're susceptible to a fungal disease. When you reach a fork, take either route, as this is the beginning of the loop trail.

After traveling through the cypress grove, you'll reach the rugged coastal headland at Pinnacle Cove with its dramatic cliffs and crashing waves. From this spot, you may see sea otters and California sea lions in the sea and on the rocks below. The otters can be seen amid the seaweed, floating on their backs, sometimes with pups on a female's chest.

Between December and May, you may also spot migrating gray whales on the headland view points on this trail. Another good place to watch for whales is Sea Lion Point. The whales pass 500 yards or more offshore, so bring binoculars. The highest concentration of whales can be seen in January and then again in April when the whales head north with their new calves.

View from Cypress Grove Trail

Take note of the rocks as you climb stairs that have been carved out of the Carmelo Formation. You can see a wide array of textures and structures in the alternating beds of sandstone and conglomerate, including large chunks of granodiorite that were incorporated during the formation of the sedimentary rock. Recall that conglomerates are composed of different types of pebbles cemented together. These layers, looking a lot like manufactured cement, are easy to identify.

When you've completed the Cypress Grove Trail, we highly recommend hiking the South Shore Trail as well, accessed via a set of stairs off of Sand Hill Trail on the south side of the parking area. On the South Shore Trail, you'll walk close to the ocean with incredible views of the rugged coastline, interesting rock outcrops of the Carmelo Formation, and turbulent wave action. This out-and-back shoreline trail will lead you past sea stacks, shore bird roosts, rugged inlets and optional beaches. At Weston Beach, stop to observe and visit if you like the character of the rocks. The beach is composed of bare rock and coarse gravel with highly observable upturned beds where the conglomerate layers have weathered out from between the sandstone layers. In a few minutes, you'll cross from this sedimentary rock into an area where the older granodiorite dominates. Continue south to one of the most beautiful spots in the park at the terminus of this trail at China Cove. There, a smooth white sand beach turns the water a striking shade of aqua. From a high point on the bluff, you can observe the smooth white sand beach and gorgeous aqua water below. Also on view here is a sturdy granite arch that, over time, was carved out by the relentless sea, first as a sea cave and then bursting completely through to form an arch.

It's easy to see the huge difference between this beach and Weston Beach with its nearly complete lack of sand. The reason this white sand beach occurs here is that the sand is composed of quartz grains weathered out of the granite. Compare that to nearly sandless Weston Beach that you passed earlier where bare rock terraces dominated. You can get down to China Cove via a very steep path. Otherwise, this is the end of the trail. Return the way you came.

If you don't have time to hike the length of the park's shoreline, you can drive to the south end of the park road, paralleling the trail, and see China Cove on a short walk south from there.

Directions: Take Highway 1 south of Carmel for three miles to the Point Lobos State Reserve. The trailhead is at the Sea Lion Point parking area.

60. Moses Spring Trail

EFFORT: Minimal
LENGTH: 1.8 or 2.0 miles
GEOLOGICAL FEATURE(S): Fault Activity, Erosional Features
LOCATION: Pinnacles National Park

Description: Pinnacles National Park is not only beautiful, but it offers a unique and fascinating geology lesson. The park road doesn't go through from one side to the other, so you have to choose which entrance you want for the day. If you have the inclination, though, you can walk about four miles between the Bear Gulch Visitor Center on the east side and the Chaparral Entrance on the west side. The driving route is considerably longer.

The two sides are like twin parks or parallel universes. They both have lots of amusing boulders and a set of caves. They both have a peaks trail, a wilderness trail, and a canyon trail. They both have visitor centers and approximately the same flora, fauna, and geology. But they also have differences. There is more surface water on the east side where our trail will turn up a natural spring and a reservoir. On the west side, there are more dramatic cliffs. We're going to hike the two cave trails in the park (this and the next trail) and have some fun climbing through the rocks.

Because the geologic history of the park is the same for both of the trails, we'll describe it only once, here.

Millions of years ago, as the Farallon Plate was subducted under the North American Plate, volcanoes erupted at the plate boundary. One of those volcanoes began its unusual journey about 23 million years ago, erupting directly on the plate boundary. It was built up into a large mountain through many eruptions until the Farallon Plate was completely consumed, and then it went silent. This volcano was located near present-day Lancaster in the western Mojave Desert. As you recall, after the Farallon Plate was gone, the Pacific Plate rammed up against the continent. But instead of hitting head-on, it slid alongside, heading northwest on the boundary we know as the San Andreas Fault. It so happened that the extinct volcano was located directly on that boundary. As the two plates ground alongside one another, the volcano was ripped apart and two-thirds of it traveled north. Over time, it was buried in sediments and ground up and generally mistreated as it emigrated to Northern California. Eventually, the sediments eroded away, revealing the core of the once active volcano. It came to light again, only to find itself nearly 200 miles from its origin within hailing distance of the Monterey Bay. Pinnacles has had a long history, but it isn't over yet. It is still moving, along with the rest of the land on the west side of the fault, at a rate of about an inch a year.

A similar phenomenon has been described at Bodega Bay, where the granite rocks of Bodega Head are in no way related to the Franciscan Complex on the east side of the San Andreas Fault. These granites are similar in composition to rocks found far to the south in the Tehachapi Mountains or even Baja California. Anomalies like the Pinnacles and Bodega Head are some of the most observable evidence we have for the speed and direction of plate movement along this dynamic boundary.

The result of this extraordinary activity is an area of intriguing rock formations for all levels of hikers to marvel at. Geologists theorize that this mountain once stood nearly a mile higher than 3,304-foot high North Chalone Peak, the highest point in the park today. Long-term weathering has broken it down to the craggy surface features that remain. Someday, even less of the old volcano will have moved on up north.

The original volcanic bedrock here was granite. Look closely and you may see pieces of the granite caught up in the overlying rhyolite as xenoliths. A *xenolith* is a pre-existing rock that is incorporated into a lava flow that solidifies around it. Sometimes, if the two rock types differ greatly in color, xenoliths are very easy to spot. Also look for a light green pumice tuff, formed from volcanic ash that shows up as a layer separating the granite from the rhyolite. In the park are examples of several volcanic rock types, including perlite (a rhyolitic volcanic glass), rhyolite, dacite, and andesite. About 60 percent of the rocks in the park are *breccia*, a conglomerate of chunks of rhyolite that can be clearly seen embedded in the mass.

Trail through the pinnacles

Even on this easy hike, make sure you bring water, especially in summer, and be prepared for cave temperatures between 50 to 60 degrees regardless of the outside temperature. Bring flashlights to explore the water-sculpted caves, the most visited attraction at Pinnacles. This area floods during heavy rains, so the trail is not always open.

From the parking area, find the trailhead for Moses Spring Trail to the south. At a fork at 0.2 miles, the High Peaks Trail heads off to the right. We'll be going left and looping back around to this junction.

You'll walk along a creek and on some moss-covered stones. The most likely wildlife you'll see will be lizards scampering over the rocks, but there are rattlesnakes, bobcats, and even mountain lions in the park.

Pinnacles is also a release site for captive-bred endangered California condors, so keep your eyes open for these huge and extraordinary birds. Trees near the water sources include live oak, buckeye, and sycamore. Blue oaks grow on hillsides, and in the drier areas, you'll find chaparral plants like chamise, buckbrush, and manzanita.

After passing into the Little Pinnacles area, you'll go through the caves on Bear Gulch Cave Trail, leaving Moses Spring Trail, which runs alongside the caves. The Bear Gulch Cave is 0.4 miles long, and not technically a cave, but rather a pocket created in a canyon where rocks have fallen. There's a bit of rock climbing required, but it is easily accomplished by most folks. If it's early spring, water will be dripping down the walls along this trail. Look for frogs and bats in the caves. The bats will begin to stir at dusk.

After exploring the cave, emerge on a path to Bear Gulch Reservoir, which is the far point of the trail and a spot to consider having lunch. You can choose to return the same way you came out for a 1.8-mile hike, or catch the Chalone Peak Trail on its way north from here to make a 2-mile loop. You can also stay on Moses Spring Trail on the return, avoiding the caves, and passing beside Moses Spring.

If you take Chalone Peak Trail back, head north on it to a junction with High Peaks Trail and turn right. Make your way 0.3 miles further to the previously encountered junction, and turn left to reach the trailhead.

Directions: For this hike, you'll want to enter the park at the east entrance. There is no road linking the east and west entrances of the park. From King City on U.S. 101, take the First Street exit, heading east. Turn onto Highway G13/Bitterwater Road, and go 15 miles to Highway 25. Go 14 miles to Highway 146 West, and proceed 5 miles to the Visitor Center, and then to the end of the road to the trailhead. An entrance fee is charged. There are restrooms and picnic tables at the parking area.

61. Balconies Cliffs and Caves

EFFORT: Minimal
LENGTH: 2.4 miles
GEOLOGICAL FEATURE(S): Fault Activity, Erosional Features,
    Caves
LOCATION: Pinnacles National Park

Description: For a description of Pinnacles' fascinating geologic history, please see the previous hike, Moses Spring Trail.

This trail will take you past imposing boulders with close-up views of the dramatic Balconies Cliffs, and then will take you through some tight, dark places in Balconies Caves. Bring a flashlight to explore the caves, which include some completely dark chambers. There is water flowing through at certain times of the year, and if the water level is high, the caves may be closed. With its many tall cliffs, like the 700-foot high Machete Ridge, this side of the park is popular with rock climbers, and you are likely to see them on your hike.

Although the trail is an easy hike, the cave portion of this route requires rock scrambling and may pose a challenge to some people.

Find the trailhead on the east side of the parking lot. Walk on the obvious path bounded by a split-rail fence to a fork and a map. Right is the Juniper Canyon Trail. Go left on the Balconies Trail.

Proceed on a wide, level gravel and dirt path, passing numbered posts. The numbers correspond to a trail brochure.

The fence ends shortly after the trail begins and your views of the pinnacles get better as you approach Balconies Cliffs. After post #3, you'll cross a wooden footbridge, the first of several, passing over the west fork of Chalone Creek, which was dry during our mid-May visit.

After the second bridge, you'll reach the impressive boulders that will accompany you all along this trail. Look at the rock closely and you'll immediately see that it is composed of lots of smaller rocks cemented together. This is pyroclastic "breccia." The "cement" holding all these bits of rock together is the hardened volcanic ash from an ancient mudflow, and the primary rock is rhyolite (which you can recognize because of its distinctive pinkish/red color). The size of the individual boulders is impressive. Imagine the force and energy involved in moving rocks that size. The sound alone would have been deafening as the massive boulders churned together in a river of mud. As the energy eventually dissipated from the moving river of rock, the mudflow slowed to a standstill, hardened, and was finally buried by more sediment and more mudflows, eventually becoming the rock you see before you today.

The trail becomes shaded as you're regaled by the chirping of cicadas and you get your first glimpse of the sheer wall of the Balconies Cliffs. If there are climbers on the face of the cliff, you should be able to spot them fairly easily, even without binoculars.

Start downhill under two large boulders creating an archway, and cross a couple more bridges and climbers' access trail going right. After 0.6 miles, you come to a junction just across one of the bridges. You can go either way at this point, as this is the beginning of a loop, but we recommend going left. There seem to be fewer uphill stretches in that direction, or at least no long uphill climbs. Also, if you're following the interpretive brochure, the numbers go clockwise.

Go left on Balconies Cliffs Trail and begin climbing up towards the Cliffs. The climb is not strenuous, but there are sections of open sun, so a hat would be helpful. Balconies Cliffs are a sheer wall of pinkish rock (the breccia) with black stripes of manganese oxide fairly regularly spaced along the face. You can see why this location is popular with rock climbers given the vertical pitch of the wall.

Make a hairpin turn and head away from the cliff as you continue climbing. It was on this stretch of the trail that we saw our first butterfly Mariposa lilies in bloom. There were just a handful of these delicate beauties at first, but we saw a few dozen on the upper portions of the Balconies Cliffs Trail. There were, in fact, many kinds of wildflowers blooming along our trail. We saw California goosefoot, suncups, wind poppies, clarkia, the brilliant red cobweb thistles, Chinese houses, Douglas wallflowers, gray mule ears, bush poppies, and shooting stars.

While we're talking about non-geology attractions, we may as well mention the fauna we glimpsed on our walk. Most happily, we saw a family of California quail with five newly-hatched chicks, tumbling through the grass trying to keep up with their parents. We saw hawks in the sky above and lizards in the rocks below, and a plentitude of butterflies, including several swallowtails. Both scrub jays and Stellar's jays made appearances in this somewhat mixed ecosystem that includes coast live oak, California buckeye, chamise, buckbrush, manzanita, and gray pine. We also saw a rattlesnake, so be on the lookout.

The trail is routed roughly along the base of Balconies Cliffs where it begins to descend to a 3-way trail junction, reached after 1.4 miles. The Old Pinnacles Trail comes in from the left. Continue straight onto the Balconies Caves Trail.

Although the geology doesn't change along this section, the trail experience certainly does. Pass beside a breccia wall on your right side to the entrance to the caves, marked with a heavy metal gate. This is a good time to locate your flashlight. You'll need it because shortly after you pass into the cave, daylight disappears entirely.

Like the Bear Gulch Cave on the east side of the monument, this is not actually a cave, in the true sense of the term. It is instead a rock-choked canyon, or talus passage, where pockets have been created between and under fallen boulders. In this case, the rocks have been packed in so tightly that the light is completely blocked out. You'll be surprised at how completely dark it is. Be very careful in the chambers, as they are sometimes low and tight. Move slowly and watch where you're going. The path through the cave is easy to spot, but requires some scrambling and rock climbing towards the end where you climb up and out. Since the rock climbing portion is near the exit where some light enters, you can put your flashlight away to free up your hands for climbing. The dark portion of this stretch of trail is quite short, just long enough to give you a sense of adventure without a fright.

After climbing out of the cave, proceed through a two-foot wide slot between rock walls. Within this narrow chasm, several boulders are caught where they fell. One enormous boulder was too large to fall between the walls, so it forms a roof across them.

Exit through another metal gate and squeeze between the boulders on the left. This completes the cave experience and you'll emerge back on the flat Balconies Trail.

Soon you'll arrive at the loop junction. Continue straight to finish out the 0.6-mile return to the parking area on the Balconies Trail.

Directions: This trail is in the west section of the park, and there is no road between the east and west, so you'll need to enter via Highway 146. From Salinas on Highway 101, go 22 miles south to Soledad, and take the Highway 146 (Front Street) exit. Drive through town, turning right on East Street to stay on Highway 146. Turn right again on Metz Road and follow it out of town. Where Metz Road continues on to King City, turn left to stay on Highway 146. Drive east 11 more miles on Highway 146 to enter the park. The road becomes one-lane with a lot of ups and downs, but is paved all the way. It is also an extremely beautiful drive in the spring past hillside vineyards and through vigorous chaparral.

Stop at the ranger station to pay the entrance fee, and drive to the end of the road for trailhead parking. There are picnic tables, restrooms, and water. The ranger station is also a small visitor center with information about the flora, fauna, and geology of the park. Note that the west entrance is closed at night.

62. Limekiln Trail

EFFORT: Minimal
LENGTH: 1.8 miles
GEOLOGICAL FEATURE(S): Mining
LOCATION: Limekiln Creek State Park

Description: Located on the Big Sur coast and named for a late nineteenth-century mining operation, this park offers beachfront, redwoods, deep canyons, and a bit of California history. There is only one trail in the park—this short half-mile trek to four enormous kilns (furnaces) that starts at the campground and takes you through Limekiln Canyon. We're going to add a side trip to a waterfall that still puts you back at the trailhead in under two miles.

Start your hike following West Fork Creek and crossing three bridges. You'll pass a small waterfall along the way. The first bridge takes you over Hare Creek. The second is over Limekiln Creek. The trail bears left from here. But, wait, there's a bonus for insiders. Just after the second bridge, you'll find an unmarked spur trail to the right along Limekiln Creek. This path will take you to the 100-foot tall Limekiln Falls in less than half a mile with a little boulder hopping along the way. The waterfall is split by a knob at the top and drops like Rapunzel's tresses over a sheer limestone cliff to the rocky gorge below. The side trip is well worth it.

When you're ready, return to the main trail and continue through a canyon occupied by redwoods, maples, sycamores and oaks.

At the end of the trail stand four large kilns alongside the creek at the base of a limestone deposit. There is very little limestone in California, so this deposit was a rare and valuable commodity.

The kilns stand tall and dark amid the redwoods and encroaching underbrush. They're made of pieces of now-rusted steel riveted together to form the cylindrical ovens. One of them has a large stone base. They're hollow and each has an opening near the base lined on the inside with brick. The lime was removed from this opening.

The limestone, calcium carbonate, was placed into the ovens, along with wood for fuel, and the lime "cooked" out. Redwood provides excellent wood for this purpose, since it burns long and steady. The heat from the fire burns carbon out of the rock, leaving lime powder (calcium oxide) behind.

These kilns were built and operated by the Rockland Lime and Lumber Company who cut redwoods in this area. It wasn't unusual for a lumber company to make lime as well, or for the two industries to coexist. The byproduct wood from the lumbering business was used to fuel the kilns. After three years of operation, most of the limestone had been used up and most of the redwoods had been clear cut, so the Rockland Company ceased production.

Return the way you came.

Directions: From Carmel, travel south on Highway 1 about 55 miles to the signed park entrance. Park in the day-use lot just past the entrance kiosk. There is a fee.

63. Oso Flaco Lake Nature Trail

EFFORT: Minimal
LENGTH: 2.2 miles
GEOLOGICAL FEATURE(S): Erosional Features
LOCATION: Guadalupe-Nipomo Dunes Preserve

Description: The Guadalupe-Nipomo Dunes, recognized as a National Natural Landmark, cover a vast 18 miles of coast in Central California. The complex contains the largest single dune in the western U.S., Mussel Rock Dune, 500 feet high. This is the second largest dune system in California. Dunes are important in understanding ancient climates and how climates change over time. They have also provided significant data used in climate change models currently in use. Discussions of sand dune formation and classification can get highly technical among geologists, but you'll be glad to hear that we're aiming for a brief overview and leaving it up to you if you want to immerse yourself in dune technicalities.

Dunes are created in dry climates where individual grains of sand (mostly quartz) are blown about by the wind and piled up based on local wind patterns. In a dune, most of the sand grains are spherical and the same size as all the others due to the long-term effects of being blasted about by the wind. Larger pieces were left behind and smaller pieces are carried forward, leaving only one size at any particular place.

One of the cool things about sand dunes is that we can observe them being formed in a way that's rare in geology. Dunes are created and recreated right before our eyes in real time. Watching this process tells us a lot about how ancient dunes, eventually sandstone deposits, were formed. Some of these ancient dunes can be seen today in the striking sandstone deposits of the Grand Canyon in Arizona and Arches and Canyonlands National Parks in Utah, as well as in many places around the globe.

In this location, some of the accumulated sand is very old, going back 18,000 years to the Pleistocene ice age. Huge amounts of sediment eroded off of the Santa Lucia Mountains and were deposited along this coast, eventually being blown, grain by grain, inland. Over time, vegetation took hold and created a somewhat more stable environment, though it is still fragile and still in flux with every gust of wind. Dunes are a unique ecosystem and many of the plants and animals living on them are rare or endangered. The Nipomo Mesa lupine, in particular, grows nowhere else, and only a few are found here.

Because of the mix of salt water, fresh water lakes, and brackish waters between, this is a good place to do some bird watching. Some of the birds are passing through on their annual migration routes, and some live here year round.

The Guadalupe-Nipomo Dunes National Wildlife Refuge is home to threatened animals, including the California red-legged frog, western snowy plover, and California least tern.

The Dunes have a varied human history. The original inhabitants were the Chumash. In 1923, the Dunes stood in for ancient Egypt in the movie *The Ten Commandments*. When the filming was complete, the massive sets were dismantled and buried on site. Occasionally pieces surface as the sands shift. From the 1920s until the 1940s, a group of mystics, nudists, artists, writers, and hermits known as the "Dunites" inhabited the Dunes. They regarded the Dunes as a center of creative energy. After oil was discovered in 1948, Unocal began drilling. Over the next few decades, huge amounts of oil were leaked under the sands of the dunes. Cleanup began in 1994. Since the 1970s, conservation and restoration have been at the forefront of human activity in the Dunes.

Bridge over Oso Flaco Lake

There are a number of different parcels of the dunes complex managed by a variety of agencies. Some of the land is off limits to visitors and some is used for recreation by OHVs. We've chosen an easy, scenic and varied trail in the Oso Flaco Lake Natural Area to provide an introduction to the dune environment for the hiker.

This trail takes you over wooden boardwalks across shallow Oso Flaco Lake to the beach. The walkways are here to allow visitors access to the dunes without harming them. Please don't venture off the trail. Not only is the plant life tenuous here, but many birds lay eggs in the dunes.

Start off through tree cover from the parking lot towards the lake, reached in 0.2 miles. Head left across a bridge to the west side of the lake, enjoying the company of many types of ducks, coots and other shorebirds along the way. Bordering the lake you can see the tops of some of the tawny-colored sand hills.

On the other side of the bridge, the trail becomes a boardwalk through the dunes where silver lupine, sand verbena and dunes paintbrush may be blooming among the coastal scrub. You'll encounter interpretive signs talking about the unique plant and animal communities of the coastal dunes. At a junction with a trail going left, continue on the boardwalk, right and enjoy views of the sandy hills all around you. Be forewarned that this trail is very close to the OHV area and the droning noise of vehicle engines may accompany your hike. If you can tune that out, you'll find this an enchanting trail.

The boardwalk terminates at a viewing platform with information signs and views of San Luis Obispo Bay.

From here, you walk a sandy path to the beach where you can play in the surf, picnic or entertain yourself as you wish. Return the same way.

Directions: From Highway 1 in Guadalupe, go north to Oso Flaco Lake Road and turn west. Proceed 3 miles to the parking lot. There is a fee unless you park outside the gate. There are portable toilets in the parking lot and a pit toilet further along the trail.

SECTION 5
THE GREAT VALLEY

The Great Valley is a vast alluvial plain making up the fertile interior of California. It's 400 miles long and up to 50 miles wide, flanked on the west by the Coast Ranges and on the east by the Sierra Nevadas, both of which offer up their rainfall and snow melt to the valley. At one time, most of that water flowed through an elaborate network of rivers that converged into the San Joaquin Delta system and flowing out to the Pacific Ocean through the San Francisco Bay. These extensive water systems create many tule-lined sloughs and marshes that teemed with wildlife. Once, vast herds of elk and antelope ranged in the valley. All of that changed with the advent of the Central Valley Project, an extensive network of dams, reservoirs, and canals built under the supervision of the U. S Bureau of Reclamation in the 1930's. Thus, the elk and antelope are now gone except for a few protected enclaves, but the waterways still provide essential habitats for huge numbers of migratory birds.

Topographically, the valley ranges in elevation from below sea level to 400 feet high, with a couple of lofty exceptions—the Sutter Buttes north of Sacramento and the Kettleman, Elk, and Buena Vista Hills in the southern region of the valley.

Geologically, the story of the valley is a story of sediment, thousands of feet of it. During glaciation in the nearby Sierra Nevadas, huge amounts of sediment accumulated at the base of the glaciers. As the glaciers melted, rivers flowed through them, carrying the sediment as glacial outwash into the trough of the Great Valley.

Beneath the recent and Pleistocene alluvium there is even more sediment and sedimentary rock, deposited a large sea that covered the Great Valley in the geologic past. It's easy to imagine how sediment filled the trough that was the Great Valley. But how did it become a trough in the first place? The answer, of course, lies in plate tectonics.

Beginning in the Jurassic, when the Farallon Plate began to subduct under the North American Plate, the Great Valley basin began to form landward of the subduction zone. Similar to today, there was a topographically high area to the east, where the Sierra Nevadas are now, consisting of a string of volcanoes now long gone. To the west lay the crumpled rocks of the leading edge of the continental margin and in between lay a deep sea. Sediment from this highland was carried into the basin by turbidity currents and landslides. The basin subsided slowly under the weight of more and more sediment filling the trough. The depth of these Great Valley sediments is unknown but estimated to be as much as 40,000 feet. The basin continued to fill with sediment until it reached a depth that caused it to emerge from the sea. In the northern area, near Sacramento, land emerged about 24 million years ago. The southern two-thirds of the valley remained a sea for much longer, gradually becoming an embayment on the coast. By about one million years ago, the San Joaquin Valley was closed off from the Pacific Ocean entirely, and became occasionally covered with large lakes. The largest of these was Lake Corcoran, which existed between 758,000 and 665,000 years ago. This lake left a formation called the Corcoran Clay, consisting of fine clays, volcanic ash, and diatomite, which covers 5,000 square miles of the San Joaquin Valley today. Those of us who live in the valley are frequently reminded of the watery history of the area by the many mollusk shells overturned in our gardens. But many more interesting marine fossils have been found in the valley, among them sharks, turtles, Mosasaurs, Plesiosaurs, walruses, even whales, which make it more than evident that the seas were considerable.

As you are probably aware, all of this rich sediment has provided one of the most fertile agricultural areas in the world, and much of the valley is devoted to farming. Possibly the most geoeconomically significant fact about the valley is that it contains rich oil and gas fields formed from ancient marine deposits at its southern extremities. Significant petroleum deposits are located in the Kettleman Hills, Elk Hills, Wheeler Ridge, Lost Hills, and Buena Vista Hills.

Because of the flat, featureless landscape, there aren't a lot of hiking opportunities in the valley catering to our theme. After all, we aren't going to take you walking through an asparagus field to look at the peat dirt. There are very good wildlife, especially birding, trails, but the geology trails are rare. One of the few places here that meets the criteria, in fact, is the Sutter Buttes, the most pronounced anomaly in the Valley. However, there is one place in this province of supreme geologic importance, the Carrizo Plain, which offers us a truly spectacular look at our old friend, the San Andreas Fault, in action. A hike devoted to the fault will be the highlight of this chapter.

Trails of the Great Valley:

64. Sutter Buttes
65. Joaquin Rocks Trail
66. Wallace Creek Interpretive Trail

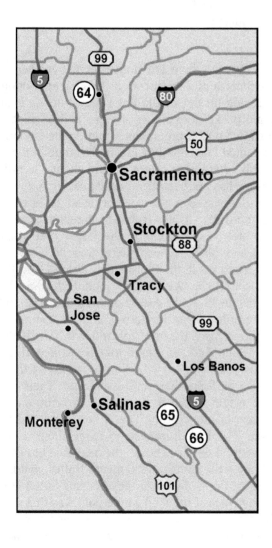

64. Sutter Buttes

EFFORT: Varies
LENGTH: Varies
GEOLOGICAL FEATURE(S): Volcanism
LOCATION: Sutter Buttes

Description: You can't help but notice them, whether you're driving along Interstate 5 north of Sacramento or looking at a topographical map of California. Rising up out of the flat valley floor is a small group of curious mountain peaks, looking mysterious and misplaced. The Sutter Buttes, which show up as a prominent bump on the smooth valley floor, have been nicknamed "the smallest mountain range in the world." They are unquestionably of volcanic origin and are about 1.6 million years old, but their genealogy has not been firmly established. Some scientists have proposed that this volcano is the southernmost feature of the Cascade Range. Others consider it an isolated, anomalous event, primarily because it does not much resemble the larger and younger Cascade stratovolcanoes, and also because there was no continuing volcanic activity after its eruptions in the Pleistocene, about 1.5 million years ago. Several peaks, North Butte, West Butte, South Butte, and Twin Peak, rise to a maximum height of 2,117 feet (South Butte). The Buttes cover an area of 75 square miles, 10 miles across, and are composed of andesite, dacite, and rhyolite. This is the only volcano in the Great Valley.

The native Maidu Indians appropriately named this unusual and sacred place "Histum Yani," or Middle Mountains of the Valley. Their grinding holes can be found here in the andesite. Their legends identify this place as the origin of the first man and woman, and as the resting place for their spirits after death. The Buttes have had various names since the Maidu. The first European to name them, Luis Arguello of Spain, called them "Los Picachos," the peaks. They have also been known as the Marysville Buttes, Sacramento Buttes, and Los Tres Picos. In 1949, the year of the Gold Rush, they became Sutter Buttes, renamed after John Sutter, owner of the land where gold was first discovered.

Almost all of the land is privately owned and permission must be obtained for hiking there. Because of this, most people simply gaze over at the oddity while driving through the valley, never getting a closer look. Also because of this, the early European history of the place has been preserved and the wild character of the land has been maintained. It's primarily grassland and oak woodland, similar to the Diablo Range in surface character, hot and dry in summer, and green, blooming, and inviting in spring. Wild animals that live on the hills include several species of bats, lizards, ringtails, feral pigs, coyotes, rattlesnakes, turkey vultures, and golden eagles.

Sutter Buttes from Gray Lodge Wildlife Area

There are historic homesteads in the canyons, valleys, and on the peaks—corrals, barns, schools, pioneer cemeteries, and other remnants of early settlers. The land is used for cattle and sheep ranching these days, as it has been since the first European settlers came. Because of the unusual circumstances of hiking this land, we're departing somewhat from our customary trail description. To experience the Buttes, you will probably do so as part of a guided tour, so we're providing tour information instead. Other groups, such as student researchers, are accommodated by some of the landowners as the need arises.

Tours are led in spring and fall by the non-profit Middle Mountain Foundation, which gives a share of the hiking fees to the landowners. Only 15 people are allowed on each guided hike, and they are popular and must be reserved. Several of the hikes are day-long events and somewhat strenuous. A "Geology Trek" is one of the conducted hikes, focusing on the natural history of the Buttes, but most of the other tours will touch on geology to some extent. The Foundation offers a variety of hiking experiences, including a full-moon evening stroll, a bat research trip, and others.

There has been talk for many years about developing land here as public parkland, and the California Department of Parks and Recreation actually purchased 1,784.5 acres in Peace Valley on the north side of the Sutter Buttes in 2003. However, at the time of this writing, no development had yet taken place and there is no access road to that parcel of land. Land owners are reluctant to open up the mountain to the public, preferring to keep it in pristine condition, an intriguing oasis in the middle of towns, freeways, and flat agricultural fields.

Directions: Visit   the   Middle   Mountain   Foundation   at http://www.middlemountainhikes.org for more information about the hikes they offer.

65. Joaquin Rocks Trail

EFFORT: Moderate
LENGTH: 9.0 miles
GEOLOGICAL FEATURE(S): Erosional Features
LOCATION: BLM Clear Creek Management Area

Description: The Joaquin Rocks are intriguing 300-foot high sandstone monoliths in a remote area on the west side of the San Joaquin Valley, visible from Interstate 5. This trail takes you to the base of those rocks and through a very special and beautiful environment. A huge expanse of public land administered by the Bureau of Land Management comprises a rugged and wild recreation area in the middle of California. The Tumey Hills (23,000 acres), Panoche Hills (35,000 acres), and the Clear Creek Management Area (75,000 acres, of which 63,000 are public land) make up this playground that attracts hikers, bikers, hunters, astronomers, rock collectors, and birders. The Clear Creek Management area was closed in 2008 due to concerns about naturally occurring asbestos (see more below), but opened again in late 2017 with many restrictions, particularly for off-road vehicle use. Be sure to check with the local BLM office before planning a trip to this area. Between the Clear Creek Management Area and I-5 lie the Joaquin Rocks, named for the notorious bandito, Joaquin Murrieta, who frequented the area (see inset).

There are numerous old mines in the area from nineteenth century chromium, mercury, and asbestos mining, including the largest mercury mine, New Idria Mine, which operated until the 1970s. Some areas are closed due to mercury and heavy metal contamination. Another hazard to be found here is naturally-occurring asbestos. This is probably more of a concern for off-road enthusiasts than those of us on foot, but BLM advises visitors to avoid the area during dry or dusty conditions. Previous asbestos mining has contributed to the dispersal of asbestos fibers into the environment. Do not drink any of the stream water, as it may contain fibers. Avoid digging or kicking up dust.

The underlying bedrock of these bare hills is the New Idria Formation, a serpentine uplift about 65 million years old. This large, friable mass is the source of the asbestos. As we have seen in other serpentine environments, the unique soils create a distinct ecosystem that harbors specialized and rare plants. The threatened San Benito evening primrose is found here, and Brewer's clarkia, coast morning glory, and the talus fritillary. The San Benito Mountain Research Natural Area nearby protects the unusual plant community and is the only place in the world where the Jeffrey pine, foothill pine, coulter pine, and incense cedar grow together. Rare animals can be found around Clear Creek also, including the southwestern pond turtle, the two-striped garter snake, the foothill yellow-legged frog, the big-eared kangaroo rat, and the prairie falcon. You also might see more common animals, such as deer, bobcats, and raccoons.

Robin Hood of the El Dorado

Although he did not give his spoils to the poor, one of the more magnanimous nicknames for the outlaw Joaquin Murrieta was "the Robin Hood of the El Dorado." The name emerged because of rumors that Mexicans throughout California gave him shelter as he fled the many lawmen and posses scouring the land for him. He was a ruthless bandit who often targeted Chinese miners, robbing and killing them. He was so feared throughout 1850s California that a special force was commissioned in 1853 to go after him, the California State Rangers.

Murrieta apparently started out in California as a miner on the Stanislaus River. By some accounts, he was dispossessed of his claim by white men who beat him and raped and killed his wife. However, there is also a story about his widow holding a religious revival at the base of the Joaquin Rocks some time later. Murrieta's identity has always been questionable, as there were apparently several Mexican Joaquins in those days with bad reputations.

The Rangers caught up to Murrieta on July 25, 1853, just southwest of present-day Fresno and killed him. To prove that they had accomplished their mission, they cut off his head, preserved it in a jar of alcohol, and displayed it in Stockton, San Francisco, and Mariposa County, asking people who could confirm Murrieta's identity to sign affidavits.

Some people still doubted that the right Joaquin was caught, and rumors continued to circulate that he was on the loose. Other stories reported that he had escaped to his native Sonora, Mexico. Whether or not Murrieta was actually captured, the reign of terror of California's most nefarious bandito came to an end.

In addition, this area is quite a draw for rockhounds. Over 150 different semi-precious minerals occur here, including the California state gemstone, the rare benitoite, a phosphorescent blue crystal. The only known commercial deposit of benitoite is mined in the Clear Creek area. Other minerals collected here include serpentine, jadeite, cinnabar, tremolite, topazite, and neptunite. Because this is BLM land, collecting is allowed, but check with the local office on current restrictions. Geology, biology, and botany field trips are regularly conducted through the area because of its many and varied characteristics. It is also extremely popular with wild pig hunters.

These hills have also yielded important fossils from the Cretaceous period when the valley was underwater, including a plesiosaur (huge lizard-like marine dinosaur) found in the Panoche Hills in 2010.

To begin our hike, from the parking area, walk past the gate on the road along the Joaquin Ridge. The landscape is typical oak woodland and bare, rolling hills. In summer, this trail can be unpleasantly hot, but in spring amid new green grass and fields of blooming wildflowers, it can be gorgeous.

Walking along the ridge road, if you have a clear day, you'll have fantastic views to the east across the valley to the Sierras beyond. After walking for four miles on this fire road, you'll reach the single-track Joaquin Rocks Trail. Take it and arrive at the base of the sandstone formations in less than a mile. There are three main rocks. They are La Piedra del Oeste (The Stone of the West), La Centinela (The Sentinel), and La Catedral Grande (The Large Cathedral). They are composed of the Vaqueros Sandstone, a soft rock that is easily sculpted by wind and water. The rocks are well weathered and pock marked with numerous depressions.

Watch out for poison oak here. If you climb up into the rocks, you may find teeming vernal pools cradled among them, depending on the time of year. The pools harbor fairy shrimp, algae, and other small organisms.

When you're finished exploring the rocks, return by the same trail.

Directions: A 4WD vehicle is required to navigate the route to this trailhead. Access is through the BLM Clear Creek Management Area, overseen by the Hollister Field Office. From Interstate 5 south of Los Banos, take Panoche Road west to Panoche, about 15 miles, then turn south on New Idria Road for 21 miles to Idria. About four miles further south, you will come to a parking area at Wright Mountain. There are no facilities. Access is free.

66. Wallace Creek Interpretive Trail

EFFORT: Minimal
LENGTH: 1.3 miles
GEOLOGICAL FEATURE(S): Fault Activity
LOCATION: Carrizo Plain National Monument

Description: The Carrizo Plain has been regarded as a special place by native peoples for thousands of years. It remains a special place today, a remote, beautiful and mysterious landscape located at the southwest edge of California's Great Valley.

The 250,000-acre Carrizo Plain Natural Area was established in 1988 to protect habitat and restore the native environment. It's the largest contiguous remnant of the ecosystem that covered most of the Valley before it was settled and converted to farmland. In January, 2001, President Clinton upgraded the Carrizo Plain to a National Monument because of its biological, geological, and cultural importance. Farming and ranching in the 1880s took a toll here as it did in the rest of the Central Valley. Cattle are now used to graze on non-native grasses and then removed when the native varieties begin to emerge. It's expected that this practice will encourage native grasses to eventually dominate.

The Carrizo Plain was formed long ago as the bordering Temblor and Caliente mountains were rising. Fault movement on the San Andreas and

San Juan faults caused the land between the mountains to sink, forming a closed basin. Runoff from the mountains created a huge inland sea and filled the basin with rich sediments. Soda Lake, a 3,000-acre playa lake, is all that remains of that vast prehistoric sea. It's the centerpiece of a large alkali wetlands environment. In winter, water accumulates in the lakebed. In summer, the water evaporates, leaving behind sulfate and carbonate salts. Each year, this cycle is repeated. Birders can take advantage of a boardwalk around the lake to observe the huge flocks of migratory birds stopping here in winter. Thousands of sandhill cranes can be seen, as well as many other types of waterfowl.

You may also spot golden eagles and other raptors, including rough-legged hawks, red-tailed hawks, kestrels, and harriers. From March through mid-July, the popular Painted Rock Trail is closed to protect nesting prairie falcons, which may be spotted at any time of year.

Other animals who live here year round include the ground squirrel, giant kangaroo rat, San Joaquin kit fox, blunt-nosed leopard lizard, antelope squirrel, burrowing owl, tarantula, California condor, tule elk, pronghorn antelope, and coyote. The elk and antelope living here now were reintroduced after being hunted to extinction in the area in the late 1800s and early 1900s.

In spring, wildflowers are legendary, including blankets of baby blue eyes and yellow blooms of locoweed amid fields of native bunchgrass, saltbush, and desert needle grass. The endangered California jewelflower, Hoover's woolly-star, forked fiddleneck, Carrizo peppergrass, Lost Hills saltbush, and Temblor buckwheat are native to the plain. Many of the plants here, however, are exotic species brought in by settlers from Europe and Asia.

All of this beauty is an added bonus to those of us here to observe the special geology on display here. The Carrizo Plain is renowned for its topographical expression of the San Andreas Fault. The fault runs along the eastern side of the plain where you can drive beside it on Elkhorn Road. At Wallace Creek, a textbook example of a fault offset stream can be observed on the Wallace Creek Interpretive Trail, and that's where we're headed.

On January 9, 1857, a major earthquake with an estimated magnitude of 8.0 occurred just north of the Carrizo Plain. This event, known as the Fort Tejon quake, caused about 30 feet of lateral offset within Carrizo Plain and ruptured the surface along the trace of the fault for about 220 miles. It was one of the most powerful earthquakes ever recorded in the United States. When people talk about "the big one" in California, this is the type of earthquake they have in mind.

Wallace Creek offers us the opportunity to observe many of the typical features of a fault zone laid out by nature in a fashion that could not be improved upon by artifice. This site has been called the best example of fault offset stream drainage in the world.

Before starting out on the trail, grab a trail guide from the box and walk east over a gently rising field toward the Temblor Range, so named for its precarious location on the San Andreas Fault. There may be wildflowers here in early spring. The hills of the Temblor Range itself are often covered with goldfields in March and April, turning the hills a nearly solid yellow.

Wallace Creek Offset

The trail begins with the numbered post 1. At this stop, looking north, you can easily see a dramatic sharp turn in the creek bed, which is dry most of the year. In the photo above, this portion of the creek follows a "Z" pattern. This shows the offset caused by earthquake activity along the fault. It's rare to see such visible evidence of movement in a fault zone. It helps that there's almost no vegetation here. Keep in mind that the creek originally followed a straight course.

Head north to see numbered post 2, another sharp bend in the channel. These two bends show where the San Andreas fault crosses the creek bed. The offset created by the fault is approximately 420 feet.

Movement along this fault averages about 1.3 inches per year. As we've said before, the movement doesn't occur continually. It occurs in spurts during earthquakes. For instance, during that major 1857 earthquake witnessed by Spanish travelers, the land jumped 30 feet all at once and tore open the ground, a scar still visible on the landscape.

Returning south, continue along the creek bed to see other evidence of dramatic changes in the landscape. Some of the sidestream channels coming down on the opposite side of the creek show how time has changed their paths. You can see where some of them suddenly stop, their lower portion showing up further to the left. In another case, there is a channel down into the creek with no corresponding channel above. This is called a *beheaded channel*. Some of these features are subtle and more easily seen from the air, but with the help of the trail guide, you should be able to get a good feeling for how the two plate boundaries are shearing this area apart. Altogether there are five numbered posts.

The trail loops back to a point just below numbered post 1. Turn left here to return to the parking lot.

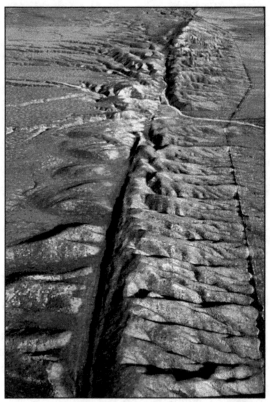

San Andreas Fault in the Carrizo Plain (USGS)

Directions: From Highway 58 in McKittrick, go west through the mountains to Seven Mile Road. Take that route west to Elkhorn Road, a good dirt road heading south along the eastern border of the Carrizo Plain. It is a short distance to a parking area on the left. If you're coming from Soda Lake Road on the other side of Soda Lake, take the long dirt Simmler Road across the plain with the opportunity to view several features of the salt plain up close.

SECTION 6
THE SIERRA NEVADAS

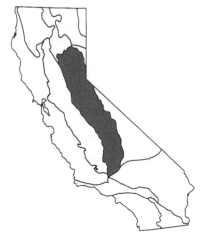

The Sierra Nevadas ("snow-capped mountain range" in Spanish) is the defining feature of eastern California, extending 400 miles north to south and ranging from 40 to 100 miles wide. It tilts westward and rises to a height of 14,495 feet (Mt. Whitney), the highest point in the continental United States. The mountains are composed primarily of granite supporting vast forests, hundreds of beautiful lakes, deep canyons, remnants of once-massive glaciers, and supreme opportunities for hiking and many other types of recreation.

The eastern side of the range drops off steeply to the eastern edge of the state, reflecting the structural tilt of the granite block that forms these mountains. That side is more barren, drier, and more harsh than the western side because it is in the rain shadow of the Sierra Nevada range. Pleistocene ice-age glaciers are responsible for many of the features in these mountains, including the incomparable Yosemite Valley. There is also visible evidence of volcanism, such as the warm waters of Hot Creek and the basalt columns at Devils Postpile. We will visit both.

On the western side of the range, the mountains descend more gradually, forming an expanse of foothills leading down into the Great Valley. Most of this foothill region is known as the Mother Lode, the mining district that spawned California's 1849 Gold Rush.

As you traverse the gold country, you'll visit many historical sites and cross paths with such colorful figures as Black Bart, Lola Montez, Lotta Crabtree, Mark Twain, Bret Harte, Kit Carson, and John C. Fremont. In addition to these notables, many ordinary folks nicknamed "49ers" made their way to California to find gold or take part in some other way in the boom. Busy towns sprang up all along the hills, including one named after two of the afore-mentioned figures, Twain Harte. People from around the world settled near the mines, and, in many cases, left them abandoned when the gold ran out.

Highway 49, a 300-mile long channel through the heart of gold country, was given its number in 1933 in recognition of its location through Gold Rush territory. If you travel this route, you'll visit many of the towns established during the Gold Rush. Some, such as tiny Chinese Camp, provide a glimpse into the multicultural composition of 1850s California, and many others now rely on tourism for their livelihood.

The Sierra Nevada mountains came about through the same tectonic forces we discussed earlier. The impact of the Pacific Plate slamming into the North American Plate was enormous. The resulting compressive stresses reached deep within the earth from Mexico to Alaska. The stresses began in the Pacific Coast area of California in the Jurassic era and culminated in the Rocky Mountains toward the end of the Cretaceous in a mountain-building event known as the Rocky Mountain Orogeny. Almost all of the geology of California can be related back to this source. Some areas of the western United States were intensely folded. Some areas were faulted with older rocks thrust over and on top of younger rocks. Other areas, such as the Sierra Nevadas, experienced a huge outpouring of magma during the violent changes occurring at the plate boundary. At about this time, around 140 million years ago, the Klamath Mountains and the Sierra Nevadas, once a continuous mountain range, separated into two distinct ranges.

Several episodes of magma intrusion took place over millions of years to form this mountain range. The molten rock cooled extremely slowly underground, miles below the surface, which is how granite forms. Each of these masses is called a *pluton* after the Roman god of fire, Pluto. Together, all of these plutons form a *batholith* (from the Greek for deep, *bathos*, and rock, *lithos*), a huge expanse of volcanic rock that extends far into the earth.

At that time, the volcanoes would have resembled those found in the Cascades, and the area of the Sierra Nevadas would have looked like Oregon does now. Then the outflow of magma ceased, the volcanoes became extinct, and a period of quiescence followed. The mountain peaks were steadily eroded through much of the Cenozoic Era, leaving only gently rolling hills.

Later, in the Pliocene, the entire area underwent faulting, resulting in the Sierra Nevada block being upthrust and tilted westward. In the Pleistocene, the temperature dropped and the mountains became subjected to the erosive power of water and ice, as glaciers carved out domes, arêtes and U-shaped valleys.

Glaciers are classified into two broad categories—valley glaciers and continental glaciers. Valley glaciers are the familiar striped ribbons of ice and debris that begin in cirques and flow down the mountainside. Valley glaciers can be seen in California at Mt. Shasta, Yosemite, and Mt. Whitney. Elsewhere in the United States, valley glaciers are abundant in Glacier National Park in Montana and in Alaska. Continental glaciers, on the other hand, are thick sheets of glacial ice that covered much of Europe and North America during the Pleistocene, such as the well-known mile-thick sheet of glacial ice that covered New York.

Continental glaciers still extant today include the glaciers that cover Greenland and Antarctica. Continental glaciation never made it to California because the Sierra Nevada mountains served as a barrier to the thick sheets of ice.

Though the Sierra Nevada mountain range is considered a single geomorphic province, it is so vast and so geologically varied and rich, we will present this chapter in three sections: the foothills, or Mother Lode, the High Sierras, and the Eastern Sierras. Topographically, they are quite distinctively different and the types of geological attractions are dissimilar as well. Put succinctly, the Mother Lode is about gold mining, the High Sierras are about glaciation, and the Eastern Sierras are about volcanism.

With all of that ground to cover, let's get started!

Yosemite Falls, Yosemite National Park

Trails of the Sierra Nevadas:

67. Diggins Loop
68. Hardrock Trail
69. Monument Trail
70. Gold Bug Mine
71. Griffith Quarry Trail
72. Black Chasm Cavern
73. Mercer Caverns
74. Moaning Cavern Walking Tour
75. California Cavern Trail of Lights Tour
76. Pyramid Creek Trail
77. Big Meadow Trail
78. Trail of the Gargoyles
79. Donnell Vista Trail
80. Columns of the Giants
81. Glacier Meadow Loop
82. Lembert Dome Trail
83. Pothole Dome Trail
84. Taft Point Trail
85. Glacier Point Trail
86. Porcupine Creek Trail
87. Hetch Hetchy Trail
88. Mono Pass Trail
89. Gaylor Lakes Trail
90. Bennettville Trail
91. Tioga Tarns Nature Walk
92. Boyden Cavern Family Walking Tour
93. Zumwalt Meadow Trail
94. Crystal Cave
95. Needles Lookout Trail
96. South Tufa Trail
97. Panum Crater Trails
98. Obsidian Dome
99. Inyo Craters Trail
100. Mammoth Consolidated Gold Mine
101. Mammoth Crest Trail
102. Devils Postpile & Rainbow Falls Trail
103. Red Cones Trail
104. San Joaquin Ridge Trail
105. Hot Creek Trail
106. Big Pine Canyon Trail

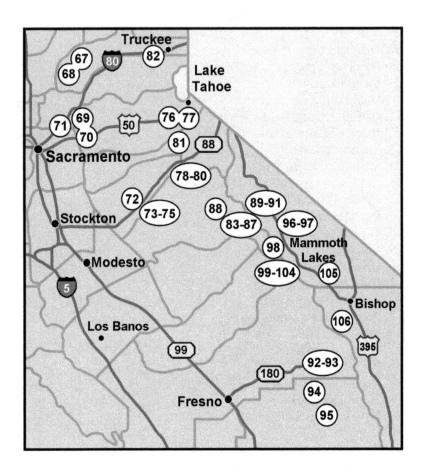

The Mother Lode

Technically, the Mother Lode is a 120-mile long belt of gold-bearing quartz veins beginning in Mariposa at the southern end and ending at Georgetown in El Dorado County in the north. Many of the gold-bearing veins are found along the major fracture known as the Melones Fault Zone. So how did the gold get here?

As the magma of the Sierra batholith cooled, it formed a thin, hard crust on the outside of the magma chamber deep within the earth. As the crust formed, it shrank and cracked as it cooled, just as any material will do. The cracks reached down into the still molten magma within the magma chamber, allowing mineral-laden steam to escape out through the fissures in the barely-solid rock material. As the steam hit the open-air cracks, the minerals carried in the steam began to precipitate out onto the sides of the cracks as a result of the change in pressure. Minerals all precipitate out at their own unique temperature, a useful tool for geologists in reconstructing earth's history. The first minerals to precipitate out typically include precious minerals made of silver, tungsten, molybdenum, and gold, along with quartz. Later minerals may include zinc, lead, and fluorite, along with more quartz. When the magmatic system is cool and close to surface temperature and pressure, the remaining quartz precipitates out, filling in all the space that remains. That's why gold is found in association with quartz veins, because at one point all the minerals existed together in the hot magma below.

In 1848, gold was discovered by James W. Marshall on John Sutter's property at Sutter Creek near Coloma. By the following year the news had spread, sparking the 1849 Gold Rush of California. And the year after that, 1850, California became a state. People hoping to strike it rich poured into the territory from around the world, establishing dozens of new, instant towns and all of the infrastructure necessary to sustain them. These hopeful folks were nicknamed Forty-Niners and their colorful tales of triumph and woe compose the tapestry of California's early statehood.

Mining operations varied from a single miner with a gold pan to large corporate mines with expensive equipment and large payrolls. The following are the types of mining that occurred in California's Mother Lode.

Hard Rock Mining: Gold-bearing ore is taken out of tunnels or open pits from the bedrock. The ore is then crushed into powder and the gold is extracted with the use of chemicals like mercury or cyanide.

Placer Mining: The gold is contained in loose deposits where tunneling isn't possible. It's removed using water to sort the material by weight. Since gold is heavier than other materials, it remains after everything else is washed away. All of the following methods of placer mining employ that concept.

Panning: Using a wide, shallow pan to collect sediment that's swirled with water to remove the lightweight material, leaving gold dust and small nuggets behind. This is a method that anybody can use with minimal expense. During the Gold Rush, miners stood shoulder to shoulder in rivers and creeks using this technique.

Sluicing: Using a sluice box, normally a wooden box with riffles in the bottom. The box is placed in a stream, then loaded with soil. The stream water washes through it, washing away the lighter materials and leaving gold trapped behind the riffles. Sluice boxes could be small or very large. They were used in hydraulic mining where massive water cannons called monitors were used to blast the soil from the landscape, a highly destructive operation that sent tons of sediment downstream, damaging ecosystems. A variation of the sluice box is a rocker box. It uses less water and employs a rocking motion to separate out the gold.

Gold Dredge (Library of Congress)

Dredging: A gold dredge is a machine that scoops up sand, gravel, etc. and sorts it using water. Most dredges employed buckets or scoops of various designs rotating on a conveyor belt to gather the sediment and dump it into the sorting mechanism. Large floating dredges were used on California rivers as late as 1962.

You won't be surprised that the majority of geology hikes in this section are centered around old mining sites. But the foothills of the Sierras are also noteworthy for their splendid show caves, four of which are included here, all within a 15-mile radius of one another. The mines are located in the granite bedrock where quartz veins harbor gold; the caves are in limestone.

67. Diggins Loop

EFFORT: Moderate
LENGTH: 1.0+ miles
GEOLOGICAL FEATURE(S): Mining
LOCATION: Malakoff Diggins Historic Park

Description: The site of the world's largest hydraulic gold mine, Malakoff Diggins, is a pit more than a mile long, a half-mile wide, and nearly 600 feet deep. The North Bloomfield Gravel Mining Company operated the mine between 1866 and 1884, and yielded millions of dollars worth of gold as well as the gravel byproduct. At the park museum, you can learn about the environmentally devastating practice of hydraulic mining. From this operation alone, 50 million tons of tailings were washed down the Yuba River, clogging streams, inhibiting boat traffic, destroying ecosystems, and ruining farmland.

Hydraulic mining is accomplished by blasting away hillsides with huge water monitors and routing the debris through sluice boxes. During full operation, eight of these devices were employed here around the clock. A couple of the monitors are on display on Main Street. The enormous amount of water that was used to sluice the gold, along with a vast amount of boulders, gravel, and sediment, combined to form a muddy stew that wreaked havoc, resulting in flooding in nearby Marysville and Yuba City. In 1884, in one of the first environmental rulings ever passed, a judge ruled that the mining company must stop flushing sediment downstream. At its height, North Bloomfield had 800 residents, including a Chinese neighborhood, but after hydraulic mining was banned, the town was all but abandoned.

Before setting out on the trail, you might want to sign up for the North Bloomfield town tour. Several old buildings are still intact and others have been reconstructed, including the drugstore, saloon, and barbershop. If you don't take a ranger-led tour, you can walk around on your own and look in windows.

For the quickest access to Diggins Loop, we suggest starting at the cemetery. Drive a short distance southwest on North Bloomfield Road. A sign for the cemetery will show you where to turn in on the right. A Catholic church stands here at the road's edge. Also located here is the old schoolhouse, worth a look. Platforms have been set up to allow you to peer in the windows of the two classrooms with their rows of antique desks. There are also two outhouses flanking the school, each with a four-holer plank inside. The outhouses are not original, but the planks look to be the real thing.

After a detour through the fence-enclosed cemetery, walk along its left side on Slaughterhouse Trail. Just past the cemetery you'll come to a trail junction. Turn left towards The Diggins. Now you are on the Diggins Loop. Enclosed in a pine woodland, you'll begin to descend steeply for a stretch, entering an area dominated by manzanita. Notice that the ground is covered with boulders. In other places along the trail you will encounter piles of gravel. These are remnants of the mining operation.

Malakoff Diggins mining operation

When the trail levels out again, it will cross over a dirt road and then come to a T-junction. A trail sign points you to either the "South Side" or the "North Side" Diggins Loop Trail. For quick access to the bottom of the giant pit, go right. The trail becomes the bottom of a gulley and is filled with loose gravel as it takes you downhill through the bleached cliffs of the mining pit. The unnaturally-exposed white and reddish sediments create an attractive setting not unlike badlands topography.

Once you bottom out, the trail disappears and you're walking on a sandy, marshy plain with a small rivulet of cool water running through it. Willows grow near the water and an abundance of songbirds occupy this spot. We saw deer tracks near the stream as well.

When you're ready, go back up the trail to the junction with South Side. To continue on the loop, go straight. If you want a short hike of about a mile, you can turn left here and return to the cemetery and trailhead.

The Diggins Trail continues around the giant pit. Another trail option is the Rim Trail, which traces the pit's rim. It's 3 miles long and offers a different perspective. Despite the devastation that took place here in the nineteenth century, this is now an attractive and enjoyable trail, especially if you're not here at the height of summer. Up at the high points, you get a good view across the pit to the sharply eroded, sparkling white spires of the cliff face. The trail rolls up and down among manzanita bushes and pine trees along the edge of the pit.

You'll come to an intersection with the Hiller Trail, which goes left past the Hiller Tunnel on its way to North Bloomfield Road. Turn around and return to the trailhead whenever you're ready or complete the loop.

Directions: From Nevada City at the spot where Highway 49 and Highway 20 diverge, proceed north on Highway 49 for 10 miles. Turn right on Tyler-Foote Crossing Road and drive about 8.5 miles to North Columbia. At a fork, bear right on Curzon Grade Road. Continue on this road for about 4 more miles, and you will then be on Back Bone Road. Turn right on Derbec Road and then bear right onto North Bloomfield Road. Proceed into town. There is a day-use fee, payable at the museum. There are restrooms across the street.

68. Hardrock Trail

EFFORT: Minimal
LENGTH: 2.5 miles
GEOLOGICAL FEATURE(S): Mining
LOCATION: Empire Mine State Historic Park

Description: This park houses the remains of one of the most successful hardrock gold mining operations in the U. S. and the most profitable in California. Hardrock mining is a method that involves digging or blasting the ore out of the earth and then crushing it into powder with huge machines called stamps. The gold is then leached out of the crushed ore using mercury or cyanide.

Gold was discovered on this site in 1850 by George Roberts, but the gold was hard to reach and the claim wasn't productive. In 1879, San Francisco businessman William Bourn took over the Empire Mine and dug deep and finally made the mine pay off. The Bourn influence in the San Francisco area was widespread, from financing the Panama-Pacific International Exposition, constructing the Opera House, and building the luxurious family estate, Filoli House, in Woodside. The Bourn Cottage here near the Empire Mine is not nearly so grand as that home, but is quite lovely and also open for tours.

The hugely successful gold mine was a combined effort of Bourn vision and hard-working Englishmen. Miners experienced in hardrock mining of tin and copper came from Cornwall, England, in the 1880s. One of their important contributions was the pumping technology that kept water out of the tunnels. The water table today lies at about 150 feet and the mine is flooded, but during its operation, the water was pumped out and the mine's tunnels reached a depth of 11,000 feet. A whopping 5.8 million ounces of gold was extracted from the mine between 1850 to 1956.

The Cornish miners seemed to have been a sour lot, as you will note when you see their pictures in the Visitor Center. While you're in Grass Valley, perhaps you'll sample a Cornish pasty, a staple in the miners' lunchboxes. These savory meat pies are still sold roundabouts.

Because the mine was operated for over a hundred years, many of the buildings and machinery are preserved on site. Our adventure here is a mixed bag. Only a small part of the walk is an actual hiking trail. The Hardrock Trail takes you to the mine shaft, old buildings, the Bourn Cottage, grounds, and outlying ruins. We will present a route that we think will be the most rewarding way to experience the park, though the official trail brochure routes you a somewhat different way.

Start at the Visitor Center. In the former carriage house, you can read about the history of the mine and see photographs of the Bourn family, the miners, etc. But the most interesting thing to see here is the scale model of the Empire Mine. It's housed in a separate room inside a glass cube. The incredible detail of the model will serve as a vivid introduction to the vast network of tunnels that made up the mine. Tunnels were blasted out with dynamite each day in a continual effort to expose and remove the gold-bearing quartz. By the time the mine was closed, there were over 360 miles of tunnels.

Exit at the back of the Visitor Center building and turn right at the junction, towards the cottage. Most times of year, the landscaped grounds leading up to the cottage are replete with blooming flowers. In the middle of summer, cascades of blue hydrangeas dominate. You'll pass by the ruins of the Ophir Cottage, the home of the mine superintendent that burned down in 1935. Ophir is a biblical place name meaning "land rich in gold," and it was from Ophir that King Solomon reportedly got the gold with which to build his temple.

On the left, the clubhouse appears. Residents and visitors enjoyed a variety of recreational activities here, and it is still used today.

After the clubhouse, the path veers right through a gauntlet of pink rose bushes towards Bourn Cottage, an 1897 English manor where the Bourn family lived. We recommend taking the half-hour tour of the inside of the cottage. On your own, you can explore the brick paths of the formal rose gardens behind the house and the reflecting pool in front on a lower level.

Leave the cottage area and walk back toward the Visitor Center, then continue straight towards the mine yard. On your right you will see a metal grate over a stone-lined tunnel entrance. Apparently, this was built to show potential investors the "mine entrance," but really goes nowhere. In the mine yard, start with the bank of wooden buildings on your left. Explore the offices where antique phones, typewriters, and bathroom fixtures will spark your imagination. You will see the furnace where the gold and mercury amalgam was heated to separate the gold. The mercury was then collected and reused. The gold was melted and molded into ingots to send to the U. S. Mint in San Francisco.

After wandering through these buildings, cross the yard to the machine shop. The mine operation is like a small village, nearly self-contained.

Next, go down into the mine shaft itself. You'll encounter a metal gate across the shaft inside. On the right sits the man-skip, the rail-riding sled that whisked the miners down the shaft for 4,650 feet. The day we visited the park, a "miner" was in the shaft to answer questions. A smithie was working in the blacksmith shop next door, and various other costumed folk were on hand to lend some historic color to the place. Check with the park ahead of time if you want to visit on one of these living history days.

Make your way past the many old rail cars, generators, and other machinery to the hoist house where the constant movement of men, supplies, ore, and waste rock was controlled.

Next you come to the stamp mill building that once housed eighty 1,750-pound stamps to crush the ore. Today these hills are peaceful, but during the mine's operation, these huge stamps ran continuously, pounding the ore with booming thunderclaps that rang out over three miles around.

Stamp Mill (Library of Congress)

Exiting the mine yard, turn right and hop on the Hardrock Trail. The trail heads into oak, Ponderosa pine and Douglas fir woods. On the right is a clear meadow surrounded by an airy woodland. You'll soon come to the site of the Orleans Mine. Poke around here for a few minutes, then continue on the trail. You'll come to a junction. To complete the short loop, go right. If you want more of a hike, there are several trails to choose from by turning left here and crossing Little Wolf Creek. You can continue on the main trail for just over a mile to reach the back door of the park, Pennsylvania Gate, a staging area for equestrians.

For the short loop, continue right on the Hard Rock Trail. The next stop is the cyanide pond on the left. This was installed in 1910 to refine the ore even more efficiently and safely than the mercury process. The pulverized rock from the stamp mills was taken to a cyanide-laced pond. The cyanide caused the gold to leach out of solution, and an electroplating step completed the process.

Continue back toward the mine yard, passing the final stop, one of the old stamps set up alongside the trail. Continue straight to return to the Visitor Center and the end of the tour.

Directions: From Highway 49 in Grass Valley, go east on East Empire Street to the park visitor center. On the way, you'll pass the Pennsylvania Gate staging area. There is an entrance fee, picnic tables, and restrooms.

WHATEVER LOLA WANTS

Eliza Gilbert (1821 – 1861), a tempestuous Irish girl raised in India, defied her mother and convention when she set out for a career as a "Spanish" dancer. She learned flamenco, changed her name to Lola Montez, invented her bizarre "Tarantula Dance," and burst forth on the biggest stages of the world. She married three times, and among her many lovers were the composer Franz Liszt and King Ludwig of Bavaria, who gave her the title, Countess of Landsfeld. It's said that Lola contributed to Ludwig's downfall through her influence on him regarding political matters.

So how did one of the world's elite celebrities end up living in the quiet Sierra town of Grass Valley? Surprisingly, it was geology. Lola had never been to California when she, like many other wealthy people of her day, invested in California's Gold Rush. She bought $9,000 worth of stock in the highly successful Eureka Mine in Grass Valley. When she did come to California in 1852, she visited the mine and decided to buy a house nearby.

The town's most notorious resident threw lavish parties and kept a monkey and grizzly bear as pets. She mentored her neighbor, Lotta Crabtree, and set the child on her path to stardom, but Lola only lived in Grass Valley two years. By 1855 she had left for Australia to scandalize the Aussies with her shocking stage performances. A huge personality, Lola was both beloved and reviled wherever she went. She died of syphilis in Brooklyn, New York, at the age of 39.

Lola's Grass Valley house still stands at 248 Mill Street and is now a state historical landmark. Nearby at 238 is Lotta Crabtree's childhood home.

Lola Montez has been memorialized in a long list of movies, songs, books and plays. There are also two lakes and even a mountain named after her in Tahoe National Forest. Mount Lola, at 9,148 feet, is the tallest point in Nevada County, California.

69. Monument Trail

EFFORT: Minimal
LENGTH: 0.75 miles
GEOLOGICAL FEATURE(S): Mining
LOCATION: Marshall Gold Discovery State Historic Park

Description: This is where it all began. On this stroll about town you'll visit the site of the gold discovery that kicked off the California Gold Rush of 1849. It happened here on January 24, 1848 when carpenter James W. Marshall found gold on the South Fork of the American River while building a sawmill for John Sutter.

Sutter's Mill, 1950 (Library of Congress)

There are a few sites you'll want to hit on this visit. One is the Sawmill Site Monument near the river's edge. Then go down to the river to the actual site of the gold discovery and a replica of the sawmill. The gold turned up in the mill's tailrace.

In summer, you'll no doubt see people rafting, a popular recreation on the American River, and you might see a few folks gold panning as well, trying to recreate that original discovery.

Next, go to Main Street and walk down it. This is part of the history tour. When you reach Sacramento Street, turn right and walk up to Church Street. Cross it and continue along Sacramento Street to the Vineyard House. Here you will find a trail on the right. This trail will take you into the park and uphill to the James W. Marshall Monument and Marshall's cabin. James Marshall, who never profited from the Gold Rush, died penniless and is buried under the monument.

From the monument, you have a good view of the valley and river. Returning to the main trail, go right to continue the loop and head downhill back to town.

Directions: From Sacramento, head east on Highway 50 towards Placerville. Turn north on Highway 49 and proceed to Coloma. Park on Main Street or in the lot at the Interpretive Center (there is a parking fee).

70. Gold Bug Mine

EFFORT: Minimal
LENGTH: 1.2 miles
GEOLOGICAL FEATURE(S): Mining
LOCATION: Gold Bug Park

Description: Gold Bug Mine is listed on the National Register of Historic Places and is one of Placerville's most visited relics from its Gold Rush origins. Placerville was first named Dry Diggins, later Hangtown, and then was renamed to put the focus back on mining and away from the spurt of hangings that took place there. As you might imagine, Gold Bug Park is a popular field trip destination for elementary school students, so you may prefer to visit on a weekend when things are considerably more peaceful.

Gold Bug Mine was opened in 1888 by William Craddock and John Dench and was originally named Hattie Mine after Craddock's daughter. In 1926, it was sold to John McKay and renamed.

Pick up a hard hat and cassette player in the gift shop and enter the hard rock mine's drift on your self-guided tour. A *drift* is a horizontal tunnel into a mine. Inside the mine, the temperature remains between 52 and 57 degrees, just as it might in a natural cave. The recording guides you step by step onto the wooden walkway. Though the mine is lighted, a flashlight will be of use to illuminate details on the ceiling and walls. The tour is informative as well as being a lot of fun. The narrator tells the story of the mine as you walk along, including old mining legends with colorful characters. You'll see quartz veins, dynamite holes, and learn the meaning of various mining terms such as "shaft" and "adit" while looking at examples.

The trail is short and flat and easily navigated. During our tour on a weekend, we were alone in the mine, which made it easier to imagine what it would be like to be inside digging out the ore with a pick.

You'll walk 352 feet through the main tunnel. At the back, an airshaft provides fresh air flowing in at around 55 degrees.

After you emerge from the mine, take the Priest Trail up the hill to the Priest Mine with its dirt floor and no lighting. This mine dates from 1849 and is available for touring by special arrangement. There are many other mines in the park, more than 250, but they're closed to the public. You'll see an airshaft and tailing piles on your walk, which brings you back after a half mile to Big Canyon Creek and Gold Bug Lane.

Turn left and walk on Gold Bug Lane to Hendy Drive. Turn right and walk a few steps to a trail that parallels Hendy Drive going north. This is Stampmill Trail. Walk on it for a short distance to the Joshua Hendy Stamp Mill, housed inside a large barn. A volunteer will be available inside to answer questions. There are eight huge stamps on the mill. You'll recall that these were used to crush the ore into powder before extracting the gold. Also in the building are various displays and artifacts from the Gold Rush era, including a working scale model of the stamp mill. The stamp mill is fascinating and not to be missed.

After touring the building, exit and return to the trail, continuing north on Silver Pine Trail. The Silver Pine Mine was one of the largest operated at this site. Follow this trail for 0.30 miles, looping back south to join the Springhill Trail, which will return you to Gold Bug Lane.

We were torn in deciding which was our favorite, the mine itself or the stamp mill. Even if you don't have time to hike the trails, do visit both of these attractions.

Directions: From Highway 50 in Placerville, take Bedford Avenue north and turn right into the park on Gold Bug Lane. There are picnic tables, restrooms, and a museum.

71. Griffith Quarry Trails

EFFORT: Minimal
LENGTH: 3.0 miles
GEOLOGICAL FEATURE(S): Mining
LOCATION: Griffith Quarry County Park

Description: Here's a mining trail in the Mother Lode that isn't about gold. This park marks the site of a historically significant granite quarry. From 1864 to 1918, a Welsh immigrant with the improbable name of Griffith Griffith operated the quarry to supply building material for the emerging cities of California. You'll find the quarry site much as it was left by Griffith when the company closed its doors. This is also a pristine natural area where native animals and plants flourish, including rattlesnakes, so be on the lookout. In 3 miles, you can explore all the trails in this small park.

The museum in the parking lot used to be the office of the Penryn Granite Works. In the town of Penryn, you can see the Masonic Hall that was built from granite quarried here. Much of the granite ended up in buildings in Sacramento and San Francisco.

Start at the interpretive sign near the parking lot. Beside the sign, on your right, are the remains of the old polishing mill, the first one built in California. There is nothing left except some stone from the foundation and part of a rock wall. To the left is an old granite-lined well. Walk past that to the gated road. The trail is the road behind the gate.

This road leads out through oak woodland and chaparral, taking in the perimeter of the park, circling around the center where side trails lead to the quarry holes. You can take any of the spur trails for overlooks to the larger holes. Keep clear of poison oak in the dense brush alongside the trail.

You'll come to your first overview of the quarry in just a minute or so, on the right. Before you is an immense pit littered with large chunks of granite. At the bottom is a scummy pond. If you make your way to the right around the pit, you'll get a view of a tunnel opening down below on the left.

On the left side of the road here, you'll see a trail marker #5 and some stone steps leading down to the Lower Trail. That footpath is an alternate route if you prefer it to the road, but it's a longer and routes you away from the main quarry. Continuing on the road, you'll curve to the right.

If you stay on the main trail, you'll make the rounds in 1.5 miles. You can then explore the central section at will, hiking the trails that wind around the various quarry holes. The smaller holes are fenced off to keep people from falling in. The trail is flanked by the occasional digger pine and lots of California buckeye trees. In fall, the toyon will be hung with bright red berries.

Between marker #6 (blacksmith's shop) and #7, you'll see steps to the right that lead down to a small loop called the Inner Trail. This is an optional side trip. At marker #7, you encounter a fork. The left side goes to the Backwoods Trail, a longer route that brings you back to the main loop on the east side, but take the right trail instead, so you don't miss any of the numbered stops. Jog out on a spur trail right to stop #8 and an overlook of another quarry. Return to the main trail and turn right to continue. The trail climbs up past stop #9 where granite tailings (waste rock) are on display and on to stop #10 where you encounter a side trail to the left. This leads to a scenic view and is worth a short detour. Returning to the main trail and the most northerly point on the loop, you'll begin heading northeast on the return trip.

At a junction with the Backwoods Trail, you have a choice go right to stay on the main trail and pass stop #11 and another overlook of the quarry. Continuing south, you'll soon be back where you began.

Directions: From Interstate 80 take the Penryn exit and proceed on Penryn Road to Taylor Road. Turn right and continue to the park on the right, on the corner of Taylor and English Colony Road. Access is free. There is a portable toilet and drinking fountains.

Show Caves of the Mother Lode

The following four "trails" are all guided underground tours through spectacular show caves. They're limestone and marble with a wide variety of structures and attractions. Limestone caves form in basically the same way around the world, but each of these caves has its own character and stand-out features that make it special and worth a visit.

There are a few things to know about visiting caves. Usually, the temperature is steady year round and unrelated to the weather above ground. If it's 100 degrees outside, it may be only 70 in the cave, so be prepared for cool temperatures. Usually, cave visitors are asked to bring only small items inside, not backpacks or anything bulky, as passages are often narrow. You'll travel single file and crowd into small rooms. Touching cave formations will damage them. There are usually a lot of stairs. If you have mobility limitations, check the details before signing up for a tour. Normally, you can take photos in caves, but you will probably not be able to use a selfie stick and may be asked not to use a flash. Set your camera for low light situations and consider attaching it to your person to avoid hearing it clatter down into a rocky abyss. Nobody's happy when that happens.

Cave formations are some of the most beautiful of nature's wonders. You'll be awestruck in any one of or all of these caves, so enjoy the adventure!

Speleothems

The crystalline formations in limestone and dolomite caves are described by many names, depending on their appearance and growth patterns—stalactites, stalagmites, flowstone, cave bacon, etc.. Collectively, these formations are called "speleothems," Greek for "cave deposits." Though these delicate structures come in many shapes and sizes, they are all made of essentially the same stuff, calcite.

Speleothems form when rain water absorbs small amounts of carbon dioxide from the soil and air, creating a weak form of carbonic acid. This acidic water seeps through the bedrock, dissolving calcium carbonate, the primary mineral in limestone and dolomite. Over time, the pits and holes created by this process carve out a cave. The water then deposits its calcium, often in the crystallized form calcite, in these air pockets as it ponds, drips and seeps, creating the beautiful crystals that beckon us to come underground. A slow drip from the cave ceiling, for instance, might create a slender helictite or soda straw.

Many factors influence the development of speleothems, including humidity, temperature, rate of water seepage, air currents, and the amount of acid in the water. A cave that has lost its source of water and is dry is considered dead. Otherwise, it's a living cave and the speleothems are still forming.

72. Black Chasm Cavern

EFFORT: Minimal
LENGTH: N/A
GEOLOGICAL FEATURE(S): Caves
LOCATION: 15701 Pioneer-Volcano Road, Volcano, CA

Description: Black Chasm is an amazingly beautiful and fragile living limestone and marble cave that was opened to the public in September, 2000. It was something of a secret prior to development, declared a National Natural Landmark in 1976, but available only to a few individuals and groups for study. Its landmark status was granted primarily due to its substantial colony of rare helictite crystals. These are unusual looping and twisting white fingers of calcite that are hollow like soda straws, but growing at every possible angle.

As recently as February 2001, a spectacular new chamber was discovered, and there may be more to come. Exploration of the cave continues, although some passages are so choked with delicate crystals that spelunkers avoid passage in order not to damage them. So far, the public tour is limited to a few rooms, estimated to be about one-sixth of the tourable cave. Great care is being taken to preserve the cave's natural state, including the construction of expensive elevated trails designed to keep visitors off of the floor. The stairs, railings, and viewing platforms are made from recycled soda bottles instead of traditional materials such as wood to avoid leaching chemicals into the environment.

Fortunately for us, visitors of earlier generations were able to enter only the first few feet of the cave, so damage characteristic of that time is limited to the area just inside the entrance. Otherwise, the preservation is exemplary.

The 50-minute Landmark Tour includes the Colossal Room, 100 feet across and 150 feet deep, and the Landmark Room, famous for its massive arrays of helictites. Be prepared for stairs, lots of them, as the tour is essentially a trip downstairs and then back up. It begins by passing through a narrow opening and descending down the first flight of stairs to a platform suspended between the walls of the fissure. You can see well-lit stalactites, stalagmites, helictites, draperies, flowstone, and other familiar speleothems.

Looking down from the first platform, you'll see a small portion of a deep turquoise lake seventy feet below, colored by naturally-occurring calcium bicarbonate. The presence of water makes this a living cave.

This is the best spot on the tour to recognize that the cave was formed along a joint, and the basic shape of the area is a narrow chasm that you'll traverse almost vertically from top to bottom. Because of the sheer vertical drop almost immediately within the entrance, this cave would not have been a viable human habitat. No archeological artifacts have been found here.

Helictites

The walkway continues through the Landmark Portal and down into the Landmark Room, which contains impressive displays of spectacular helictites in the walls and ceiling. *Helictites* are formed under unusual conditions, which include water under pressure and the presence of certain trace minerals. As water droplets emerge through the rock to an exposed, vertical wall, they cling to it by surface tension. Rings of calcite are formed where the droplets make contact and build up into hollow tubes. These tubes begin in a more or less horizontal manner and then twist and turn in bizarre shapes as random crystals grow. Since helictites must battle gravity, they don't usually grow much longer than a few inches, but at Black Chasm there are many long helictites, including one near the entrance to the cave that measures twelve inches long.

The Landmark Room also contains one of the most beautiful flowstone formations you will come across.

Your guide will point out some of the small passageways that may eventually host cave-cams. You can easily see that these crystal-choked passages will not allow for visitors, walkways, ladders, etc., without significant destruction.

This is the end of the tour, from which you retrace your steps up to the entrance, squeezing past the next tour group along the way.

Directions: From Stockton, take Highway 88 east to Pinegrove. Turn left at Volcano-Pinegrove Road and continue three miles to the bottom of a big hill, make a steep right turn onto Pioneer-Volcano Road and continue about 1500 feet. Turn right at the Black Chasm National Natural Landmark entrance. You'll come to a parking area alongside the road. This is overflow parking. Continue past it to the main parking area and visitor center. The cave is open daily for public tours. Expect a reasonable wait of about an hour for your tour time, the perfect opportunity to sit down to that picnic lunch. There is a fee for the tour.

73. Mercer Caverns

EFFORT: Minimal
LENGTH: N/A
GEOLOGICAL FEATURE(S): Caves
LOCATION: Sheep Ranch Road, Murphys, CA

Description: Tours of lovely Mercer Caverns are 45 minutes long, descending to a depth of a 16-story building into the limestone. On view are typical cavern formations—stalactites, stalagmites, flowstone, soda straws, cave popcorn, etc.

This cave system is noted for its collection of rare aragonite *flos ferri*, a type of aragonite that grows in a dendritic, or treelike pattern. Your guide will point these out to you.

The first people to use Mercer Caverns were the native Mi-Wuk, for whom it was a mortuary between 1,500 and 2,000 years ago. They brought their dead here and rolled them through the opening, so imagine the gruesome underground scene when prospector Walter J. Mercer rediscovered this cave in 1885.

Tours were given to the public almost immediately after Mercer explored the cave, making this the longest continually operated commercial show cave in California. In the earliest days, the first paying visitors descended into the cave with ropes and candles. You, however, will walk on stairs with the aid of electric lighting.

While you're in Murphys, you may as well take a side trip for another geologic wonder. In the last decade, the Mother Lode has emerged as an extensive wine producing region, replacing gold mines with wineries. The beautiful Kautz Ironstone Vineyards is one of the finest. The winery is modeled after a 19th-century gold stamp mill. In the mining museum and jewelry store, you can walk into a bank-style vault that houses an astounding 44-pound gold nugget unearthed by the Sonora Mining Company in nearby Jamestown in 1992 and purchased by John Kautz in 1994. It was valued at 3.5 million dollars at that time and is an amazing thing to behold. It is sights like this one, such a vivid reminder that there is still gold to be found, that rekindle gold fever in the minds of visitors.

Cave Popcorn (National Park Service)

Directions: From Highway 49 in Angels Camp, turn left on Murphys Grade Road. If you reach the junction with Highway 4, you've missed it. Continue toward Murphys. As soon as you enter town and just before you get to the historic Murphys Hotel, turn left on Sheep Ranch Road and proceed to the Mercer Caverns parking area. There are restrooms and a gift shop. There is a tour fee. The cave is open daily for tours.

74. Moaning Cavern Walking Tour

EFFORT: Minimal
LENGTH: N/A
GEOLOGICAL FEATURE(S): Caves
LOCATION: 5350 Moaning Cave Road, Vallecito, CA

Description: Moaning Cavern's claim to fame is its massive main chamber, large enough to hold the Statue of Liberty. Discovered in 1851 by gold miners, the cave's "moaning" is created by water drops falling into holes in a bottle-shaped flowstone formation and echoing through the cave.

There are three tour options available for this cave. The easiest is the 45-minute walking tour. The guided tour begins through narrow marble passageways to the enormous main chamber. From here you descend on a spiral staircase, taking 235 stairs to a depth of 165 feet. At the bottom of the chamber, excavations have uncovered the remains of prehistoric people who fell into the cave thousands of years ago. As you descend, your guide will discuss the geology and history of the cave. The way out is back up the stairs.

For the more daring, there is the 2-hour Wild Cavern Adventure Trip that takes you through some of the deep chambers and passages in the cave. Wearing lighted helmets, you'll climb and crawl your way through undeveloped sections with an experienced guide. All clothing and equipment is provided.

The cave rappel, a popular experience inside the main cavern, is currently closed as of this writing. The operators are attempting to comply with state requirements that have classified it as an amusement park ride. If and when that happens, the rappel will reopen. Check the website for updates.

Meanwhile, there are multiple opportunities for fun at the park if you want to make a day of it, including zip lining, geode cracking, and panning for gold.

Directions: From Stockton, take Highway 4 east to Angels Camp and stay on Highway 4 until you see the sign to turn onto Parrotts Ferry Road. Turn right on Parrotts Ferry Road and go one mile. Turn right on Moaning Cave Road at the Moaning Cavern Park sign. The cavern is open every day, year round. There is a fee for the tour.

75. California Cavern Trail of Lights

EFFORT: Minimal
LENGTH: N/A
GEOLOGICAL FEATURE(S): Caves
LOCATION: 9565 Cave City Road, Mountain Ranch, CA

Description: Opened to the public in 1850, California Cavern was the state's first show cave and is State Historic Landmark #956. It contains many striking crystalline formations that can be observed on the 60 to 80-minute Trail of Lights Walking Tour. In the wet season, winter and

spring, this tour is called the Trail of Lakes tour due to the presence of pools of water. Two other tours are offered, which are described below.

The walking tour trail is nearly level and well lighted as it takes you through the cave, visiting several rooms, including the recently-discovered Jungle Room, named for the crystalline "vines" covering the ceiling.

Another offered tour is the two to three hour Mammoth Cave Expedition where you crawl and squeeze through passageways. Participants must be at

Dripstone (National Park Service)

least 8 years old and reservations are required.

A more rigorous tour option is the 3 to 4-hour Middle Earth Expedition, where groups are led through about 80% of the cavern system from the east entrance to the west exit. The trail is a mile long and consists of crawling and squeezing through narrow passageways in the Mammoth Cave area. Next you will go through the Middle Earth area, discovered in 1980, in which you will walk through deep, sticky clay. You'll then examine horizontal fissures in the Cave of the Quills and pass by raft across Tom's Lake. After exploring more chambers with beautiful crystalline formations, climb ladders to the world above. Participants must be at least 16 for this trip. Reservations are required.

For the last two tours, call for reservations. The Trail of Lights/Trail of Lakes tour does not require advance reservations. Check the web site for tour schedules.

Directions: From Stockton, take Highway 99 north to Lodi, then Highway 12 east to San Andreas. Turn left on Mountain Ranch Road and go approximately 8 miles. Turn right on Michel Road at the California Historical Landmark sign that says "California Caverns." Follow the signs for approximately 2 miles to the driveway on the left. The area has a nature trail and picnic area. There is a tour fee.

The High Sierras

Yosemite National Park

Making your way east from the golden, oak-studded hillsides of the foothills, you leave the valley haze and heat behind and enter the blissful high country. The High Sierras are characterized by thick conifer forests, glacial lakes, smooth granite, alpine wildflowers, cool, clear streams, and plenty of solitude.

The two people we most associate with this area of the state are naturalist John Muir and artist Ansel Adams. Both have wilderness areas named after them. There are several other wilderness areas in the Sierras, as well as three national parks and plenty of national forest for public recreation. There are trails of every length and description and a whole lot of hiking going on. The iconic Pacific Crest Trail makes it way steadily along the top of the range, traversing its entire length. Our paths will cross the PCT on occasion on our exploration of High Sierra geology, primarily a story of magma, volcanoes and the sculpting power of glacial ice.

As a reminder, the Sierras are a massive granitic batholith that has been uplifted by tectonic action to form the 400-mile long mountain range. The bedrock geology consists of metamorphosed sedimentary and volcanic rocks, intruded by the granites, or granodiorites, of the Sierra batholith, all of which are capped by the remnants of volcanic activity that occurred between 4 and 20 million years ago, depositing lava, ash and mud. In the last million years, during the Pleistocene, ice over 1,000 feet deep covered all but the highest peaks of the Sierra Crest. You can see evidence of the power of ice to sculpt rock everywhere in the Sierras, in the bowl-shaped cirques and U-shaped valleys, on the surfaces of polished stone and in the rocks and sediments that were shifted and moved by the ice. We'll see all of these things and more on the beautiful trails of the High Sierras.

Sierra Nevada Granite

Whenever you're hiking in the High Sierras, smooth light gray bedrock dominates and defines the landscape. It formed from molten magma cooling deep underground between 120 and 85 million years ago during the Jurassic and Cretaceous periods.

This igneous rock is commonly called granite, but may technically be granodiorite, tonalite or diorite, depending on the exact combination of minerals. In any case, granitic rocks are defined as being rich in quartz.

The rock of the Sierras is composed of the light-colored minerals quartz and feldspar and the dark-colored minerals hornblende and biotite. The combination of these mainly white and black components give the rock a salt and pepper appearance. The color of the rock may be lighter or darker depending on the percentage of each mineral. In the Sierras, you'll commonly see a light pink mineral. That's feldspar. Another variation you'll observe in the granite is crystal size. Differing temperatures during cooling affect how large the crystals grow. For example, on one of our hikes, you'll see some extremely large feldspar crystals in the granite domes near Tuolumne Meadows in Yosemite. Geologists speculate that this rock formed while undergoing episodic heating and cooling.

Sierra Nevada Granite Mineralogy

Quartz
Gray-white, Glassy
Amorphous

Hornblende
Black or gray
Blade-shaped

Biotite
Black or dark brown
Book-shaped

Feldspar
White or pink, Opaque
Rectangular prism-shaped

76. Pyramid Creek Trail

EFFORT: Minimal
LENGTH: 2.6 miles
GEOLOGICAL FEATURE(S): Glaciation
LOCATION: El Dorado National Forest

Description: For low-effort day-hikers like ourselves, this trail offers something not easily found, a fairly painless access route into beguiling Desolation Wilderness. Horsetail Falls is the destination, 300 feet of whitewater plunging over the cliff in a dramatic series of cascades and cataracts. Come in the late spring or early summer to see the waterfall at its most robust, but autumn is also an excellent time to visit when the worst of the heat is past and the trees near the creek are turning yellow. Whenever you visit, bring a picnic to enjoy in this charming forest setting.

The bare granite cliffs surrounding Pyramid Creek are considered to be one of the best examples of Pleistocene glaciation in the Sierra Nevada range.

Before you begin, sign in at the trailhead. Wilderness visitors must register, even for a day hike. You'll start at 6,100 feet in elevation. Head out in an easterly direction, roughly parallel to the highway, which is within earshot. You'll travel through sparse tree cover, ducking in and out of shade. Throughout the entire route, Pyramid Creek will remain on your right.

The trail climbs up into a spacious, circular canyon with high walls on three sides. Shortly after starting out, the trail makes an abrupt turn left, leading you up a stone staircase to a trail sign. Turn right to proceed across granite slabs near the creek. The trail will become indistinct here, but just continue along the creek to a serious swath of whitewater. It's around this point that the roar of the creek begins to drown out the roar of Highway 50 below. Looking towards the back of the canyon, you'll get your first view of Horsetail Falls as it wends its way over and down the sheer granite cliff face.

A glacier moved through here about 12,000 years ago, scooping out the valley and leaving behind the long waterfall of Pyramid Creek, a "hanging" valley. Besides the riveting waterfall and the canyon itself, several other features of geologic interest can be found here. While you're enjoying the trail, pause to examine them. Look for evidence of *frost wedging* where hefty boulders have been split apart by the continual freezing and thawing of water within their joints. Also be on the lookout for many good examples of *differential weathering* (variance of discoloration, disintegration, etc., of rocks of different kinds exposed to the same environment), often easily seen in the presence of xenoliths (foreign rocks) and dikes in the granite. A *xenolith* is a pre-existing rock that was incorporated into igneous rock when it was molten. A *dike* is sort of the opposite—later rock that cut across a pre-existing body of rock, forming in a fracture. Along this trail, resistant xenoliths protrude from the bedrock that has eroded around them. Many aplite *dikes* cut across the rock. You'll see these as whitish stringers of quartz and feldspar running through the granite. These, too, are often protruding somewhat, indicating that they are more resistant to weathering than the surrounding ground mass.

Frost Wedging

Pyramid Creek falls over the cliff at the back of the canyon and then winds around the east side of it to meet up with Highway 50 on the south. Our trail climbs gently beside it for the first 1.3 miles over rocky, uneven ground.

If you lose the trail on bare granite, you'll probably pick it up again when it turns back into dirt. There are occasional signs reading "trail" to put you back on course. There are also cairns placed by other hikers. More often, there are little hiker symbols nailed to tree trunks, so look up to find these. But if you can't always locate the trail, just head on your own route toward the back of the canyon and the waterfall, which frequently comes into view.

Along the way, take the time to veer off the trail to explore the creek. There are numerous idyllic spots along its banks to enjoy that picnic lunch. As the trail routes you north, you'll enter a section that's mostly dirt, mostly shady, and mostly level. A few ferns can be found growing here.

After a half mile you'll reach the boundary of Desolation Wilderness. At an unmarked trail junction, paths fork left and right. To the left the trail will soon reach a signed junction with Twin Bridges Trail. You can make a loop out of this hike by taking that narrow path back, but it is somewhat overgrown with manzanita and not nearly as pleasant as Pyramid Creek Trail, so we recommend making this an out and back trip. Turn right at the unmarked junction to continue climbing toward the waterfall. It will be another half mile to Lower Falls.

As you climb, you get better views of the surrounding terrain. Looking back toward Highway 50, to the southwest, you can see Lover's Leap, a popular rock climbing location.

Once you reach the waterfall, you can cool off in its spray and contemplate how a river of ice created this magnificent place.

This is the end of the trail for us, but many people find the idea of climbing to the top irresistible. It's a steep climb with some rock scrambling. Give it a try if you feel like it, since the view from above is heady. Follow a route marked by spray-painted green arrows over granite slabs. Once you reach the top, you come out onto a flat area with incredible views to the valley below. There are many small streams up there heading for the falls, and several pools suitable for swimming. However, you should exercise extreme caution at the top of the falls. Several people have died here. At the time of this writing, the waterfall has just claimed another victim, a woman who slipped and was carried over the cliff.

Return via the same route or just head back over the bare granite slabs in the center of the canyon. The geological features we came to see are quite abundant there.

Directions: You'll find this trailhead on Highway 50 18 miles southwest of Lake Tahoe and 80 miles east of Sacramento. Park in the lot north of the highway near Twin Bridges. The lot is signed, "Pyramid Creek Trailhead." This lot fills up quickly on weekends. There is limited parking along the highway, but be careful to heed No Parking and Tow Away signs. There is a fee to park in the lot and there are restrooms at the trailhead.

77. Big Meadow Trail

EFFORT: Moderate
LENGTH: 5.2 miles
GEOLOGICAL FEATURE(S): Volcanism
LOCATION: El Dorado National Forest

Description: This is the site of one or more ancient volcanic eruptions and the resultant mudflows, but it's not all about geology on this trail. Wildflowers are excellent here as well, as you might have guessed from the name of the trail, so time your hike in summer to make the most of the blooms.

Start out going south on a portion of the Tahoe Rim Trail through pine and fir forest, and shortly enter Big Meadow after a half mile. Cross a wooden bridge and walk through the meadow, then begin a gentle climb through a sparse forest. Keep an eye out for wildflowers along the way, including blue lupine, Indian paintbrush, brown pinedrops, pink monkeyflowers, purple columbine, and aster growing in open places within the forest.

After about 1.5 miles, you come to a creek and a meadow rich in blooms. Continuing, you climb up and over a ridge and on through a volcanic environment where ancient mudflows are on view. A volcanic mudflow is known as a *lahar*, and these secondary effects of volcanoes can be far more devastating than the lava flow itself. Lahars can also be caused by intense rain falling on newly-deposited volcanic ash after the eruptive activity has ceased. A disastrous lahar occurred in the Philippines after the eruption of Mt. Pinatubo in 1991, burying entire villages and destroying everything in its path. The word "lahar" is now commonplace among the Filipinos; it's a geologic term they know all too well.

After two miles, you descend to reach a junction. The trail to the right leads to Dardanelles Lake. You'll bear left instead and negotiate some ups and downs through distinctive rock outcrops. Notice that the rocks look like chunky cement, and in a way, that's what they are. During the mudflows created by volcanic eruptions, the ash and mud mixture caught up existing rocks of varying sizes and "cemented" them together as it cooled. This sort of composite rock is known as a *conglomerate*, something we've already observed on a few of our earlier trails.

Continue along a level stretch of trail through a fir forest until reaching the north shore of rock-rimmed Round Lake. Look to the east side of the lake to see another of those mud flow formations. Walk around the shore until you find the perfect spot for a picnic. After enjoying the lake, head back the way you came.

Directions: From Highway 50 at Highway 89, proceed south on Highway 89 for 5.2 miles to Big Meadow trailhead. Park in the lot on the left just past the trailhead. Access is free.

78. Trail of the Gargoyles

EFFORT: Minimal
LENGTH: 3.0 miles
GEOLOGICAL FEATURE(S): Volcanism, Erosional Features
LOCATION: Stanislaus National Forest

Description: This hidden gem of an interpretive trail is worth driving a mile on a bumpy dirt road. It's a beautiful and amazing spot that dramatically displays the process of erosion upon soft volcanic deposits. Somebody in the Forest Service seems to have taken some delight in trail naming. In this area, other intriguingly-named interpretive trails include Columns of the Giants, Trail of the Survivors, and Trail of the Ancient Dwarfs.

From the parking area, walk up the dirt road to the trail register and a startling overlook of a deep, forested canyon and the mountains beyond them in the distance. Even if you didn't come to hike the trail, this view alone would be worth the stop. To the north and south, tall cliffs circle around the canyon. There is not much tree cover on this trail, so wear a hat and carry water. What trees you'll find are Jeffrey pine, white fir, lodgepole pine, and western juniper. Manzanita bushes also grow among the sparse ground vegetation.

There is evidence here of several volcanic events—lava flows, lahars (mudflows), and ash deposits. You can see immediately that the cliff edges are fragile and highly eroded. Stay away from the edge. The South Rim Trail follows the south canyon wall, and the North Rim Trail follows the north canyon wall. This is not a loop. You start in the middle, walk to the end of one trail, come back, and walk the other direction. The two sides of the trail are similar, but they do have different formations, and it's worthwhile hiking both.

There are numbered posts corresponding to the guide, but the trail is not in the best condition. Some of the posts seem to be missing. Nevertheless, we didn't have much trouble identifying the important features. You can start with either the north or south rim. For this description, we're heading south.

You're walking on the remnants of a lahar, rock formed by a mixture of volcanic ash and snow or water that flowed as hot mud, collecting smaller rocks and debris along the way. Once the mudflows cooled, the resulting material resembled concrete. You can see the rocks embedded in the ash where they were gathered up.

The dark band of rock around the canyon, below the rim, called the River of Stone by the brochure, is an ancient lava flow that filled a river channel. Above and below the lava are lahar deposits. As you approach the south canyon wall, you get a good view of the "Wall of Noses." Stop and enjoy the metaphor. It's easy to see that the noses were formed by water erosion on the soft ash flow deposits.

Wall of Noses

Continuing on the footpath, you head downhill and swing around a tall block of stone that you can see well once the trail takes you back to the canyon rim. Look back at the eroded stone wall you just detoured around. It looks a bit like a castle. The trail continues only a little further, ending at an overlook of the canyon.

Return the way you came to the trailhead, and then continue on the North Rim Trail. At stop #2, you can see the tops of a series of basalt columns fifty or sixty feet tall. Such columns are a natural result of lava cooling at a uniform rate. Cracking patterns form similar to those in a mud flat baking in the sun. If you're interested in such columnar formations (of course you are), you can drive further up Highway 108 to the Columns of the Giants Trail (Hike #80) where a much more impressive example can be seen. And an even better example not far away is at Devils Postpile (Hike #102).

Erratics

On either leg of this trail, you'll notice many granite boulders, or *erratics*, transported to their current location by glaciers. These big rocks, caught in the ice, acted like grinding stones, polishing and gouging the landscape as the glacier moved through. After the ice retreated, the boulders were left behind. You can recognize erratics as rocks that look out of place, as if they were just dropped there by a giant, which, in essence, is exactly what happened. Another clue that a boulder is an erratic is if its composition is different from the surrounding rock. Identifying the source of erratics gives geologists clues to the size and direction of historic glaciers.

At stop #7, you'll see evidence of how frozen water in the crevices of the lava enlarge the cracks over time and create a fragmented surface. This process is called *frost wedging*.

The Gargoyles at stop #9 are the interesting columns that have been carved by erosion of the mud flow deposits. Such natural sculptures are formed fairly rapidly in the soft lahar material by wind, rain, and snow.

The trail ends at stop #11. Turn back and return to the trailhead.

Directions: From Highway 108 in Sonora, travel east to Strawberry, continuing a couple of miles before turning right on Herring Creek Road. Proceed 6 miles to the trailhead. This paved, two-lane road will narrow after a couple of miles to become a paved one-lane road, after which it becomes a rough dirt road for the last mile. When we visited, the only marker for the trail was a piece of paper stapled to a tree. The paper may not be there when you visit. If you reach a signed fork in the road, you have just passed the pullout for this trail. It is on the left side of the road, an open dirt area with a sign reading, "No Camping Beyond This Point." Hopefully, both the trailhead and trail itself will get a signage update at some point. Stop at the Summit Ranger Station just before you get to Strawberry and ask for a trail pamphlet. This is also a good place for a restroom stop, as there are no facilities at the trailhead. Access is free.

79. Donnell Vista Trail

EFFORT: Minimal
LENGTH: 0.5 miles
GEOLOGICAL FEATURE(S): Glaciation, Volcanism
LOCATION: Stanislaus National Forest

Description: Take fifteen minutes out of your drive across the Sierras to walk this short trail to a grand overlook with superb views of the Dardanelles and the Stanislaus River canyon.

Located at 6,240-feet high, this paved, accessible trail winds past huge granite boulders and low-growing manzanita. Take your lunch along, as there's a picnic table with a heady view alongside the trail.

The Dardanelles is a nine million-year-old eruption that covers a huge area up to 1,000 feet thick, flowing out seventy miles as far as Knight's

Ferry in the foothills to the west. On your drive up from the west, you may have seen remnants of this lava flow on either side of the highway. It appears as flat-topped, black hills. At the time the lava flowed, those hills used to be lower than the surrounding landscape and were possibly flowing within a river bed. Over time, the softer sediments that originally contained the volcanic rock have eroded away.

Continue on the easy trail to the overlook at the end where a railing separates you from a lengthy drop north into the Stanislaus River canyon. Peer down at the river far below and to the west to Donnell Reservoir and its curving dam, then east to the Dardanelles. You can easily see the profile of the ancient lava flow from this angle, including the Dardanelles Cone, the source of the lava. It's a breathtaking vista, and you'll want to gaze at it for a while.

Donnell Reservoir

Recall the geologic history of this area. The bedrock granite formed underground and was uplifted to create these mountains. Volcanoes then erupted, covering the granite with lava. Later, the ice age glaciers traveled through, scraping away some of the volcanic deposits and exposing the granite once again. There's evidence of this history all around you.

When you can tear yourself away from the view, take a moment to walk over the smooth granite and peer at it more closely. You'll see a few incipient potholes left by the rocks swirling in flowing water under the glaciers. There are also many huge xenoliths (pre-existing rocks engulfed by magma) incorporated into the granite.

Take the same trail back to the parking area.

Directions: From Sonora, take Highway 108 east to the Pinecrest exit, and then go about 18 miles further east on Highway 108 to the Donnell Vista Point on the left. There are restrooms and picnic tables here. Access is free.

80. Columns of the Giants

EFFORT: Minimal
LENGTH: 0.5 miles
GEOLOGICAL FEATURE(S): Volcanism
LOCATION: Stanislaus National Forest

Description: This is an easy walk on a well-worn trail to a cliff of 150,000-year old Pleistocene basalt formations known as the Columns of the Giants, an example of *columnar jointing*. These fascinating columns are similar to those found at Devils Postpile National Monument (Hike #102) near Mammoth Lakes, but are more weathered and a little less distinct. The basalt is about 400 feet thick and located in the Middle Fork of the Stanislaus River canyon.

You can see the column formation from the parking area. It's the black wall of rock across the river. To get an up close look, walk south on the trail signed "Trail" and cross the river over a sturdy wooden bridge. When we were here in October, aspens provided bright yellow strokes of color near the water's edge, and a couple of amusing water ouzels dove into the frigid water looking for aquatic insects.

Although this is a spectacular geologic wonder and extremely easy to get to, we were alone on the trail except for a squirrel dashing ahead of us and a few Stellar's jays hopping on nearby branches.

The landscape is fairly open with well-spaced pine trees as you walk beside the river for a short distance and then turn right away from it.

Head gently uphill and you'll soon come upon the huge talus (rock debris) slope of broken columns, above which stand columns that are still intact. Some of the columns are standing vertically, which is how they form. Some, especially at the top of the cliff, are tilted to a nearly horizontal position by the shifting of the earth's crust. Others are bent and bowed by the same forces occurring slowly over a long period of time.

Columns of the Giants

This lava flow originally covered five square miles. The later passage of glacial ice carved it down to two. If you could look down on top of the columns you'd be able to see the polished tops, indicating the passage of glaciers. There is explanatory information about how these columns form at the end of the trail. The geometric shapes are created naturally by slow, uniform cooling and cracking of the basalt. Given enough time and enough mass, basalt flows always shrink and crack into a hexagonal pattern, as the hexagon represents the most energy-efficient geometric shape in nature. This pattern propagates down through the thickness of the lava, resulting in rows of upright columns. In columnar jointing, columns may form with as few as three sides and up to eight, but six is the most common.

Walk to the right along the base of the wide slope. The trail will turn away from the columns and loop back to the river, but this return leg of the trail is more challenging, especially near the end when you have a steep descent to the bridge. If you want to avoid that, you'll lose nothing by returning along the same path you originally traveled out.

Although there is a picnic table here, a more inviting lunch spot is just west at the Donnell Vista Point (see previous hike). It too is well worth the visit.

Directions: On Highway 108 heading east from Pinecrest, note when you reach Clark Fork Road. Drive 5 miles further to the signed Columns of the Giants trail. Turn right into the parking area. There are toilets. Access is free.

81. Glacier Meadow Loop

EFFORT: Minimal
LENGTH: 0.5 miles
GEOLOGICAL FEATURE(S): Glaciation
LOCATION: Tahoe National Forest

Description: This is an easy walk on an interpretive trail showcasing the glaciation of the area. It is also extremely easy to get to, beginning at the Donner Summit rest stop off Interstate 80. This is the perfect diversion on your way over the hill, to get out of the car, stretch your legs, and use the facilities. Although you can hear the traffic from the freeway throughout most of the walk, it is only mildly distracting. This is also the trailhead for many other longer trails. For that reason, we've hiked it numerous times, but always enjoy this section at any time of year.

As we write this, the trail is unsigned. The Forest Service is working on new signs to replace those badly vandalized and removed some years ago.

Start the trail from behind the building at the rest stop, on the right side just past the picnic tables, or on the northeast side of the Sno-Park parking lot from the Pacific Crest Trail access trail.

You'll walk through an alpine forest decorated with huge granite boulders. The trail is fairly easy, but can be wet in spring, and will be buried in snow throughout the winter and into May. In autumn, you will enjoy the colors of the changing season in the surrounding aspens.

On your right, you'll encounter a huge sloping slab of granite, well fractured and open like a beckoning ballroom dance floor. Go ahead and frolic on it. While you're dancing, look at the many xenoliths (foreign rocks) caught up in the granite. Recall that a xenolith is a pre-existing rock that is incorporated into magma that solidifies around it. There are many good examples here. There are also potholes made by the swirling of stones in streams under the glacier. And look for striations, scratches made from the scraping of rocks along the surface of the slab as the glacier moved above it, grinding it smooth with the gravel caught up in the ice.

Xenoliths in Granite

When you're finished at this playground, return to the trail and cross a seasonal creek. There's a large roundish boulder beside the trail that shows a good example of frost wedging. The boulder has been split into four pieces by the continuous freezing and thawing within its fractures. You can tell by the clean surface of the break that this occurred in the relatively recent geologic past.

Heading south, you'll come to the edge of a pond which, when rimmed with snow, is an enchanting little stop in the woods. A sign here marks the trail junction where the south path follows alongside the pond and leads to the Pacific Crest Trail. You can explore it a bit if you like. This is a pretty little pocket of solitude.

Our loop trail continues to the left (north), heading up through more granite boulders on its return to the rest stop. The trail takes you up one section of stone steps, and then down another, where you emerge behind and just east of the rest stop building, completing the loop.

Directions: From Interstate 80 immediately west of Donner Summit, take the Castle Peak Area/Boreal Ridge Road exit. Look for a sign reading "Tahoe National Forest Trailhead/Donner Summit/Pacific Crest Trail." After exiting the freeway (and going under it if you were traveling west), turn left and proceed to the Sno-Park. Park near the trailhead at the northeast edge of the lot. The trail actually starts and ends at the eastbound Donner Summit Rest Area, but unattended parking is not allowed there. Access is free.

Yosemite National Park

What can we say about Yosemite, except that we are grateful to have it practically in our backyard. Spectacular waterfalls and gorgeous granite amid evergreen forests are the main attractions here. Some people consider many spots in this park sacred. For rock climbers all over the world it is a shrine, home to magnificent, unrivaled landmarks like Half Dome and El Capitan. The majestic granite domes and monoliths will imbue the most jaded travelers with awe.

For us, the granite would be enough to justify the national park classification. But Yosemite has more superlatives to offer. It has the deep, glacier-carved Yosemite Valley with its lovely meadows and long-distance vertical views. It has numerous dramatic waterfalls as part of its glacial legacy. And it has three groves of giant sequoias, the largest trees in the world.

Yosemite is a crowded park, especially in summer, but as in most national parks, the crowds tend to cluster together on the main road and not venture out on the longer trails. As soon as you walk more than a mile, you'll leave most of the people behind and find remote seclusion and breathtaking beauty. To ease the road congestion, a free shuttle takes visitors through Yosemite Valley year round.

If you want to see the water shows, come in spring or early summer when the snowmelt is at its height. If you want to avoid the crowds, come in autumn before the snows arrive. Or, if you ski, winter is the season to take in some of the wonders of cross-country trails. Tioga Road, which passes through the park west to east, and Glacier Point Road are closed in winter, but the heart of Yosemite is open all year.

There are over 800 miles of trails in this park. We've chosen just a few, those that demonstrate the geology of the park, a story that centers around glaciation. Like the Sierra trails we've already explored, Yosemite occupies part of the Sierra batholith, granite bedrock that was uplifted and later covered by ice. On display here are some of the same features of glaciation we've already seen, but when it comes to rocks, everything in Yosemite is on a grander scale.

Directions: These directions to Yosemite National Park will not be repeated in the details for each hike. There are several routes in: Highway 120, heading east from Central California, leaves Highway 99 in Manteca, south of Stockton. Coming from further south on Highway 99, take Highway 140 northeast from Merced. From the eastern side off of Highway 395 in Lee Vining, take Highway 120 west through Tioga Pass (closed in winter). The south entrance is on Highway 41 from Fresno. There is a fee for entering Yosemite, but it's good for seven days.

82. Lembert Dome Trail

EFFORT: Minimal
LENGTH: 2.0 miles
GEOLOGICAL FEATURE(S): Glaciation, Erosional Features
LOCATION: Yosemite National Park

Description: Yosemite is known for its massive granite domes, most famously Half Dome, but domes are plentiful here. You can easily climb a few of them—Lembert and Pothole in the Tuolumne Meadows area, and Sentinel near Glacier Point. The domes are a result of the natural weathering exhibited by granite. Exposed to rain, wind, and cold, they shed layers in a process called *exfoliation*, or sheeting. The result, after several layers are shed, is a round boulder. This can be observed throughout the Sierras and anywhere that granite is present. But you don't often see boulders as immense as those found in Yosemite. The boulder in the photo below, for example, isn't as tall as a human, but Lembert Dome is 800 feet tall. Both exhibit the same weathering patterns.

Exfoliation

Before heading out on the trail, take a moment to look around and imagine the geologic history of the area. During the glacial ice age, this valley was inundated by a giant river of ice up to 2,200 feet thick. The thickness of a glacier can be determined in part by observing where it did not leave its mark. In this case, the top 200 feet of Cathedral Peak to the southwest was left untouched by the ice. The mountain below that height shows evidence of glaciation.

The trail is short but steep, with an average grade of twelve percent, and climbs relentlessly to a height of over 9,000 feet. If you're prone to altitude sickness, don't make this climb. In any case, make it slow and stop to catch your breath often. Having said that, the sheer face of the dome where experienced climbers may be clinging is deceptive. You will be climbing up the other side, which is much easier and requires no climbing equipment.

This dome is name for Jean Baptiste Lembert, a sheepherder and hermit who lived and was murdered here in the 1890s. His body was found in a cabin in Yosemite Valley, but his murderer was never found.

Start out on the trail by the restrooms, the trail for both Dog Lake and Lembert Dome. Climb around the dome and to the back side through lodgepole pine. The dirt path will give way to bare rock after 0.8 miles. From here, choose your route and climb up onto the granite. There is no trail onto the dome. Just make your way up it the safest way you can, being careful to get good footholds. Although the coarseness of granite makes it relatively easy to climb, loose material can prove treacherous.

If you look for them on your way up, you'll see the striations (scratches) left by the passing glaciers. Also notice the conspicuous glacial erratics left here on top of the dome.

Your reward for the climb is the stunning, panoramic view. Look out over Tuolumne Meadows with its meandering streams and the surrounding mountains named for notable scientists (Lyell, Dana, Gibbs) from your high perch. Sir Charles Lyell was an important early geologist who wrote the first geology textbook, *Principles of Geology*. James Dwight Dana was professor of geology at Yale at the time of the peak's naming and wrote the first book on minerology, still used today. Oliver Wolcott Gibbs was a chemist at Harvard and the founder of the National Academy of Sciences.

The return trip is on the same path.

Directions: Find the Lembert Dome parking lot at the east end of Tuolumne Meadows off of Tioga Road. This trailhead is shared and signed for Lembert Dome, Dog Lake, Soda Springs, and Glen Aulin Trails. The trail starts near the restrooms.

83. Pothole Dome Trail

EFFORT: Minimal
LENGTH: 2.0 miles
GEOLOGICAL FEATURE(S): Glaciation, Erosional Features
LOCATION: Yosemite National Park

Description: This is a short hike to an easily reached granite dome that formed about 85 million years ago during the Cretaceous when the magma cooled from the Cathedral Peak pluton. There are several domes you can climb in Yosemite (see previous hike), and all of them are fun, but this one is an especially good lesson in geology.

From the parking area, look directly across the meadow to the granite dome you're about to climb. In summer, the meadow will be green and blooming red with Lemmon's paintbrush. In autumn, it's dry and golden. These meadows are extremely fragile and easily damaged. Although it would be quicker to cut across the meadow to the dome, don't do it. This trail is short enough as it is.

Take the trail to the left of the parking area along the edge of the meadow, west and then north. The trail turns east and becomes a narrow track between the base of the dome on your left and the meadow on your right. A few young conifers grow here along the trail.

At 0.3 miles, the trail turns northeast. You'll see where other hikers before you have left the trail to walk up the gentle east side of the dome. You do the same. There is a pronounced joint (open space, like a fault, but without any up/down or side-to side movement) running all the way to the top, defining a sort of trail if you want something to follow.

Pothole Dome

Once upon the smooth granite, the geologist in our party was wriggling with glee. A number of interesting features leap out at you right away. First, the differential weathering is highly pronounced, where little knobs of perfect pink potassium feldspar crystals stick stubbornly out of the bedrock granite. The protuberances are harder than the granite matrix, which erodes away around them. The feldspar crystals are called *phenocrysts*. They're striking and hard to miss. Even when the feldspar crystals aren't sticking out of the granite, they are remarkable for their incredible size. Feldspar is a ubiquitous component of granite, but never have we seen it so large. These rectangular crystals were two to three inches in length and are typical in the Cathedral Peak granite *porphyry*, the type of rock you'll find here. A porphyritic rock is one that has

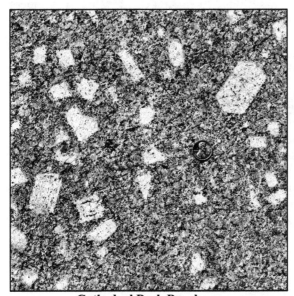

Cathedral Peak Porphyry

prominent phenocrysts set in a groundmass of smaller crystals, which means the original melt cooled in two distinct stages. If you're lucky enough to have a sunny day, the crystal faces and cleavage planes will be sparkling all over the dome, dazzling you. The impressive size of the crystals indicates that the original pluton cooled very slowly, allowing enough time and space in the magmatic chamber for the true shape of the crystal to form.

Continue upslope. As you approach the high point, the climb gets a little steeper, but continues to be easy. As you gain elevation, you'll also get better and better views of your surroundings. The next part of this geology lesson comes about two-thirds of the way up where the polished surfaces of the granite are more and more evident. The rock is as smooth as a kitchen countertop, polished by the grinding action of rocks carried within the glacier. You'll no doubt catch the glint of these surfaces if the sun is shining. You may think of glaciers as pure ice, but in fact the bottom of a glacier is mainly rocks and soil held by the ice. Be sure to run your hand over the smooth surfaces to feel just how effectively glaciers can grind.

Nothing grows on this bare granite except in the occasional cleft where the rock has fractured and a bit of soil has accumulated. One such crack can be seen near the summit and a few small trees have rooted themselves there. The trees help to create the soil that sustains them, breaking down the rock with their root systems.

The top of the dome contains boulders called erratics that were brought here by glaciers. They are easily identified because they stand out clearly against the symmetry and smoothness of the dome. Roundish boulders sitting on the dome like goose eggs on a platter were carried within the ice and then left here when the ice melted. You can look westward from the summit to see several erratics on the smooth dome across the way. They stand out in profile on the horizon.

Pothole Dome is named for the many potholes on it, mainly on the south slope. Most potholes are found in streambeds, created by boulders jostling around in a depression and eventually deepening it. These potholes, in contrast, were probably created by rocks swirling in waterways flowing under the glacial ice.

Once you attain the dome's high point, you'll have sweeping views in all directions, including the Cathedral Range. To the east is Tuolumne Meadows spread out with its narrow waterways in clear relief.

When you're done exploring the dome (and you can drag your geologist away from it), head back down to its base and take the same trail back to the parking area.

Directions: From Tuolumne Meadows Information Center, proceed 1.5 miles west on Tioga Road to a signed turnout at the west end of Tuolumne Meadows. The parking area is on the north side of the road.

84. Taft Point Trail

EFFORT: Minimal
LENGTH: 2.4 miles
GEOLOGICAL FEATURE(S): Erosional Features
LOCATION: Yosemite National Park

Description: Unbelievable views can be had from Taft Point, and the fissures are a geologic marvel.

Descend from the parking area to the trailhead shared with Sentinel Dome and turn left where the two trails diverge. Walk into a sparse, mixed conifer forest, keeping a lookout for a couple of sightings of Sentinel Dome on your right. Soon you'll reach Sentinel Creek, which you cross by boulder hopping. In autumn, it will be dry.

The trail continues to a junction at 0.5 miles. The trail to your right heads back toward Sentinel Dome. You'll continue straight. Past the junction, descend into a moister area where water seepage provides habitat for bracken fern and wildflowers. The trees become more dense as well along this section and their limbs are trimmed with bright green lichen. You won't be seeing much in the way of views through this section, but this is a good place for spotting wildlife. Stellar's jays dart through the trees and deer may wander along for the green grass growing here. We were lucky enough to spot three grouse scratching among the ferns directly beside the trail. They were wary, but didn't bolt and let us take their picture.

As you approach your destination, the trail becomes somewhat rockier and you can see that the trees open up ahead. Climb down some natural rock stairs beside friendly granite boulders and then walk out of the forest and across bare granite. A short distance ahead the ground drops away quite suddenly and dramatically.

Soon you arrive at the edge of a chasm above the first of the Fissures, five vertical fractures in Profile Cliff, extending 3,000 feet straight down to the valley below. The Fissures were created by successive freezing and thawing of the rock, which wedged it apart. Stay a safe distance back and make sure you have firm footing. Standing on the edge of this cliff, looking so far straight down is the perfect way to make yourself teeter. However, we couldn't resist lying on our stomachs and looking over the edge.

One of the narrower fissures has two boulders wedged into it, caught where they fell from above.

Rocks caught in a fissure

Just beyond the Fissures, as you walk near the edge of the cliff, enjoy the expansive views of gray granite domes for miles around. Taft Point has a railing that will provide a safer opportunity for looking over from your dizzying 7,500-foot height. El Capitan stands looming before you across the way, a 4,000-foot tall granite monolith, and Yosemite Valley is spread out far below.

This is probably a good spot to stop and reflect on just why El Capitan is here. Or why any of the features of Yosemite turned out as they did after the patient forces of ice, wind, and water whittled away at them over time. Although we've been talking about the granite as though it's just a single type of material, it actually comes in many different compositions. The great batholith that forms the Sierra Nevadas is composed of several different *plutons* (bodies of intrusive igneous rock) emplaced at different times. In 1930 after an exhaustive and still definitive geologic mapping project, F. C. Calkins of the USGS published a paper describing the Yosemite bedrock in which he named the different rock types, such as the El Capitan Granite, the Sentinel Granodiorite, Taft Granite, etc. The differences are mainly in crystal size and the ratios of quartz, feldspar, hornblende, and biotite.

Taft Point looking across at El Capitan

These small differences in composition can lead to dramatic differences in the rate and pattern of erosion. El Capitan is composed of Taft and El Capitan Granites, both rich in quartz and resistant to weathering. Less resistant types of rock which used to stand around it have given way, leaving it as a hulking mass on its own. El Capitan, Half Dome, and other big hunks of stubborn rock are largely unjointed. Without joints for erosional forces to gain a foothold, these rocks present a formidable defense against the elements.

However, even these seemingly immutable landmarks aren't immune to erosion. Every once in a while, a section of rock, pried loose by weather and gravity, will fall. The most recent events as of this writing were September 27 and 28, 2017, on El Capitan. A massive chunk of rock gave way, crashing to the valley below and killing one man. The following day another rock fall occurred in the same location. From the observation platform at Taft Point you have an excellent view of the scar left by that event. The fresh face of the newly-revealed rock is light gray, lighter than the surrounding rock, and easily distinguished as a long, narrow swath descending to the base of the monolith (see photo).

Observing that missing mass across the way might make you a little nervous about standing here on the edge of Taft Point 3,000 feet above the valley floor. It did us. But the view was irresistible anyway.

You can continue walking west near the edge of the gorge to a dramatic ledge with a single small tree growing on it, and then a little further along to a view facing westward, giving you another perspective. Any of the granite slabs up here make a great picnic table. You'll feel like you're on top of the world and will want to stay a while to enjoy the majesty of your surroundings. When you're ready, take the same route back.

Directions: From Wawona Road/Highway 41, turn onto Glacier Point Road. Proceed 13.2 miles to the Sentinel Dome/Taft Point parking area, two miles before the end of the road. This road is closed in winter. There is a single pit toilet. After your hike, visit Glacier Point at the end of this road for an even better view (yes, it's possible) of Yosemite's most famous landmarks.

85. Glacier Point Trail

EFFORT: Minimal
LENGTH: 0.5 miles
GEOLOGICAL FEATURE(S): Erosional Features, Glaciation
LOCATION: Yosemite National Park

Description: This short, paved trail offers about the biggest payoff for the smallest effort you will ever find, anywhere. From the gift shop, walk out on Glacier Point Trail to an overlook where a small stone building sits. From the balcony of this building or the viewing deck below it, you get the view of a lifetime. There is no way to oversell this one. This view can bring you to your knees, and, in the process, it will reveal to you all that the word "Yosemite" can evoke.

You stand on the edge of the south cliff above Yosemite Valley where tiny cars are parked in lots dotting the flat valley floor. Instead of looking up at Half Dome as usual, you're looking directly across at it. Bring your binoculars and try to spot climbers on the face of that magnificent landmark. We saw a string of five of them on a trip in October, appearing as tiny black specks, not visible without magnification.

You'll also want to train those binoculars on the waterfalls on view— Upper and Lower Yosemite, Vernal, and Nevada Falls. And feast your eyes on other landmarks—Basket Dome, North Dome, and Clouds Rest.

From this vantage point, it's easy to see that domes are the natural shape of Yosemite peaks. Looking left from Half Dome, domes too numerous to count jut up off into the distance. Almost all of the exposed rocks on view have the same rounded crowns that occur after long-term erosion by the process called *exfoliation* or sheeting, previously described.

Yosemite Domes from Glacier Point

When you can tear your gaze away from this view, the little hut behind you has information explaining the geology of the glacially-carved valley and the impressive granite formations. We've already covered most of that information leading up to this hike, but it's a good refresher, especially while you're smack dab in the midst of this grandeur.

Continue to the end of the trail and another such view, this time angled a bit differently. It will be hard to leave this spot, so perhaps you should plan your picnic here. When you're ready, return the same way.

Directions: From Wawona Road/Highway 41, turn onto Glacier Point Road. This road is closed in winter, usually by November. Proceed to the end of the road, past Washburn Point (stop here too), to the Glacier Point parking lot. It's a large parking lot, but is often full. There are restrooms and a gift shop located here.

86. Indian Rock Trail

EFFORT: Difficult
LENGTH: 6.0 miles
GEOLOGICAL FEATURE(S): Erosional Features
LOCATION: Yosemite National Park

Description: This trail eventually leads to North Dome after 8 miles and a gain of 1,420 feet in elevation, but since exfoliated domes are not rare in Yosemite, and since we've included others that are easier to get to, this trip will focus on something much harder to find in the Sierras, a natural stone arch called Indian Rock.

Head south on North Dome Trail through a red fir forest to drop down to a paved road. Follow it downhill for about a half mile until you cross a tributary of Porcupine Creek and leave the road. Then cross Porcupine Creek itself and continue uphill for a short distance before descending again. Enjoy wildflower blooms in season as you walk through forest and then meadow.

After the first mile, you cross another creek and then walk a flat trail through tree cover. You climb up to a saddle and a trail junction. The left arm goes to Yosemite Valley. The right goes to North Dome. Go right and meet up with another trail junction right away. Right is for Yosemite Falls. Bear left towards North Dome.

Begin climbing up Indian Ridge. Ford a stream after two miles and then climb through thinning tree cover on a fairly steep route up to a trail junction at 8,140 feet and about 2.7 miles from the trailhead. Right, the trail continues to North Dome, along with most of your fellow hikers. Take the left trail towards Indian Rock. The trail is steep and open over a sandy path up to the arch, reached in another 0.3 miles and 400 feet in elevation.

The granite arch is rough-hewn, as though chiseled by a blind giant. You'll notice right away that this is nothing like the smooth, elegant sandstone arches of the Utah parklands. This arch is believed to be the only granite arch in the entire Sierra range, and we have to wonder how long it will continue to stand. Like rock arches everywhere, it will continue to erode until it collapses. If you climb up to the arch, you can see Half Dome through it.

After checking out the arch, return to the main trail and decide if you want to continue out to North Dome. The views from that vantage point are spectacular. If you don't want to go that far, turn right at the junction and return the way you came.

Directions: On Highway 120, 22 miles west of Tioga Pass, locate the Porcupine Creek Trailhead parking area on the south side of the road. Note that Tioga Pass Road is closed in winter and early spring until the snow is cleared.

87. Hetch Hetchy Trail

EFFORT: Moderate
LENGTH: 5.0 miles
GEOLOGICAL FEATURE(S): Glaciation
LOCATION: Yosemite National Park

Description: Hike this beautiful and special part of Yosemite and know that you've had a rare experience. Very few of Yosemite's many visitors ever see or even know about Hetch Hetchy. That's mainly because there are no roads within the park connecting it with Yosemite Valley or Tuolumne Meadows. Many visitors to Hetch Hetchy come just for the view from the top of the dam, from which you look out over the reservoir to the wispy Tueeulala waterfall and the raging Wapama Falls, your destination for this hike. If you come on a spring or summer weekend, you'll probably see other hikers here, but no crowds.

Hetch Hetchy Valley, now flooded by the damming of the Tuolumne River, was named from the Native American word "Hatchhatchie," a species of grass with edible seeds that once grew here. The history and character of this valley are similar to that of its more famous neighbor, Yosemite Valley. Before the dam, the valley was a spectacular U-shaped gorge carved out by a glacier about 10,000 years ago. Evidence of the polishing action of the glacier is abundant along the trail. Before the glacier, the valley was V-shaped, created by the erosional force of the river. The narrow, steep canyon walls made this spot perfect for building a dam, a project fiercely opposed by naturalist John Muir and others and approved by Woodrow Wilson in 1913. The movement to remove the dam is still extant, led by the Sierra Club.

O'Shaughnessy Dam, named for Michael O'Shaughnessy, San Francisco's city engineer at the time, was built between 1915 and 1923. At 312 feet tall, it was at that time the largest structure on the West Coast. Between 1935 and 1938, it was raised another 80 feet. The reservoir supplies San Francisco with drinking water. For that reason, swimming and boating are not allowed. Fishing is allowed, but live bait cannot be used.

Start out walking on top of O'Shaughnessy Dam. From atop the dam, look out over the reservoir and see the two striking waterfalls on the north cliff faces. In the accompanying photograph, the falls are visible coursing down to the valley floor before the dam was built. The wider waterfall is Wapama Falls, which you may have seen while driving in. Even from this vantage point, you can see its abundant spray. The slimmer, more delicate Tueeulala Falls can be seen here as well. It too has a drop of more than a thousand feet. Tueeulala dries up in summer, so come in late spring for the best show.

Hetch Hetchy Valley, 1908

Look for Hetch Hetchy Dome on the north side of the reservoir, and Kolana Rock, Hetch Hetchy's El Capitan, on the south side. Although the view from the dam is impressive, it doesn't compare to walking across the granite or standing in the spray of the waterfall.

After crossing the dam, you enter a tunnel where a flashlight would be helpful, but if you don't have one, you can allow your eyes to adjust and walk carefully towards the light at the other end. There may be some puddles of water on the floor of the tunnel. Upon exiting the tunnel, you'll reach the trailhead with a trail map and some informational panels.

The trail begins as a wide, sandy path along the northern edge of the reservoir with Wapama Falls visible in the distance. Vegetation includes big leaf maple, Ponderosa pine, incense cedar, black oak, and poison oak. Wildflowers bloom in spring, including shooting stars, Sierra leisiga, lupine, buttercups, and California fuchsia. Among wildlife you may see are mule deer, black bear, squirrels, rattlesnakes, and king snakes. When we were here, we saw squirrels, a handsome lizard, and several types of butterflies, including Monarchs and Swallowtails.

At the edge of the trail, notice the piles of grüs, the name given to small bits of disintegrated granite. The trail travels through patches of shade and open sunshine. About the time you lose sight of Wapama Falls, you begin to climb up a gentle grade. Soon you cross a seasonal stream through a fern-lined gully. Much of the charm of this trail comes from its continuously changing character. It will alternate between bare granite to shady oak woodland to moist meadow grasses. The reservoir will be on your right all the way, and the steep north cliff will remain on your left. As you look up the side of the cliff, notice the dark vertical stripes. These are manganese oxide deposits marking the path of groundwater seeping out of the cliff face. They are most pronounced along the uppermost portion of Tueeulala Falls.

After 0.7 miles, you reach a T-junction. Turn right onto a narrow rocky trail. From here, the path gets more difficult, rising and falling, studded with rocks. Hiking boots are definitely an asset along this trail and watching your step is critical. You'll cross a couple of sections of bare granite. These are excellent spots to observe the glacial polishing and striations (scratches). Recall that these were caused by gravel and boulders carried by ice and acting as grindstones. Striations tell geologists the direction the ice was moving.

A bridge crosses over a boulder-filled ravine where Tueeulala Falls flows into the reservoir. Looking up, you'll see the wispy spray drifting leisurely down. By June, you may not see any water here, depending on rainfall. It will be seeping through the lower rocks or be gone altogether.

In 2.4 miles, you reach the first of four bridges spanning the gush of water at the base of Wapama Falls, a huge and impressive 1,200-foot torrent. The waterfall is on Falls Creek, a tributary of the Tuolumne River. From your perch on a footbridge across the base of the falls, feel the spray from the powerful white water leaping off the granite cliff. You will want to spend some time here, cooling off in the spray. The time of year of your visit will determine how wet you get.

Both of these waterfalls, like those in Yosemite Valley, were created by the glaciers. Imagine a time before the ice when the creeks fed into the river canyon, running in an ordinary course down the hillsides. When the glaciers arrived, they filled the canyon and moved along the same course as the river, widening and deepening the original channel, changing its shape from a V to a U. Ice also filled the channels of the creeks feeding into the river, but the amount of ice, and thus its power, was much less than the ice in the main channel. When the ice melted and the streams flowed again, the river was far below its original course and the side streams were left hanging high above the river on the precipice of steep canyon walls, creating what geologists call "hanging valleys." Waterfalls were the result.

When you've had enough of this impressive natural spectacle, return via the same route.

Directions: The road is open in May until the first snows in November. On Highway 120, just before the Big Oak Flat Entrance Station of Yosemite National Park, take Evergreen Road north 7.4 miles to Camp Mather. Turn right on Hetch Hetchy Road and drive into the park. Proceed 6.5 more miles to the end of the road at O'Shaughnessy Dam. Stop at Inspiration Point along the way for great views and to get your bearings. Just before you reach the dam, you'll pass a comfort station on your right. There are restrooms and a picnic area there, a good place to stop because, although parking is available at the dam, there are no other facilities there.

88. Mono Pass Trail

EFFORT: Moderate
LENGTH: 8.0 miles
GEOLOGICAL FEATURE(S): Mining
LOCATION: Yosemite National Park

Description: It's often said that the true legacy of the Roman invasion of the British Isles was the system of roads they built. The same can be said of the Great Sierra Consolidated Silver Company during its brief enterprise in the High Sierras. The Great Sierra Wagon Road was a huge and energetic undertaking driven by the lure of silver in the high country.

Though the silver remained elusive, the road would endure, eventually becoming a major trans-Sierra route through Yosemite National Park. This hike, along with the following two (#89 and #90) take you to the primary sites of the 1880s Great Sierra mining venture in Yosemite.

The Mono Pass Trail is an ancient route over the crest of the Sierras, one that was historically used by the Mono Basin Paiute who traded salt and obsidian for acorns and berries with the Yosemite Mi-Wuk. It was later used by prospectors and fur traders. In 1859, a miner named George "Doc" Chase came through Mono Pass and found silver-rich ore near Tioga Lake. He etched a message on a smashed tin can and left it on the site as his claim marker. He then struck it rich in another location and never came back. A sheepherder named Bill Brusky found the tin can in 1874 and had the ore assayed, discovering that it was rich in silver. He staked four claims. The silver vein was named the Sheepherder Lode in his honor.

Geologically speaking, what Chase and Brusky had discovered was a skarn deposit with silver mineralization. *Skarn* is a general term for pre-existing metamorphosed rocks that are adjacent to plutons (a body of intrusive igneous rock). It was the heat from the pluton that metamorphosed the original sedimentary rock and allowed for crystallization of precious minerals like gold and silver. The ancient seafloor that once covered the granite batholith of the Sierras has been largely stripped away over time. The remains of the sediments, which have been twisted and crushed, are the "roof pendants," remnants of the ancient "roof" that covered the granite. Pockets of these roof pendants can be found throughout the Sierra Nevadas and are often the site of mining operations like this one.

By 1881, the Great Sierra Consolidated Silver Company, headed by Thomas Bennett, had bought up all the silver claims in the area, including Brusky's, and had begun work on the Great Sierra Mine (see Hike #89). In support of its mining operations, the company established the town of Bennettville as its headquarters. In 1882, word got out and a boom broke out in the Tioga area, attracting a swarm of miners who staked 350 new claims and went to work with picks and shovels.

The Great Sierra Company, however, was after the main silver vein and needed to bring in heavy equipment to get to it. Without a road, that was nearly impossible, so they set out to build a road from Oak Flat 56 miles to the west to the mining district. It was a massive undertaking for the location and conditions of the area. A large, well-paid force consisting mostly of Chinese laborers, carved out The Great Sierra Wagon Road in record time, putting down a half mile of road a day. The road was completed in 1883.

Once big equipment could be brought in, mining began in earnest. The company established three additional mines: the Golden Crown, Ella Bloss, and Ella Bloss #2. After spending over $50,000 building the road, the company spent another $300,000 of investors' money on drilling, but the main silver vein remained out of reach and the company's funds eventually dried up. The Great Sierra Company halted mining in 1884 after drilling down 1,784 feet into the mountain. By 1890, the area was abandoned, having never yielded its riches. The briefly vibrant town of Bennettville was likewise deserted, a rotting testament to lost dreams.

Presumably, the silver is still there, but after the Great Sierra Company failed, no large-scale mining was ever again attempted.

The Great Sierra Wagon Road fell into disrepair, but people continued to use it to travel from Big Oak Flat to the upper reaches of Yosemite for sightseeing, fishing and camping. Several people observed that it would be terrific if the road were improved and pushed through a little further east to create an eastern entrance to the park. After a lot of government red tape, that finally happened and a through road was completed in 1909. That was Tioga Road, the only through road in Yosemite and the road you drove up on to reach this site.

Thomas Bennett and his colleagues may have failed at their mining venture, but they gave us one of the most breathtaking drives in California, not to mention access to dozens of spectacular hiking trails, including this one.

What you'll see on this trail, in addition to gorgeous views, are the remains of miners' log cabins and some tailing piles from the best preserved mining site in Yosemite. You'll head up to a breathless height of 10,600 feet, gaining about 1,000 feet along the way.

Beginning at Dana Meadow, the trail routes you through a lodgepole pine forest. About a quarter mile along, you break out of the tree cover to enter a small meadow. After a half mile, cross Dana Meadows Creek. You then begin to climb a moraine and cross a couple of small streams feeding Parker Pass Creek before reaching an old cabin.

At just over two miles, you come to a junction. Stay on the Mono Pass Trail. The last 1.5 miles, the trail climbs with some steep stretches. It breaks out of the mature lodgepole pine forest onto a broad, westward dipping plain mantled by a green meadow with lots of wild onions. Flowers along this trail include lupine, Indian paintbrush, phlox, and mountain mint. After passing another old cabin, you'll come to a small lake. It was here that Orlando Fuller built his cabin after discovering silver here in 1879. Like the others, he didn't have much luck with the mining, but he did have a fabulous front yard.

A spur trail heading south from here takes you 0.3 miles to a group of five well-preserved cabins. These whitebark pine structures housed the miners of the Golden Crown and Ella Bloss mines.

You can head back the way you came to the trailhead after visiting the mine site, but why not finish the trail to Mono Pass? It's only 0.7 miles further on the main trail. Head east to Summit Lake with willows growing at its west end, then hike on to the pass itself where grassy meadows give way to bare rock and scattered, windswept whitebark pines.

From these heights, you get a great view of Mono Basin and Mono Lake to the east. Angular granitic peaks of the Kuna Crest rise to the west. This is the end of the Mono Pass Trail. The trail leading down the east side of the range goes through Bloody Canyon, an alternate and more difficult route up to the pass. Its gruesome name was earned for the many horses that were injured or killed going through it. The canyon is lined with sharp rocks that cut the flanks of horses and pack animals. After enjoying the views, return on the same path.

Directions: From Tioga Road at Tuolumne Meadows, travel east to the Mono Pass trailhead at Dana Meadows. There's a pit toilet in the parking lot. Note that Tioga Road is closed in winter.

Who Was Ella Bloss?

Hiking Mono Pass Trail to the mines, two of which were named "Ella Bloss," it seems logical to ask, who was she?

Ella Stone Bloss (1855 – 1893) was the wife of George Samuel Bloss, an early resident of the area of California that would become the town of Atwater in Stanislaus County. Ella and her family moved to California from Connecticut in 1883, at exactly the time that the Great Sierra Consolidated Silver Mine was operating near Tioga Pass. They were following the lead of Ella's uncle, John William Mitchell, who had come out much earlier, during the Gold Rush. But Mitchell wasn't a miner. Instead, he bought property, and by the time his niece arrived, he was an extremely wealthy landowner in the San Joaquin Valley and the founder of the town of Turlock.

With the Great Sierra Company in desperate need of funding to get at that silver vein, they tapped Mitchell to invest. Okay, he said, as long as they named a mine after his favorite niece. It turned out they named two mines after her. Did they go back to Mitchell a second time for more money? Possibly.

Mitchell died in 1893, a widower who had no children, and left the bulk of his estate to his three nieces. Unfortunately, Ella Bloss also died in 1893. Her husband George bequeathed some of the money to build the Ella Stone Bloss Memorial Hospital in Atwater. Throughout the years, the Bloss family has continued to donate money to the building and renovation of community health care facilities.

Ella Bloss was buried in Turlock Memorial Park.

89. Gaylor Lakes Trail

EFFORT: Difficult
LENGTH: 4.0 miles
GEOLOGICAL FEATURE(S): Mining, Glaciation
LOCATION: Yosemite National Park

Description: This popular trail leads to Middle and Upper Gaylor Lakes and then on to the ruins of the Great Sierra Mine, an unsuccessful silver mine owned by the Great Sierra Consolidated Silver Company and worked in the 1880s. For background information on the Great Sierra enterprise, see the previous hike (#88). The first lake is reached in a mile and the mine site in about two miles.

Start out at over 9,000 feet on a rocky trail through forest and meadow, switchbacking up a roof pendant (see previous hike) of metamorphic rock to a ridgetop at about 0.75 miles. Views all around are spectacular here in the high country of Yosemite with Gaylor Peak to the north and the Cathedral Range and Mammoth Peak to the south. You can also see Granite Basin and its two sparkling lakes ahead in the distance.

Below you is Middle Gaylor Lake. Descend on a treacherous, rocky trail to its shore after a mile of hiking. Middle Gaylor Lake is at 10,334 feet high. Continue around Middle Gaylor's northern shore about a quarter mile further. A creek leading uphill from Middle Gaylor leads to Upper Gaylor. There is a trail junction here. The left path leads around Middle Gaylor Lake. The right path follows its connecting stream to Upper Gaylor Lake. Follow the stream up through lovely meadows dotted with glacial erratics.

Everyone agrees that hiking in Yosemite is sublime. On this trail, you'll enjoy a feast of treats that reinforce that conviction. Views west into the heart of Yosemite are superb.

You'll reach Upper Gaylor Lake after 1.7 miles. It's a rocky bowl (glacial cirque) with almost no vegetation around it. If you like bare rock (you do, of course), then you'll be quite at home sitting here with the snow-capped granite peaks surrounding you and reflected in the still surface of the lakes.

After two enchanting alpine lakes, we're not yet done. There's more climbing to do, so rest a while and then continue along Upper Gaylor's west bank. At the north end of the lake, you'll come to a run-off stream and a trail fork. You want to go north here.

Leaving Upper Gaylor behind, climb steeply for another 0.3 miles to a height of 10,760 feet. You'll come to an old stone building with three-foot thick walls, its chimney still intact. This is one of the buildings left after the Great Sierra Mine was abandoned in 1884. Explore the area to see other remains, including some mineshafts and tailing piles. This mine, like the other silver mines in the area, was unsuccessful. To this day, the fabled Sheepherder Lode has never been found.

From the mine site, you can look back down along your hiking route to Middle and Upper Gaylor Lakes, Gaylor Peak, and mountains beyond. This is a great place to savor a snack and the endless views of the Sierra high country before returning along the same route.

Great Sierra Mine building

Directions: From Highway 120 (Tioga Road) immediately west of the Tioga Pass entrance, park in the lot on the north side of the road. There is an entrance fee to the park. Tip: you can catch this trail from outside the park, just east of the Tioga entrance station, parking in a pullout and walking cross-country to join it. This will enable you to avoid the entrance fee and shorten the hike.

90. Bennettville Trail

EFFORT: Moderate
LENGTH: 2.5 miles
GEOLOGICAL FEATURE(S): Mining
LOCATION: Inyo National Forest

Description: This trail takes you to the site of the historic mining town of Bennettville, named for Thomas J. Bennett, president of the Great Sierra Consolidated Silver Company (see Hike #88 for background information). When the company bought up several silver mining claims in the area in 1881, it created Bennettville as a company town. In its day, Bennettville was a modern town with a telegraph line and sophisticated mining equipment. The residents were primarily from New England and were responsible, along with Chinese laborers, for the building of the old Tioga Road, then named the Great Sierra Wagon Road. When the silver mines turned out to be unproductive and were closed after only a few years in existence, the town dried up and blew away. At that time, the road from Big Oak Flat to the west dead-ended here, as it was built to service the mines. It was only later that Tioga Road was pushed through to Mono Lake to make it a useful route for tourists. By then, Bennettville was mostly a memory and today is just one of many mining ghost towns in the Sierras.

At the trailhead, an informational panel will give you some background on this town and the mines that supported it. Start out by crossing Lee Vining Creek and going right on the trail to a fork. Bear left here to go to Bennettville. Climb up above Junction Campground with views of Mount Dana and Tioga Peak. Take note that these mountains are not granite like most of Yosemite. They're metamorphic, originally sedimentary rock that underwent changes through contact with the granitic pluton. Recall that it is this metamorphic process that created an environment conducive to the occurrence of precious minerals.

The trail follows Mine Creek to the town site amid flowery meadows. Your introduction to the mining operation will be tailings, mining machinery, and wooden buildings, reached after 0.75 miles. The buildings here—barn, bunkhouse and assay office—are reconstructions built in 1993. The machinery, however, is from the mining period. It was brought up here from Lundy Canyon to the east before there was a road, pulled over the snow in winter, as getting it here over the rugged bare rock would have been nearly impossible.

Explore the site at your leisure before continuing.

A short distance further, you'll come to a junction with a faint trail to the right where the main trail crosses the creek. Follow the spur trail to reach Shell Lake, the perfect spot for a lunch break. Returning to the main trail, continue south (right) for another quarter mile to reach a large tailings pile and the Great Sierra Mine tunnel, blocked off with a fence. This is the end of our route. Retrace your steps to return.

Directions: From Highway 395 in Lee Vining, go south to Tioga Road and turn west. Turn right (north) on Saddlebag Lake Road, and then left into the Tioga Junction campground. The trailhead is on Junction Campground Road just before site #1. Toilets are available.

91. Nunatak Nature Trail

EFFORT: Minimal
LENGTH: 0.5 miles
GEOLOGICAL FEATURE(S): Glaciation
LOCATION: Inyo National Forest

Description: This is a short, paved, self-guiding loop trail explaining the natural history found in this breathtaking high alpine environment. The glacial features you see here will be found all over the high Sierras, so this trail makes a good introduction. It's also a sweet little diversion if you want to take a walk but don't have time for one of the longer trails in the Yosemite area.

As you know by now, the Sierras have been subjected to a number of glacial periods since their uplift, and both Yosemite and Hetch Hetchy Valleys were carved out by the glaciers. We've seen granite polished smooth and observed scratches (striations) in the bedrock made by the movement of the ice. We've seen huge boulders that were carried vast distances by the ice and dropped far from their source (erratics). We've seen tons of sediment that were pushed ahead of the glacier to create new land features where none existed before (moraines). On this trail, we'll concentrate on two other glacial features: tarns and nunataks.

Leaving the highway behind, the trail begins at a pond, or tarn. *Tarns* are small bodies of water that occupy glacially-carved basins, or *cirques*. There are several of them on this trail, ranging in size from small ponds to lakes.

A feature of glaciers we haven't talked about previously is introduced on this trail. When the glacial ice flowed over this area, the highest peaks of the mountains that rose above the ice became islands of plant and animal life (*nunataks*). All life was devastated where the ice covered the ground, but the nunataks allowed pockets of life to survive. Once the ice melted, the surrounding area was recolonized by the flora and fauna that occupied the nunataks.

Walk the loop and read the signs to learn about other natural features of this area. You'll enjoy tree cover from lodgepole pines and summer wildflowers, as well as views of the surrounding mountain splendor. At the east side of the loop, you'll circumnavigate Nunatak Lake, the largest of the tarns on this trail.

The short loop ends back at the highway's edge before you know it.

Directions: From Highway 395 in Lee Vining, go west on Highway 120 towards Yosemite National Park. The trailhead is just east of Tioga Lake on the north side of Highway 120 where a long pullout allows parking on the side of the road. There are no facilities.

Kings Canyon & Sequoia National Parks

Sequoia National Park, designated in 1890 to protect the giant sequoias (*Sequoiadendron giganteum*) from logging, was the second national park created in the United States. One week later, General Grant National Park next door was created. In 1940, Kings Canyon National Park was created, subsuming General Grant.

Kings Canyon is a spectacular 8,000-foot deep gorge originally carved by the Kings River and later deepened and widened by the flowing of glacial ice. This river was given the name *Rio Los Santos Reyes* (River of the Holy Kings) by Spanish military commander Gabriel Moraga in 1805. It was later simplified to Kings River.

Like Yosemite National Park, Sequoia & Kings Canyon are located in the Sierra Nevada mountains and are therefore composed of huge granite monoliths and domes that were subjected to glacial ice at least four times in the historic past. But there's also some interesting metamorphic rock on display, especially in Kings Canyon. For example, on the long drive down to the valley floor, you'll pass some magnificent chevron folds in the rock walls beside the road. Don't miss these, as they're fabulous. It may be hard to imagine solid rock being able to bend into these shapes without crumbling, but given enough time, heat, and pressure, it does happen.

Kings Canyon Chevron Folds

Another metamorphic rock in these parks is marble. Marble is metamorphosed limestone, the stuff that caves are made of, and Sequoia and Kings Canyon together contain more than 270 marble caves, including the longest cave in California, Lilburn Cave, with nearly 17 miles of surveyed passages.

Though these two parks showcase many natural wonders from the biggest trees in the world to the deepest canyon in North America, they are remote and lightly visited compared to their northern neighbor Yosemite or that other fantastic gorge, the Grand Canyon.

Some of the highest peaks in the Sierras (14,000 feet) are here in Kings Canyon and Sequoia National Parks, and these form the remote and rugged Great Western Divide, the largest and highest subrange in the Sierras. The most southerly glaciers in North America still exist here at those impressively high elevations.

You might be getting the idea that the southern Sierra range is a place rife with superlatives—biggest trees, highest peaks, deepest canyons. It's true! Be prepared to be impressed.

92. Boyden Cavern Walking Tour

EFFORT: Minimal
LENGTH: N/A
GEOLOGICAL FEATURE(S): Caves
LOCATION: Kings Canyon, Giant Sequoia National Monument

Description: Boyden Cavern, a magnificent show cave, is located in the deepest canyon in the United States, the spectacular Kings River Canyon, and lies beneath the massive 2,000 foot high marble walls of the Kings Gates beside the Kings River.

Boyden Cavern was formed in Mesozoic marble and contains a variety of speleothems, including unusual shield formations, the type of cave ornamentation that Lehman Caves in Great Basin National Park is famous for.

Shields consist of two round or oval parallel plates with a thin medial crack between them. Shields grow at all sorts of angles from the ceiling, walls, and floor of the cave. They form when water under hydrostatic pressure moves through thin fractures in the limestone. As it enters the cave passage by means of capillary action, the water deposits calcite on either side of the crack, building plates of calcite with a thin, water-filled crack between them. Shields may be further decorated with popcorn or helictites on the top and along the medial crack, and draperies and stalactites on the bottom. Sometimes the speleothems on the bottom plate get so heavy they pull the shield apart. Be on the lookout for these various formations as you walk through the cave.

The 45-minute tour begins with a steep five-minute walk to the cave entrance. From there visitors travel deep within where the temperature is a constant 55° F. Groups follow a well-lighted and hand-rail equipped trail as guides point out many natural formations. Reservations are not required. Tours leave approximately every hour on the hour.

Popular features include The Pancake Room, a stalactite group called the Upside Down City, the Bat Grotto where bats spend summer days sleeping, and a flowstone formation called Mother Nature's Wedding Cake. The Drapery Room contains massive drapery-style stalactites, long soda straws and twisting crystalline helictites. As usual, the cave guide will point out cave formations that appear to resemble familiar, everyday objects such as the Taco Shell formations, the Baby Elephant and Mom stalagmites, and the Christmas Tree. There is also a subterranean stream and many other unique features in this beautiful cave.

Shield formations

Directions: From Fresno, take Highway 180 east into Kings Canyon National Park. Follow this road to the bottom of the canyon where the road meets the Kings River. The parking lot is just off the road next to the bridge. The cave is open daily May through October. There are toilets and picnic tables near the parking lot. There is a fee for the tour.

Note: Boyden Cavern was closed at the time of this writing due to fire damage to an access bridge and a controversy over who should pay for its replacement. A reopening date has not yet been determined. Check the cave's web site for the latest information.

93. Zumwalt Meadow Trail

EFFORT: Minimal
LENGTH: 1.0 miles
GEOLOGICAL FEATURE(S): Erosional Features, Glaciation
LOCATION: Kings Canyon National Park

Description: This scenic trail offers a lush meadow, wildflowers, and spectacular views of the granite cliffs and the South Fork Kings River. It is a self-guiding 18-stop nature trail with brochures at the trailhead. The meadow is located on the south side of the river, and the trail will take you along its edge and into the surrounding forest.

You'll enjoy views of some of the largest rocks in the park on this trail. Grand Sentinel is 8,504 feet high and North Dome is 8,717 feet. Pinecones litter the landscape where, in season, lupine blooms in a pink profusion.

Zumwalt Meadow was originally carved by a river. Later, it was subjected to the sculpting power of glaciers that were as much as 1,600 feet deep and modified the shape of the valley into the characteristic U. As the glaciers advanced, widening the canyon, they also pushed enough rock and sediment through to create at least thirty moraines. One of these formed a natural dam that blocked the flow of the river. A lake formed behind it. Eventually, that lake filled with sediment to become Zumwalt Meadow.

The trailhead is located on the northeast side of the parking lot. Cross a footbridge to begin. As you start out on the trail, Grand Sentinel stands tall across the river. Head toward the river lined with cottonwoods, willows, alders and sugar pines. You'll walk through a forest of incense cedar and ponderosa pine.

At stop #4 you'll find bedrock mortars used by the native Monache Indians to grind acorns from black oaks into meal.

After stop #5, cross over the river on a bridge and turn left at a junction with River Trail. Look across the river to see North Dome and notice its sheer wall, created by the passing glacier that shaved off some of the rock.

Continuing, you'll come to the site of a destructive avalanche that occurred in the winter of 1968, the result of heavy snowfall. Just past stop #6, you'll encounter a fork. This is the beginning of the loop trail. Bear right to go counterclockwise in the order of the numbered stops.

Pass into the shade of Grand Sentinel and a forest of white fir. On your right, a cliff rises up. On your left is the moist meadow, visited by numerous songbirds and dotted with wildflowers in early summer. Deer and black bear also visit the meadow. At the base of the cliff is a talus (debris) pile, created by rocks falling from the cliff face. The trail has been routed through the talus pile at the meadow's edge.

As you come to the western end of the meadow, you'll encounter a trail junction. Turn left to continue the loop. Walk along the south side of the meadow with the river on your right. When you return to the beginning of the loop, turn right to return to the parking area.

Directions: From Cedar Grove Village, go east on Highway 180 4.5 miles to Zumwalt Meadow parking area.

94. Crystal Cave

EFFORT: Moderate
LENGTH: 1.5 miles
GEOLOGICAL FEATURE(S): Caves
LOCATION: Sequoia National Park

Description: Crystal Cave was discovered in 1918 by park employees, but wasn't opened to the public until 1941. It's named for the extensive crystal formations within. To explore the rich offerings of this beautiful cave, you'll need to take a tour. The standard tour is 50 minutes and takes you on a half mile loop on lighted pathways to view the typical formations—stalactites, stalagmites, drapery, flowstone, cave pearls, and soda straws. This is a living cave; that is, it is wet and still forming.

Once you arrive at the cave parking lot, you'll walk a steep half mile trail along Cascade Creek to the cave entrance. For this reason, people in poor physical condition are discouraged from taking the tour.

The tour starts at the Spider Web gate, a metal grate built in a web pattern that blocks the entrance to the cave. The temperature within the cave is a steady 48° F. Dress accordingly. Backpacks are not allowed in the cave, but cameras are.

Your guide will lead you through the chambers and point out items of interest. This cave began as limestone that was metamorphosed through high temperatures and pressures into marble, and then gradually eroded by groundwater. This type of cave is common in Kings Canyon and Sequoia National Parks, but this one is among the most spectacular with its crystalline structures and beautiful banded marble. It is estimated that there are 10,000 feet of passageways in the cave, maze after maze of tunnels and the occasional expansive chamber, like the Marble Hall, which is 175 feet long and 40 feet high. You'll also tour the Organ Room and Dome Room.

Two other tours are offered at Crystal Cave: the Discovery Tour, which is one and a half hours and more in depth, and the four and a half hour Wild Cave Tour, a spelunking adventure involving belly crawling through narrow passages, given on Saturdays during the summer.

Directions: From Highway 99 in Visalia, take Highway 198 east through Three Rivers to the Foothills Visitor Center. From Highway 99 in Fresno, take Highway 180 east to Sequoia National Park and the Lodgepole Visitor Center. Purchase tickets at one of the Visitor Centers (not at the cave), and then drive on the Generals Highway to the cave parking lot where there are restrooms and water.

95. Needles Lookout Trail

EFFORT: Moderate
LENGTH: 5.0 miles
GEOLOGICAL FEATURE(S): Erosional Features
LOCATION: Sequoia National Park

Description: Beginning at a substantial elevation of 8,150 feet, you don't have much climbing to do to get to the 8,245-foot high lookout tower and the Needles, dramatic granite formations rising up from the North Fork of the Kern River. The Needles range in height from 400 to 1,000 feet. With their smooth sheer sides, they're a world-famous rock climbing destination, and the most massive rocks (Magician, Djin, Charlatan, Sorcerer, Wizard, Witch, Warlock, and Voodoo Dome) were named by climbers. We've talked a lot about the ice age glaciers that flowed over the Sierras. This spot and these boulders are exceptions. They have never been glaciated.

The lookout tower was built in 1937-38 by the Civilian Conservation Corps, a sturdy structure atop a granite spire named The Magician with incredible views of the southern Sierras. Used to spot forest fires, the tower itself fell victim to a fire in 2011 and was destroyed. As of this writing, there is a plan to rebuild the tower, but as yet there is no established timetable for the project. For now, hikers can take this trail to the Needles, but the lookout tower is closed.

The trail winds eastward up and down fairly easily, starting out on an old logging road. After a few hundred yards, the trail narrows to a hiking path and enters a mixed forest of fir and pine. Climb up to a saddle and then over a hill. Drop down to another saddle to reach the lookout tower location. A series of steep stairs leads to the top of The Magician where the tower was and will be located once rebuilt.

If you've chosen a clear day, the payoff up here will be spectacular. You look down into the Kern River canyon, over to Dome Rock to the southwest, Olancha Peak to the west, and Mt. Whitney northeast. The Kern River flows about 3,000 feet below at the bottom of the canyon. Return by the same route when you're ready.

Directions: From Porterville in Tulare County, go east on Highway 190 for 40 miles. Turn south on the Western Divide Highway (107). About a half mile south of the Quaking Aspen Campground, take Needles Road (Forest Road 21S05) east for about 3 miles to the end where you will find the trailhead. Access is free. There is a toilet. This road is closed in winter.

Needles Lookout Tower on fire (USFS)

The Eastern Sierras

On the eastern side of the Sierra Nevada Range, in the rain shadow of the mountains, everything looks different. Here, the land is a desert. Not much precipitation occurs and because of sparse tree cover, much of the rich volcanic history of the area is sitting on display like a museum exhibit. For the geology hiker, this place is a playground of the first order.

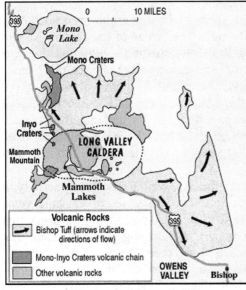

Long Valley Caldera (USGS)

The Long Valley Caldera, the largest volcano in the continental United States, is responsible for much of the landscape in the Eastern Sierras and for many of the sights we'll visit in this region. In the accompanying figure, you can see the major eruptions and the extent of this volcanic field,

Here on the east side of the mountains, the Sierra Nevada province gives way to the Basin and Range. Technically, a couple of the locations we'll visit are in the Basin and Range, such as Mono Lake. But the lake is clearly part of the Long Valley Caldera region, so we're treating all of the associated locales together for the sake of continuity and won't repeat these sites when we get to the Basin and Range province in the companion guide, *Geology Hikes of Southern California*.

The Long Valley has been a place of volcanic activity for the last 3.6 million years. Although earliest lava flows were basaltic in composition (meaning not too much quartz), that changed about two million years ago to eruptions of lava that had a higher silica (quartz) content. The significance of a high silica lava is that an increase in silica makes the lava more explosive. A shallow chamber of high quartz magma began developing underground until the roof of the magma chamber ultimately collapsed about 760,000 years in a catastrophic eruption, one of the largest volcanic eruptions on Earth. Afterward, the surface sunk more than a mile into a 10 by 20-mile depression created by the emptied magma chamber.

Major fallout associated with this event was the extrusion of massive amounts of volcanic ash. Approximately 150 cubic miles of ash flows occurred in Long Valley. Airborne ash fell as far east as Nebraska and Missouri. The Mono Basin, Owens Valley, and parts of the Sierras were covered in 600 to 3,000 feet of ash. The blankets of ash, which fell over 580 square miles of California and Nevada, subsequently solidified into a light, porous igneous rock known as *tuff*. The pinkish Bishop Tuff is so famous and important to geologists that geology students throughout the United States are familiar with this rock and often make pilgrimages to the area to observe it for themselves.

After this colossal eruption, a series of smaller eruptions ensued over the next few hundred thousand years. The center of the caldera rose in response to new magma filling in below, creating a resurgent dome, a broad, dome-shaped highland of post-caldera lava domes that stands above the surrounding lower lands. Mammoth Mountain on the southern edge of the caldera was one of these later volcanoes. It's believed to have originated about 180,000 years ago with its first eruption and will likely erupt again in the future. Although there have been no eruptions from this volcano for the last 100,000 years or so, the magma is likely still beneath the surface.

The Long Valley Caldera is not the only source of volcanic activity in this area. The Mono-Inyo volcanic chain is a series of volcanic vents located close by. These vents are so close that some geologists argue that the Mono-Inyo volcanic chain is part of the Long Valley Caldera, not separate. These volcanoes are much more recent, however, with the Inyo Craters erupting only about 600 years ago. The only known younger eruption was Negit Island in Mono Lake, believed to be only 150 years old.

All of that magma underground generates heat, and some of that heat has been tapped by the Casa Diablo Geothermal Plant, built in 1984. Wells 600 feet deep reach into the geothermal field to produce electricity. The plant is part of the Mammoth Geothermal Complex built on BLM land, and consists of three separate power pants. The BLM closely monitors groundwater and approved a groundwater monitoring and response plan for the project in January, 2017. You can tour the plant if you're interested. You can also experience some of that hot water firsthand at the Hot Creek Geothermal Area where it reaches the surface and creates warm pools in the creek.

Earthquakes occur daily in this area, most of them small and uneventful, but frequent reminders of the volatility of the earth beneath our feet. Most of the quakes are centered near the junction of Highway 395 and Highway 203.

The Long Valley Caldera is considered a highly active volcanic area that will certainly produce major volcanic events in the future. Episodes of heightened activity have occurred over the last few decades (earthquakes, ground uplift, and/or volcanic gas emissions). As a result, the USGS manages a dense array of field sensors providing the real-time data needed to track unrest and assess hazards.

From dramatic granite peaks to young volcanic craters and weird mineral deposits, there are endless wonders in the Eastern Sierras for geology buffs like us, so let's get started.

96. South Tufa Trail

EFFORT: Minimal
LENGTH: 1.0 miles
GEOLOGICAL FEATURE(S): Erosional Features, Volcanism
LOCATION: Mono Lake Tufa State Reserve

Description: Situated at the base of the Eastern Sierras the fascinating Mono Basin is associated with the Long Valley Caldera. The basin contains murky Mono Lake and its strange growths of tufa. Tufa towers such as these occur in one other place in California, at the Trona Pinnacles in the Mojave Desert, and they will be covered in our Southern California guide.

Mono Lake is old for a lake, maybe as old as one million years. About ten million years ago, as the Eastern Sierras were lifted, Mono Basin moved correspondingly down, eventually becoming a catch basin for several streams running down the eastern side of the Sierras. The lake has no outlet, so any minerals running into it are trapped there. As a result, the water of the lake is three times saltier than the Pacific Ocean.

Even though the salty water cannot support a varied marine population (there are no fish in the lake), it is an important ecosystem for California's migrating birds. The California gull nests here on the lake's islands in huge numbers. You may also see eared grebes, loons and many other types of birds that feed on the lake's brine shrimp and alkali flies. The brine shrimp here are unique to Mono Lake; they are found nowhere else on earth.

As you approach the lake, you'll be drawn to the knobby, putty-colored spires standing at its southern shore. They look a little like piles of candle wax or perhaps cave stalagmites, and are related to cave formations in that they're mineral deposits resulting from the precipitation of minerals from water. But the conditions and composition of tufa is different than that of cave deposits (calcite).

Tufa is formed through a reaction between calcium carbonate in fresh water and the briny lake water, caused by the abundance of chloride, carbonate, and sulfate in the lake. The resulting material is aragonite, a calcium carbonate mineral that forms commonly in areas of hot springs. Recent research has suggested that algae also contribute to production of tufa by extracting carbon dioxide and thereby reducing calcium carbonate solubility.

Mono Lake Tufa

As you wend your way through the tufa towers, you'll get the sensation of being on another world. These irregular bumps and spires rise up all around you like bizarre sand castles. The towers were once underwater, but the level of the lake has been drained over the years as water from surrounding creeks was diverted to Southern California (an action that inspired the movie *Chinatown* and is further described in the non-fiction book, *Cadillac Desert*). By 1981, the lake level had dropped 45 feet and the salinity had doubled due to the redirection of water. In 1994, a lawsuit resulted in the finding that the lake ecosystem had been damaged by the water diversions. The Audubon Society and the Mono Lake Committee have worked tirelessly to stop the drain on the lake and have been successful in their efforts. The water is no longer being diverted and the lake has risen 12 feet from its low point. Today, Mono Lake is an 8 by 13 mile body of salt water, a most fetching shade of greenish blue. For the last several years, the lake level has remained stable.

You can make your own trail among the towers, so you can spend as little or as much time as you like admiring them. The featured trail is an interpretive trail that will explain the formation of the tufa towers and the lake's food chain. A paved path starts at the payment booth and heads towards the lake. About halfway along, the pavement ends and a wooden boardwalk completes the trail to the shore of the lake, making this section of the trail wheelchair accessible. The remainder of the trail, going right along the lake shore, loops through the formations and back to the parking lot, and can only be made on foot.

In addition to the tufa mineral deposits, there is volcanic activity on display here as well. Each of the volcanic features here has a unique story. Black Point is the low, black hill on Mono Lake's northwestern shore. It's a volcano that erupted approximately 13,000 years ago during the last ice age. At the time, Mono Lake was 900 feet deeper than it is today and completely submerged Black Point's eruption. The weight of hundreds of feet of water is responsible for its flat top. Now exposed by the receded shoreline, Black Point is an excellent specimen of something we normally don't see—a recent underwater volcano.

The islands within Mono Lake are also volcanic, relatively new additions to the lake's topography. The black island is Negit, a volcano that first erupted 1,600 years ago and flowed as recently as 270 years ago. It's composed of dacite.

The youngest member of the Mono Basin volcanic family is Paoha, the white island in the middle of the lake, only 300 years old. Since its volcanic and so young, you might wonder why it looks so different in shape and color from Negit. White and rolling, Paoha resembles the sediment that covers that bottom of Mono Lake. Paoha is, indeed, exposed lake-bottom sediment, pushed up above the surface of the lake in a volcanic upheaval that lacked the momentum to fully erupt and therefore did not cover the surface with lava. Although there have been a few small lava flows on the north end of the island, Paoha has yet to let go in a full-scale eruption. Still, steam vents and fumaroles on the island indicate its potential for future activity.

Before or after your hike, you may want to visit Mono Lake Vista Point 12 miles north of Lee Vining on Highway 395. From that vantage point, you can see the Mono Basin quite well for what it is, a depression with streams draining into it. Another good place to view Mono Lake is on the Rim Trail atop Panum Crater to the south. The next hike will take us there.

Directions: From Highway 395 in Lee Vining, travel 5 miles south. Go east on Highway 120 for 5 miles to the turnoff for the South Tufa Area/Mono Lake Tufa State Reserve. Turn left and go 1 mile to the parking area. There are restrooms and picnic tables in the open sun. An entrance fee is charged. Note that there is also a trail to tufa formations on the north shore of the lake, but it isn't as extensive as this one.

97. Panum Crater - Rim & Plug Trails

EFFORT: Minimal
LENGTH: 1.0 miles
GEOLOGICAL FEATURE(S): Volcanism
LOCATION: Inyo National Forest

Description: This route takes you around the rim and then down into Panum Crater, a young, rhyolitic volcano located in the Mono Craters area of the Long Valley Caldera. The trail offers majestic views of the Sierra Nevada and Mono Basin and makes a good companion hike for exploring the tufa formations at Mono Lake (Hike #96).

Panum Crater is the youngest mountain on the American continent and the last of the Mono Craters to erupt, only 640 years ago. Mono Craters began erupting about 40,000 years ago, producing 21 peaks. Their dramatic, unglaciated shapes indicate that most of them erupted during the 12,000 years since the last ice age. They form a string along the east side of Highway 395 south of Mono Lake, looking somewhat like a moonscape with their light gray pumice and ash-covered flanks devoid of trees.

Panum Crater (USGS)

The well-defined structure of Panum Crater is easily seen in the aerial view shown in the accompanying photograph. It's a tephra (volcanic ejecta) ring around an inner rhyolitic plug dome that rises above the rim in the center of the crater sort of like a castle surrounded by a moat. The moat is dry, though, so we can walk through it to that castle of volcanic rock.

The intriguing landmark you see today was created in a two-step process. First, magma rising underground came into contact with groundwater, flashing it into steam and causing a huge steam-driven explosion. This produced the crater and the debris thrown out around it. After that, the magma slowly rose to the surface, emerging as viscous rhyolitic lava above the vent. The lava hardened and was pushed up and apart by further emerging lava until a substantial pile of volcanic debris stood inside the crater. The crater has a diameter of 4,000 feet and is littered with pumice, lapilli (Latin for "little stones"), obsidian, and granite ejecta.

Wear a hat and sunscreen and carry water. There is no shade on the Rim Trail.

From the parking lot, head up the loose gravel trail past the signboard to the rim of the crater where you'll have excellent views of the rest of the Mono Craters to the south. Mount Lewis and Mount Gibbs can be seen in the Sierras to the west. Look between Mount Gibbs and Lewis to see two lateral moraines near the mouth of Bloody Canyon. Recall that Bloody Canyon is the eastern route up to Mono Pass (Hike #88) in Yosemite.

At the rim you'll encounter a sign that directs you right for the Rim Trail and left for the Plug Trail. We've chosen a route that combines the two for the optimum experience of this crater, although you may choose to do both trails completely if you have time. There will be no surprises along this trail because you can see exactly where you'll be going along the entire route. But the views will change and your proximity to certain features will bring them more sharply into focus as you circle the mountain.

Go right to follow the Rim Trail, a wide gravel and sand path that contains volcanic material, including lots of obsidian. Find some good samples and observe the conchoidal fractures in the black glass. If you're old enough to remember broken glass of the old Coke bottles, you'll recognize the concentric half-rings that typify a conchoidal fracture. Native Americans took advantage of this natural fracturing pattern to fashion sharp arrowheads. Obsidian was highly valued and extensively traded among tribes.

Also, be on the lookout for *breadcrust bombs*, chunks of lightweight rock with surface cracks. These were formed by molten lava flying into the air and cooling to form an outer skin around still hot centers. As the lava within cooled, the surface cracked in a fashion similar to a crusty French bread or Dutch crunch rolls.

Look up on the plug from the south rim and locate a chunk of rock with alternating dark and light stripes on it. This is *flow banding*, evidence of the course the lava took while liquid. Another good example of this can be found on the north side of the crater sitting just beside the trail.

As you circle the crater in a counterclockwise direction, you will come upon superior views of Mono Lake and the South Tufa Area. From this vantage point, you get a feeling for what the Mono Basin is all about. Also, you can observe the layout of the tufa formations in a way that is impossible walking among them. They form arcing chains in a pattern that is clearly not random. Since the tufa is built upon natural spring water emerging from the lake bed, the pattern represents the location of faults where the water escaped from underground.

From here also you get good views of Mono Lake's two islands, Negit (the black one) and Paoha (the white one). Both are the result of volcanic eruptions. More details about Mono Lake, its islands, and history can be found in the description of the South Tufa Trail (previous hike).

On the east side of the rim where the trail dips briefly, you can observe birds flying over the low point from their nesting area on the plug dome. From this low point, you'll climb somewhat steeply, a process made more difficult by the loose gravel of the trail. On the north edge of the crater, you go steeply down, your feet sinking into the sand with each step. You will almost be skiing down this slope. You can certainly see why it would be hard for plants to grow in this loose debris.

As you reach the northwest corner of the crater, the rim trail goes steeply uphill to the high point. It's a tiring climb, and there is an alternative. A narrow path leads down and south from here. Take that one and drop into the ring at the bottom of the crater. These two trails will meet up back where you began. You'll enjoy the new perspective inside the crater, walking alongside the inner plug. Because of the more compact soil, there's some vegetation down there and you may be in the shade of the crater itself, depending on the time of day. Continue along the west side of the dome and then up, out and back to the Rim Trail. This completes the circuit. Turn west and go back down the slope to the parking area, where you can dump the sand out of your boots before leaving.

Directions: From Highway 395 south of Lee Vining, take Highway 120 east 3 miles and then turn left on a dirt road to Panum Crater (there is a small sign). The road is suitable for passenger cars. Continue about a mile to the parking area. There are no facilities. Access is free.

98. Obsidian Dome

EFFORT: Minimal
LENGTH: 0.5 miles
GEOLOGICAL FEATURE(S): Volcanism
LOCATION: Inyo National Forest

Description: From Highway 395, if you're paying attention, when you reach the exit for Obsidian Dome Road, you can look west and see the high piles of boulders that make up this mile-wide, 300-foot high volcanic glass flow. Better yet, if you pull off the road and drive less than a mile, you can walk right up to it. The only other place in California you can see something like this is at Glass Mountain in the Modoc Plateau.

This obsidian formation was made from highly viscous rhyolite lava that was forced up through a small opening, creating a sort of mushroom shape above ground. The dome is the cap of the mushroom and the stem is the lava in the throat of the eruption. You can get a much better sense of the structure of this flow from the aerial view in the accompanying photo.

This eruption took place between 1,000 and 5,000 years ago, cooling too quickly to allow crystals to form, thereby creating glass. It's composed of flow-banded obsidian and rhyolite.

Aerial view of Obsidian Dome (USGS)

From Obsidian Dome Road, walk uphill on the dirt 4WD road through a forest to a massive, sparkling jumble of boulders. As you near the boulders, you'll notice that they are primarily black glass, obsidian, a glassy form of rhyolite. You'll see bands of non-glassy rhyolite interspersed with the obsidian. The patterns in the rocks are stunning. The variation of size and abundance of gas bubbles present created the differing colors and textures as the lava solidified. The pure glass pieces had very little gas. Take a small sample for your rock collection if you're inclined.

While we were admiring the gas bubble depressions in the glass, another visitor was climbing up to the top of the flow. If you climb, be very careful. A fall could result in serious cuts. This fellow made it to the top without mishap, while his companion below hollered up, "Do you see the dome?" "No!" he hollered back. He was standing on it, of course.

Wander the perimeter of the flow until you're ready to return the way you came.

Directions: From Highway 395 and Highway 203, drive north on Highway 395 to just past Deadman Summit. Take the Obsidian Dome Road/Bald Mountain Road exit. Go west on dirt Obsidian Dome Road for 0.7 miles. A 4WD dirt road takes off to the left. If you have the proper vehicle, you can drive right up to the obsidian flow. Otherwise, pull safely off the road to park.

Access is free. There are no facilities.

99. Inyo Craters Trail

EFFORT: Minimal
LENGTH: 0.7 miles
GEOLOGICAL FEATURE(S): Volcanism
LOCATION: Inyo National Forest

Description: This short trail leads to a series of fascinating, young volcanic craters, two with lakes in them. The Inyo Craters are one of the most recently active eruptive centers in the area, dating from only about 500 to 600 years ago.

There are three main craters—North, South, and the crater at the summit of Deer Mountain. There are several associated smaller craters and domes in the chain that runs along a north-striking fault system and extends northward to the Mono Craters.

Inyo Crater

From the parking area at 8,000 feet, head out on a pleasant trail shaded by pine trees. You'll climb about 300 feet along the way to the rim. The trail passes between two picnic tables just as you emerge from the forest, approaching a slight rise towards the edge of a huge pit in the ground. When you reach the south crater rim after a mere quarter mile, use the viewing platform to look inside the 600-foot wide hole, over 200 feet deep. The steep sides are only sparsely vegetated, so this crater is much easier to view than the north crater. At the bottom is a murky-looking turquoise lake.

The Inyo Craters were created by hydrothermal explosions when the magma rising underground met groundwater, creating a steam explosion that blew off the overlying crust and threw debris outward. This was not a lava eruption because the magma never broke the surface.

Walk right along the rim to a second viewing area. This area was closed when we visited because the edge of the crater had eroded back to start gobbling up the railing's feet. As a matter of fact, one plastic warning sign lay far below inside the crater. Either it fell in or some rude person threw it. Either way, let this be a caution to keep back from the lip of the crater.

Continuing around to the north side of the south crater, you will notice, suddenly, that there is another crater on your right. You're standing on the narrow rim between the two. Turn back and walk east and then north along the rim of the north crater. It's forested and inhabited by many birds and small animals. You can't see the crater's features as well as the other crater, but you can see how large it is. It too is about 600 feet in diameter and is somewhat shallower than the south crater at 150 feet deep.

The trail heads up steeply for about 400 yards to the north towards the top of Deer Mountain and the Summit Crater. It has no lake in it. We'll leave it up to you to decide if it's worth the struggle to visit that one. There are good views from up there and we know how the high points beckon.

Return by the same route.

Directions: From Mammoth Lakes on Highway 203 (Main Street), turn right where it becomes Lake Mary Road and proceed to Mammoth Scenic Loop (Forest Service Road 3S23). Turn right onto it and drive to a dirt road signed for Inyo Craters on the left. Follow this dirt road and the signs for 1.5 miles to the trailhead. The road is passable for all vehicles in good weather. Access is free. There are no facilities.

100. Mammoth Consolidated Gold Mine

EFFORT: Minimal
LENGTH: 0.5 miles
GEOLOGICAL FEATURE(S): Mining
LOCATION: Inyo National Forest

Description: This is a self-guided walking tour of the remains of a historic mining camp established in 1927. Tour the old buildings left from the activity surrounding the operation of the Mammoth Consolidated Gold Mine. A brochure is available at the Mammoth Ranger Station.

Long before becoming a ski resort, the Mammoth area supported intensive mining. Known as the Lake Mining District, it was established in 1877 when gold and silver were discovered. This strike came to be known as the Mammoth Lode and prompted a gold rush to the area. A twenty-stamp mill was in operation by 1878, and the towns of Mammoth City, Mill City, and Pine City sprang up. By 1881, the area was all but abandoned, miners moving on to the next promising site.

Several years later, in 1927, A. G. Mahan, his son Arch, and partners bought up claims on Red Mountain and formed the Mammoth Consolidated Mining Company. They employed between six and fourteen workers on site and built this camp to house and feed them.

The trail is through a shady pine forest that leads you quickly to a trail junction. Forward is the path to Heart Lake. Left is the mine site. Go left. A loop with numbered stops begins with the bunkhouses and travels in a clockwise direction.

The equipment and buildings that currently occupy the site are from the last major mining effort to take place here. It lasted from 1927 to 1933. There are wooden bunkhouses, remains of a cook house, assay office, a sturdy log cabin, a couple of outhouses, a rusty old stove and several other remnants of the mining camp to look at. After exploring the ruins here, continue on the trail from the top of the loop, following the sign saying "Mine" to climb up to stop #11, the lower adit of the mine, a 729-foot horizontal tunnel. On this section of the trail, you'll gain enough elevation to get good views of Mammoth Mountain and Lake Mary.

After peering into the mine shaft, come back down to the loop and finish the other side of it, passing a couple of air compressors that were used to run air-powered drills, then return to the trailhead. If you have the brochure, you'll be able to locate a couple of outlying items of interest, including the upper adit of the mine.

A lot of ore was taken out of this mountain, but getting the gold out of it was expensive, so this mine was only marginally successful. Money ran out in 1933 during the Great Depression when no further financing could be procured.

Arch Mahan bought the Reds Meadows resort in 1934 and ran horseback trips to Devil's Postpile (Hike #102), tapping into what would become a new economic boom for Mammoth—recreation. In the 1980s, the Mahan family donated the buildings and equipment on the mine site to the town of Mammoth Lakes.

Directions: From Highway 395, exit on Highway 203 towards Mammoth Lakes. Continue on Lake Mary Road southwest. Turn off at Coldwater Campground and park in the Duck Pass Trailhead parking lot.

101. Mammoth Crest Trail

EFFORT: Difficult
LENGTH: 5.5 miles
GEOLOGICAL FEATURE(S): Volcanism
LOCATION: Inyo National Forest

Description: This scenic hike will take you to the Mammoth Crest, a long ridge dominating the Mammoth Lakes region, through a colorful volcanic landscape, and then to the summit of a cinder cone with a total elevation gain of 1,425 feet. Lots of big rocks and bald mountains reveal themselves on this trail.

From the Crystal Lake/Deer Lakes trailhead on the north side of Lake George, hike above Woods Lodge cabins through a mixed pine and fir forest. You'll climb up some long switchbacks and then emerge into the open to a surprising view of Lakes Mary and George. As you continue to climb, the views get better. Crystal Crag, a prominent granite spire, appears to the south.

After about a mile, you'll duck back into tree cover and then come to a trail junction. The left path goes to Crystal Lake; the trail to Mammoth Crest goes straight ahead. Go left if you want to visit the lake. It's only about a quarter mile to get there, and it will be a lovely rest stop before you begin the grueling part of this day.

Otherwise, head right towards Mammoth Crest and begin climbing, sometimes steeply, until you emerge at a level patch with astonishing views. All of the peaks of the surrounding ranges are within your sight, from the mountains of Yosemite to Mammoth Mountain, the White Mountains, Red and Gold Mountain, the town of Mammoth Lakes, Crystal Crag, and several of the area's lakes. You'll also see the Minarets, characterized by distinctive pointy spires. Stop walking to take it in or you may trip yourself up.

The trail continues to climb as the tree cover diminishes and the landscape starts to get really interesting. You're now entering young (2,000 years old) volcanic terrain with pumice, loose cinders, and sparse vegetation.

After 2.5 miles you reach a sign announcing that you're entering John Muir Wilderness. Then you arrive at the top of a ridge and are on the Mammoth Crest. Descend to the west side of the crest and a volcanic landscape surrounds you. There is a classic red cinder cone to the west and underfoot you'll see red lava rock interspersed with the Sierra Nevada granite. We've already discussed the formation of cinder cones in depth, and this one is typical.

At a fork in the trail, you'll take the right arm. The main trail continues left, but our destination is the cinder cone. Let those others head for the lakes; we are in it for the rocks. Make your way up the slope as it rises steeply up the side of the cone. This is the tough part of this hike, a slow climb in open sun.

The summit of the cone is 10,480 feet and worth every gasp it took to reach it. What spectacular views! All of the mountains sit solidly around you in a 360-degree panorama. The view around your boots is also entertaining with its myriad of lava colors.

After a good rest, return the same way.

Directions: From Mammoth Lakes, head west to the intersection of Highway 203/Minaret Road and Lake Mary Road. Go straight on Lake Mary Road for almost 4 miles to a fork signed for Coldwater Campground. Bear right to stay on Lake Mary Road. Continue past Lake Mary to a junction where a road off to the left is signed for Lake George. Turn left and pass Lake Mary Campground. At the next junction, go right towards Lake George, continuing to the lake and trailhead parking lot. Don't take the road on the right to Woods Lodge, but you'll find the trailhead beside it. Access is free. There are restrooms near the trailhead and a picnic area at Lake George.

102. Devils Postpile & Rainbow Falls Trail

EFFORT: Moderate
LENGTH: 5.0 miles
GEOLOGICAL FEATURE(S): Erosional Features, Volcanism
LOCATION: Devils Postpile National Monument

Description: Located in Ansel Adams Wilderness, this national monument was established in 1911 to preserve the geological formation known as Devils Postpile as well as the magnificent Rainbow Falls. Like many sites in the Sierras, the Postpile exhibits a history of assault by the transforming forces of fire and ice.

The Postpile is a remarkable basalt column formation about sixty feet high sitting at an elevation of 7,600 feet. The columns formed when basaltic lava erupted in the valley of the Middle Fork of the San Joaquin River about 100,000 years ago. The valley was filled with lava 400 feet thick, which cooled at an uneven rate with the outermost edges cooling first while heat was retained in the insulated middle areas. As the lava cooled, it shrank and cracked into these geometric shapes. The columns were exposed 10,000 years ago when a glacier flowed down this river gorge and scooped away one side of the Postpile, revealing this splintered cliff face to the world. This is one of the finest examples of columnar jointing you can see anywhere and is the best example in California. Another such formation can be seen at Columns of the Giants in Stanislaus National Forest (Hike #80) and the Machado Postpiles in Eldorado National Forest. We haven't included the Machado Postpiles in this book because there's no trail to the site, but dogged geology buffs may score a guided hike cross-country as we did. The most famous example of columnar basalt in North America is the spectacular Devil's

Tower in Wyoming. In all of these cases, the columns formed in the same way.

You'll find the trailhead beside the ranger station. Pick up a park brochure there before setting out. It has a map that you may want to use to create your own hiking route, especially if you're taking advantage of the shuttle service and don't need to return to the same trailhead. We'll be taking the most popular out and back trail to the Postpile and continuing to the waterfall.

The trail is wide, level, and well-marked. Fortunately, most people can make the less than half mile trek to the Postpile without difficulty. You'll walk around a meadow blooming with wildflowers in summer. At a signed trail fork, go left for the Postpile.

Other nearby evidence of recent volcanic activity includes Soda Springs on a gravel bar north of the Postpile. Gases from deep in the earth combine with groundwater to produce carbonated mineralized springs. The iron in the water stains the gravel a rust color.

Devil's Postpile

When you reach the Postpile, walk along its base and marvel at the symmetry that nature exhibits. Each column has from three to eight sides, polygons that occur with some frequency in nature, from salt crystals on the floor of desert playas to mud cracks in a dry pond.

The columns standing up straight are in place as they formed. Those on the edges that are bowed and angled towards vertical have moved over time. Amazingly, many of the bowed columns have not broken, as the movement occurs so slowly that the rock has time to adapt and bend. At the bottom, lots of broken column pieces lie in a jumbled pile. Many good examples in this talus slope are immediately beside the trail so you can get an intimate view of them. Take advantage of several split log benches to sit and admire the formation.

When you're ready, return to the left side of the Postpile to take the steep uphill trail to the top. Once you're standing on the flat top of the columns, you'll be amazed. It looks like a hexagonal tile floor, each "tile" highly polished and scratched by glacial ice. The evidence of scraping ice is easy to read on this smooth surface.

Look around the hill behind this floor and you'll see more exposed sections of the basalt formation. You'll also see a trail heading up, signed for Rainbow Falls. Take this trail even if you're not continuing to the waterfall. It circles the back of the Postpile formation and comes around the other side back to the main trail. On the way, you'll see more columns, and the south side of the pile is quite interesting. Coming down on this loop, turn left to continue to the falls.

Walk south on the trail through lodgepole pine and red fir to Rainbow Falls on the Middle Fork of the San Joaquin River. Watch for the small Belding ground squirrel and Stellar's jays. The trail slopes gently downhill over its entire length. After about a mile from the start of your hike, you'll cross a creek on a log bridge. The trail parallels the river bank, coming close enough in a couple of places to give you lovely views of the water and, in autumn, the yellow leaves of aspen and cottonwood. A lightning-sparked forest fire in 1992 burned out many of the trees along the trail. Their blackened trunks cover the hillsides. One memorable dead tree trunk stands beside the trail, its interior completely gutted by fire, leaving only a shell.

You'll pass a trail junction where the left arm goes to Reds Meadows. Continue straight for the falls. Across the river are the volcanic formations known as the Buttresses, exposed basalt that is believed to be the oldest volcanic rock in the Monument area. This basalt is different from that of the Postpile in that it has abundant pyroxene crystals, indicating a different magma source.

Cross another plank bridge on the way over Boundary Creek. You'll briefly enter Ansel Adams Wilderness, and then cross back into monument land. At a junction with Fish Creek Trail, turn right and descend a dirt and log stairway. You'll hear the tumult of the waterfall to the right before you see it, and then you'll reach the viewing area above the falls. It's an exquisite 101-foot drop over volcanic rock, which, in the right light, produces rainbows in its mist. When we were here, we saw a rainbow from the second viewing platform just above this first one.

Similarly to the Buttresses, the rock of the waterfall cliff is different from the basalt of the columns, indicating a different magma source or, possibly, magmatic differentiation. That will be immediately apparent. This is andesite and rhyodacite, light gray and fine-grained, exhibiting horizontal thinly-spaced joints giving a platy appearance.

Walk down to the second platform and take a look, and then continue to a long, steep flight of granite stairs down to the base of the falls where the continuous mist creates an inviting habitat for moss and ferns. Using the numerous rocks in the river, you can walk out on a gravel bar to a well-positioned tree trunk at the edge of the waterfall's emerald pool. This makes a perfect spot to sit and watch the falls, the spray gently raining down on you. We were here in October when the volume of water is not at its height, but the waterfall was still running voluminous and magnificent. Along the right side of the main fall, the water skips down a natural stone staircase in a delicate descent to the river below.

You can continue another half mile to Lower Falls, if you're inclined to extend your trek. Either way, hike back the way you came. There is also an option of hiking back on another trail to Red's Meadow at the junction we passed on the way out, where the shuttle also stops. There's a store and restaurant there if you haven't packed a lunch. There's a hot spring near Reds Meadow, attesting to the continuing volcanic activity in the area. Allow extra time for the transportation to and from the trail if you're taking the shuttle. We ended up spending four hours on this trail. There was a lot to see!

Directions: Some of the roads traversing the Sierras are closed in winter, so check road conditions. From U.S. 395, take the Mammoth Lakes exit and proceed to the Mammoth Mountain Inn (where a woolly mammoth statue stands beside the road). From June to September, you'll have to take a shuttle bus to the Postpile and pay a fee for the trip. Buy tickets at Mammoth Mountain Inn, the departing point. If you come off-season or very early in the morning or in the evening, you can drive to the trailhead. Proceed past Mammoth Mountain Inn and past Minaret Vista Point. Continue seven miles to an intersection and turn right, then another quarter mile to the parking lot. The trailhead is next to the ranger station. Access is free. There are restrooms.

103. Red Cones Trail

EFFORT: Moderate
LENGTH: 6.0 miles
GEOLOGICAL FEATURE(S): Volcanism
LOCATION: Inyo National Forest

Description: On a section of the John Muir Trail, you'll climb about 1,000 feet to reach the unimaginatively, but aptly named Red Cones, two young, ruddy-colored cinder cones. There's an optional scamper to the top of one cone.

Red Cones

There are many hiking trails in this area, and there are other routes to the cones. You might want to study a map to determine the best use of your day. An alternate route can be started from Horseshoe Lake, for instance, off of Lake Mary Road, which is a longer hike, but will give you an excellent swimming hole when you're done

From Reds Meadow Pack Station, take the trail south through a sparsely wooded area toward Rainbow Falls. Shortly, you'll reach the John Muir/Pacific Crest Trail junction. Continue uphill on a sandy, pumice-covered trail. There was a major fire here in 1992, and the damage is quite apparent. This has allowed some of the lower-growing plants such as lupine to thrive. If you hike this trail in summer, you'll be rewarded with wildflower blooms.

After two miles, you cross Boundary Creek and then go up a wooded hillside. After three miles, you reach Crater Creek along Crater Meadow and the base of the northern cone. This eruption is the most recent in the Devils Postpile area, younger than the event that created the Postpile. The cones, about 8,500 years old, formed after the last ice age, and have therefore never been glaciated. A basalt lava flow that issued from the base of the southern cone extends down Crater Creek to within one mile of the Middle Fork of the San Joaquin River.

You can easily identify Red Cones from any of the viewpoints in the area. They are the classically-shaped conical peaks protruding above the forest, two symmetrical mounds, reddish in color. The cones are covered by loose cinders blown out of the center of each when they erupted. Pick up some of the rocks to note their light weight and porosity. As we've seen before, this type of volcano produces scoria, a volcanic rock with a high gas content that leaves it riddled with holes.

The Red Cones are vents of the Mammoth Mountain lava dome complex on the southwest rim of the Long Valley caldera, a system that includes over 35 vents, all of them mineralogically similar, producing rocks with large amounts of magnesium and iron (mafic), which are often reddish due to the oxidation of the iron (rust). In the case of these two cones, the red color is pronounced.

If you want to make the effort, you can climb to the top of the northern cone to see the depression left around the volcano vent. You'll notice several trails worn by others who have come before you. The 9,000-foot perch at the top will give you fantastic views of Mammoth Mountain, the Mammoth Crest, and the Ritter Range.

Whether or not you climb the cinder cone, retrace your steps on the return trip.

Directions: Some of the roads traversing the Sierras are closed in winter, so check road conditions. From U.S. 395, take the Mammoth Lakes exit and proceed to the Mammoth Mountain Ski Area, right, and park there.

From June to September, you'll have to take a shuttle bus to area trailheads and pay a fee for the trip. Buy tickets at Mammoth Mountain Inn, which is the departing point. If you come off-season or very early in the morning or in the evening, you can drive to the trailhead. Proceed past Mammoth Mountain Inn and past Minaret Vista Point. Continue past the Devil's Postpile exit to Reds Meadow Resort. Access is free.

104. San Joaquin Ridge Trail

EFFORT: Moderate
LENGTH: 4.6 miles
GEOLOGICAL FEATURE(S): Volcanism, Erosional Features
LOCATION: Inyo National Forest

Description: The trail is a rough dirt road atop the San Joaquin Ridge with unequaled views in all directions and great wildflower displays in summer. Be prepared for thin air, gorgeous rocks, terrific views, windy exposures, and a gain of 1,080 feet in elevation.

Before starting on the trail, take a few minutes to munch on the view from the vista, one of the best viewpoints around and an awesome place to begin a hike. The information there will identify the major features on the horizon. Look west to see the spiky Minarets, Banner Peak, and Ritter Peak. Below is the upper San Joaquin River drainage. It is a wide, sweeping, fabulous view that will prepare you for the sort of breathtaking journey you're about to undertake.

From the Minaret Vista, the trail is a blocked jeep road passed on the right as you drive the entrance road to the vista parking lot. Walk back to this road to begin and head north. There is also a path east of the restroom that will take you downhill to the trail if you don't want to walk on the road.

The San Joaquin Ridge marks the Sierra Divide, the border between water runoff to the east and runoff to the west. You'll be walking over volcanic soil with chunks of light-colored pumice from eruptions that occurred about 20,000 years ago.

The Minarets, those pointy peaks to the west, are the remnants of an ancient lava flow. Their sawtooth appearance was caused by the repeated cycle of freeze and thaw, winter after winter, which cracked the rock, chipping away at it over time.

At a fork, bear left, continuing on the 4WD road. Where Mountain View bike trail branches off right, you continue on the road called "Hard Corps" trail. This same road will be our route for the duration of the hike.

As you gain some height, you'll begin to get those promised westward views. You'll also have the company of some colorful blooms alongside the trail.

After 1.25 miles, the trail starts to climb steeply for about a quarter mile before leveling off. A little further along, at a fork, continue on the Hard Corps Trail by bearing left. Begin climbing again, pushing on to the 2-mile mark, and earn views to both east and west. You're now walking along the knife-edge in an incredibly dramatic location, and you'll feel that drama in your lungs.

Minarets

Up ahead you'll see your destination, Deadman Peak, the high point you'll shortly enjoy. In 1868, a headless man's body was found near Deadman Creek, the source of the name of both the creek and the peak.

The Ritter Range sprawls to the west and Long Valley lies below to the east. As you push on to the summit, take your time to enjoy this top of the world feeling (and catch your breath). Deadman Peak tops out at 10,255 feet. Your views here are endless and unobstructed. Sit down for a while and enjoy it.

The way back is the same, only in reverse.

Directions: From Mammoth Lakes on Highway 203, turn right onto Minaret Road and proceed past Mammoth Mountain Inn heading west to Minaret Summit. Turn right on Minaret Vista access road and park in the large Vista parking area. Access is free. There are restrooms.

105. Hot Creek Geological Site

EFFORT: Minimal
LENGTH: 2.0 miles
GEOLOGICAL FEATURE(S): Geothermal Activity
LOCATION: Inyo National Forest

Description: This trail leads to the Hot Creek Geological Site, a spot where hot water bubbles up through fissures, warming the pools in the creek and creating a fascinating geothermal marvel. There's plenty of boiling water in the area, so be extremely cautious when coming into contact with it. The conditions here can change rapidly when earthquakes alter the patterns of water seepage and produce new hot spots and occasional geysers. This happened significantly in 2006 when increased geothermal activity raised the temperature of the surface water enough to cause the closure of the previously temperate swimming holes in Hot Creek. Prior to that, this area was enjoyed by bathers who found natural hot tubs at the end of this trail. Now the pools are fenced off, too hot to safely bathe in. In addition, there had already been numerous injuries and fatalities (over a dozen) of people who accidentally came into contact with scalding water. At this time, you can look and smell, but you can't take a dip.

Magma not far beneath the surface provides the heat for these features. Most of these hot springs originated on August 24, 1973, in a single event that produced at least five springs, two of them starting out as geysers. The geyser activity dwindled off almost immediately, but the hot springs remain productive. There is no real evidence to explain the appearance of these springs, but some have suggested that a small earthquake zone located 25 miles southeast might be responsible. The springs erupted almost immediately following that seismic activity. However, even prior to that significant event, there were hot springs in the area. Native Americans used the mineral-rich hot pools as sources of medicinal water.

This site is somewhat unique in that the hot water emerges into a cold mountain stream, producing an unusual environment where water temperature varies greatly from spot to spot. When trout were first introduced here many years ago, it was unknown if they would survive, but they've thrived, apparently being smart enough to avoid being cooked alive.

At the parking lot you'll find bathrooms, picnic tables, interpretive panels and plenty of safety warnings. You can get an overlook of the trail from the parking area before setting out. Look for steam, best observed in the cool morning hours. You're also likely to get a whiff or two of sulfur.

Take a look around at the mountains and the larger landscape to remind yourself that you're standing in the middle of the huge volcanic caldera. The magma chamber of this volcano is underfoot, and in the creek, it's very close to the surface.

Hot Creek begins its life in the Eastern Sierras as Mammoth Creek, flowing out of Twin Lakes and fueled by snow melt. Like any mountain stream, it's naturally cold until it reaches this spot and is heated by hot springs.

Walk down to the creek on a paved trail and then across a bridge to the north side of Hot Creek. Turn left and follow the dirt path towards the blue-green hot pools. Geothermal activity can be observed along a 2-mile section of the creek, but these features are in constant flux, so we can't tell you their exact location. Look for steam, either coming off the creek water or along the shore. There are springs in the canyon that don't mix with creek water, and these create mineral-rich, turquoise-colored boiling pools. In some place, hot water emerging into the creek can be found where you see bubbles coming to the surface. These indicate escaping volcanic gases from below. You'll also see areas where hot springs once occurred, but are now absent. These can be identified by mineral-stained rocks surrounding sometimes obvious holes in the ground. Don't go barefoot here, but if you did, you'd find places where the ground is warm. Some of the escaping hot steam emerges through fissures, even tiny cracks that can't be easily seen, but will give you a surprise if you step on them.

This geothermal activity is harnessed by the nearby geothermal plant to produce electricity and the Hot Creek Fish Hatchery that uses the warm spring waters to maintain its artificial environment at optimal conditions for raising young trout.

The canyon is narrow and full of interesting rock formations. Pay close attention to the rocks on the trail. Hydrothermal activity has altered the rhyolite in the canyon, producing a bleached appearance. You'll also see evidence of intense folding in the colorful bands of the metamorphic rocks. Sulfur deposits and moss add splashes of color as well. All in all, this is a beautiful and special place and one of the more unusual volcanoes you'll ever walk inside.

Return by the same path.

Directions: On Highway 395 east of Mammoth Lakes, continue south to the Hot Creek Fish Hatchery exit. Turn left and proceed 3 miles on Hot Creek Hatchery Road, past the Fish Hatchery to the Hot Creek Geothermal Area. Turn left into the parking lot. Access is free.

106. Palisade Glacier Trail

EFFORT: Difficult
LENGTH: 16.0 miles
GEOLOGICAL FEATURE(S): Glaciation
LOCATION: John Muir Wilderness

Description: You know you're going to have to work if you want to touch a California glacier. There is nothing equivalent here to Alaska's Mendenhall where you hop off the cruise ship onto glacial ice. This narrow, rocky trail takes you into the John Muir Wilderness and on to one of the largest glaciers remaining in the Sierras, the Palisade Glacier. From the Owens Valley east of the Sierras, you can see the glaciers atop the tallest peaks to the west. But that's nothing like hiking up to them in the stark and stunning domain they inhabit. This is one of the most beautiful trails in California, but is also one of the most difficult, climbing 4,000 feet to a height of over 12,000 feet. Completing this trail will qualify as an epic adventure for most people.

This trail climbs from Big Pine Canyon to several high-elevation glacial lakes unimaginatively named First, Second, Third, etc. However, there are several possible destinations along this trail for less determined hikers, and in autumn, the colorful foliage is exceptional. An easy and rewarding 3-mile trip can be made by visiting two pretty waterfalls (unimaginatively named First and Second Falls) along North Fork Big Pine Creek. All of these destinations will be out and back hikes. It is possible to hike the full length of this trail as a day hike if you start early, but camping overnight is a popular option. A permit is required for overnight camping in the John Muir Wilderness.

Pass a locked gate at the end of the road and walk beside Big Pine Creek past summer homes. The road tapers off to a footpath and climbs up a hill. You'll come to a bridge over the creek at just over a quarter mile and your first point of interest. The cascade here is First Falls nestled among aspens and Jeffrey pine. Take a moment to enjoy it before passing over to the other side of the creek and continuing to a junction. Turn right for North Fork Big Pine Creek. Switchback steeply up the main trail until you meet up with a road at 0.6 miles. Turn right onto the road and cross the creek on a bridge. Soon you're at another junction with two of the routes heading for the second waterfall. Upper Trail heads right and climbs through manzanita bushes above the road. For the easier route, take the road left for a level path with spur trails leading off left, providing stream access and shaded by abundant trees.

Second Falls, a lovely tumbling cascade, will soon come into view ahead as the trail narrows and routes you uphill. At 1.5 miles, you reach a junction with Upper Trail. You can go left on the trail to the top of the falls if you wish. And just beyond that you'll enter a meadow beside the creek which, in season, will have wildflower displays.

Continue beyond the falls and through the flowery meadow. After 2.7 miles and 1,700 feet, you pass a trail leading left to Big Pine Creek Wilderness Ranger Camp, a 1929 stone building that was commissioned by horror-film actor Lon Chaney, Sr., who enjoyed this tranquil retreat only briefly before he died in 1930. Detour there for a look if you want.

Continuing on the main trail, emerge into a sunny stretch with intermittent lodgepole pines and granite outcrops. Ford the stream at four miles and again shortly thereafter. Switchback uphill to a trail junction. The left fork is your trail. This route takes you to a chain of seven lakes. Thankfully, the trail reenters tree cover and passes a side trail left that leads to a camping area on the shore of First Lake, a lovely glacial tarn.

At 4.5 miles you reach a viewpoint above First Lake at 10,000 feet in elevation. Continuing, you'll reach Second Lake about 100 feet higher at 4.75 miles. There's a picnic area here overlooking Second Lake, and glacial erratics will be apparent nearby.

After passing Third Lake, colored a milky turquoise by glacial meltwater, you'll climb steeply to a meadow with sweeping views of the icefield. Along the way, you'll see many signs of glaciation, such as striations on the rocks along the creek. A half mile above Third Lake, the Palisade Glacier trail goes left (don't take the trail to Upper Lakes— Lakes Four through Seven). Switchback over grassy benches to boggy Sam Mack Meadows, reached in about 7.5 miles. You're now at 11,000 feet in elevation and enjoying spectacular views. The terrain here is wet, mostly treeless and mossy. Backpackers often use this as their overnight campsite. Be prepared for mosquitos.

From here, the trail crosses the stream and goes up to a ridge with views to the east of First through Third Lakes.

The last half mile of the route involves boulder hopping and some scrambling along an indistinct trail marked with cairns. Note that you're making your way through the glacier's moraine and you can tell this by the jumbled size of the rocks underfoot, ranging from very small to boulders. Once you can see the glacier and its lake, it's up to you if you want to make the tough climb down to it or be content with a view.

The glacier is your final destination on this gorgeous high-country trail. It flows off of four peaks, including its namesake North Palisade, at 14,242 feet, the third highest peak in the Sierras. The jagged peaks above this tongue of ice are Mt. Sill, Mt. Gayley, Thunderbolt Peak, Starlight Peak and North Palisade. This glacier, the largest in the Sierras, is a remnant of the Little Ice Age that occurred worldwide between the sixteenth and nineteenth centuries, but these mountains have been glaciated numerous times in the historic past. The remaining glacier is 0.8 miles long and 0.5 miles wide. Palisade Glacier is unusual in that it terminates in a proglacial lake dammed by its former moraine. The lake is turquoise colored from the sediment suspended in the water.

Return via the same path.

Directions: From Highway 395 near Big Pine, take Glacier Lodge Road west about 11 miles to the end, just past the entrance to Glacier Lodge where there is trailhead parking. Access is free.

ABOUT THE AUTHORS

Robin C. Johnson, a native Californian, is a retired computer software designer and webmaster. She is the author of several novels and nonfiction books about California's natural and human history. Among her nonfiction books are *Fearless: Gutsy Gals of a Bygone Era* and *Enchantress, Sorceress, Madwoman: The True Story of Sarah Althea Hill*. When not writing, Robin enjoys hiking, theater, chasing down historical landmarks and savoring culinary adventures.

Dot Lofstrom, CHMM, RG, is now retired, formerly the Division Chief for the California Environmental Protection Agency, Department of Toxic Substances Control. She has a Master of Science degree in geology, and has held wide-ranging positions in state and federal government, environmental consulting, and community college education and has gained a wealth of geologic experience throughout California.

Both are avid hikers and enjoy the varied trails of California and the desert Southwest.

APPENDIX A – THEMATIC INDEX

Fault Activity

44. Earthquake Trail
54. San Andreas Fault Trail
60. Moses Spring Trail
61. Balconies Cliffs and Caves
66. Wallace Creek Interpretive Trail

Volcanism (see Caves for lava tubes)

12. The Whaleback
13. Avalanche Gulch Trail
14. Brewer Creek Trail
15. Black Butte Trail
16. Squaw Meadows Trail
17. Burney Falls Trail
19. Spattercone Nature Trail
20. Cinder Cone Trail
21. Lassen Peak Summit Trail
28. Mammoth Crater
31. Black Crater Trail
32. Fleener Chimneys
33. Schonchin Butte Trail
35. Captain Jack's Stronghold Trail
36. Whitney Butte Trail
38. Burnt Lava Flow
39. Medicine lake Glass Flow
40. Spatter Cone Loop
51. Round Top Loop
64. Sutter Buttes
77. Big Meadow Trail
78. Trail of the Gargoyles
79. Donnell Vista Trail
80. Columns of the Giants
96. South Tufa Trail
97. Panum Crater Trail
98. Obsidian Dome
99. Inyo Craters Trail
101. Mammoth Crest Trail
102. Devils Postpile & Rainbow Falls Trail
103. Red Cones Trail
104. San Joaquin Ridge Trail

Caves

8. Samwel Cave Nature Trail
9. Lake Shasta Caverns
11. Pluto Caves
18. Subway Cave
29. Valentine Cave
30. Big Painted Cave & Symbol Bridge
34. Heppe Ice Cave
37. Cave Loop Road
60. Moses Spring Trail
61. Balconies Cliffs and Caves
72. Blask Chasm Cavern
73. Mercer Caverns
74. Moaning Cavern Walking Tour
75. California Cavern Trail of Lights
92. Boyden Cavern Family Walking Tour
94. Crystal Cave

Fossils

45. Petrified Forest Trail
48. Fossil Ridge Trail
50. Castle Rock Trail

Geothermal Activity

22. Bumpass Hell Trail
23. Cold Boiling Lake Trail
25. Devils Kitchen Trail
26. Boiling Springs Lake Trail
27. Terminal Geyser
105. Hot Creek Trail

Glaciation

4. Heart Lake Trail
13. Avalanche Gulch Trail
14. Brewer Creek Trail
16. Squaw Meadows Trail
76. Pyramid Creek Trail
79. Donnell Vista Trail
81. Glacier Meadow Loop
82. Lembert Dome Trail

APPENDIX B – GEOLOGIC TIME SCALE

Years Ago	Era or Eon	Period	Life and Environment
0 to 2 million	CENOZOIC ERA	QUATERNARY	Modern humans evolve.
2 to 67 million	(Age of Recent Life)	NEOGENE	First large mammals appear. Abundant mammals; first
		PALEOGENE	hominids. Grasses and modern birds also appear.
67 to 140 million	MESOZOIC ERA	CRETACEOUS	Heyday of dinosaurs until their extinction at end of period. First flowering plants.
140 to 208 million	(Age of Medieval Life)	JURASSIC	Earliest birds appear. Giant dinosaurs (sauropods) flourish. Plants: ferns, cycads and ginkos.
208 to 250 million		TRIASSIC	Age of dinosaurs begins. First mammals. Mollusks are dominant invertebrate.
250 to 290 million	PALEOZOIC ERA	PERMIAN	Age of Amphibians. Supercontinent known as Pangaea forms. Greatest mass extinction ever at end of period. Trilobites go extinct.
290 to 365 million	(Age of Ancient Life)	PENNSYLVANIAN AND MISSISSIPPIAN (CARBONIFEROUS)	Widespread coal swamps. Large primitive trees. First winged insects and reptiles. Many ferns. Amphibians common.
365 to 405 million		DEVONIAN	Age of fishes. First shark. Land plants abundant and diverse. Earliest amphibians, ferns and mosses.
405 to 430 million		SILURIAN	First insects, jawed fish and vascular plants (with water conducting tissue) on land.
430 to 500 million		ORDOVICIAN	First corals. Primitive fish, fungi and seaweed. Non-vascular land plants (moss) first appear.
500 to 570 million		CAMBRIAN	Age of Trilobites. Cambrian explosion of life occurs. All phyla existing today develop. First vertebrates and earliest fish. First shells appear on mollusks, echinoderms, brachiopods, trilobites.
570 to 2500 million	PROTEROZOIC (Early Life)	Commonly known as the PRECAMBRIAN	First soft-bodied invertebrates and colonial algae. Oxygen build up: Mid-proterozoic.
2500 to 3800 million	ARCHEAN (Ancient Life)		Life appears. First bacterial and blue-green algae begins to free oxygen to atmosphere.
3800 to 4600 million	PRE-ARCHEAN		Earth molten.